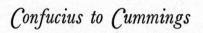

Confucius to Cummings

Confucius to Cummings

An Anthology of Poetry

Edited by Ezra Pound & Marcella Spann

A NEW DIRECTIONS BOOK

New Directions Books are published for James Laughlin
by New Directions Publishing Corporation,
333 Sixth Avenue, New York, 14.

Acknowledgments

The Editors are grateful to the following poets and publishers for permission to reprint copyright material in this collection:

Estate of Richard Aldington for "Triumph of Bacchus and Ariadne" from *Fifty Romance Lyric Poems*. Copyright 1928 by Crosby Gaige.

Basil Bunting for "Gin the Goodwife Stint" and "The Complaint of the Morpethshire Farmer."

Padraic Colum and The Devin-Adair Company for "I Shall Not Die for Thee" from *The Collected Poems of Padraic Colum*, published 1953 by The Devin-Adair Co., New York. Copyright 1953 by Padraic Colum.

Mrs. E. E. Cummings and Harcourt, Brace and Company, Inc. for "XIII from *One Times One*." Copyright 1944 by E. E. Cummings. Reprinted from *Poems 1923-1954* by E. E. Cummings by permission of Harcourt, Brace and Company, Inc. and the author.

T. S. Eliot, Harcourt, Brace and Company, Inc., and Faber & Faber Ltd for "Whispers of Immortality" from *Collected Poems 1909-1935* by T. S. Eliot. Copyright 1936 by Harcourt, Brace and Company, Inc.

Miss Janice Biala, Executrix, Estate of Ford Madox Ford, for four poems from *Collected Poems*. Copyright 1936 by Ford Madox Ford, published by Oxford University Press; and the translations of Walther von der Vogelweide's "Under the Lindens."

Grove Press, Inc. and Norman Holmes Pearson for "Never More Will the Wind" by H.D., from *Selected Poems*. Copyright © 1957 by Norman Holmes Pearson, published by Grove Press.

The Executors of the Hardy Estate, Macmillan & Co. Ltd. (London), The Macmillan Company (New York) and The Macmillan Company of Canada Limited for the poems and translation from *The Collected Poems of Thomas Hardy*. Copyright 1925 by The Macmillan Company.

Harvard University Press for the translations from *The Confucian Odes* by Ezra Pound. Copyright 1954 by the President and Fellows of Harvard College.

Miss Eva Hesse for her German translation of Cummings' "XIII from *One Times One*."

Mrs. Wyndham Lewis for the excerpt from "One-Way Song."

Miss Marianne Moore and The Viking Press for "O to be a dragon" from *O To Be a Dragon* by Marianne Moore. Copyright © 1957 by Marianne Moore. Reprinted by permission of The Viking Press, Inc. and of the author.

Dallam Simpson for his translation from Aeschylus.

Mrs. William Carlos Williams for "The High Bridge above the Tagus River at Toledo" from *Pictures from Brueghel*. Copyright 1962 by William Carlos Williams, published by New Directions.

Mrs. W. B. Yeats, The Macmillan Company (New York) and The Macmillan Company of Canada Limited for the poems from *Collected Poems* of W. B. Yeats. Copyright 1906, 1912 by The Macmillan Company, 1934 by W. B. Yeats, 1940 by Bertha Georgie Yeats; published by The Macmillan Company.

and to Professor Vincent Miller of Wofford College for his valuable collaboration.

Preface

Courses in English literature can arouse curiosity and give the student a taste for reading things she or he would like to remember in later life. As an English instructor I have found it almost impossible to stimulate such curiosity through the use of the textbooks available. One is often forced to run a mimeograph machine, or to require students to purchase paperbacks, of which only small portions prove suitable.

One of my teachers, Professor Vincent Miller, insisted that his students learn to *read,* i.e., to understand the meaning of poems. When a student examines poetry as closely as this teacher insisted on our examining it, he begins to distinguish the real from the sham. No one textbook served Professor Miller's purpose.

In collecting material for the present volume, the teacher's dilemma was the first which Mr. Pound and I had to consider. But is the teacher really in a different box from the student or the most casual reader? The problem is universal: to arouse curiosity, not kill it, and this without implying false values or false views of proportion.

As this volume is intended for those who read only English, we have been limited in our selection to poems written in English, or those translated or adapted into it. William Cookson has said that it would be nearly impossible to assemble a body of writing in any language that "for wisdom and continuous beauty" would stand against the *Classic Anthology Defined by Confucius;* in choosing the poems included here we have kept this challenge, and the example of the Confucian collection, in mind.

We have also been mindful of the difference between the occidental and the oriental approach to instruction. Su-Lung Wang, in *A Daughter of Confucius,* tells us that when she began to learn English she read that "the cat can see the rat." Thinking of her first day in her Chinese family school, where she had learned that "the nature of man is originally good," she concluded that "education in English seemed less philosophical."

The arrangement of this volume is—with one exception, ex-

plained in a note on page 278—chronological, by the date of
the poems' original composition rather than of their translation
into English. This arrangement is adopted for convenience only,
and need not interfere with the reader's approach to individual
poems. Professor Norman Holmes Pearson, to whom we owe so
much, has written privately: "The best way to start kids on po-
etry is *not* in reference to the history of its development, that is
the period racket, but by showing them poems, especially by hav-
ing them listen to the reading of same. The process is much like
that of learning language, and how to understand what one hears
spoken."

What matters in poetry, as Coleridge would have agreed, is
the intensity of the emotion, and the depth of comprehension
registered by the writer. It is our hope that the poems assembled
in this volume will, to use a Celtic phrase which Yeats has con-
tributed to current critical aspiration, "make the soul," even if
it cannot fulfill his larger hope for "a new sacred book of the
arts."

As Pound wrote in *Canto LIX*, Chun Tchi prefaced the Con-
fucian Odes:

"less a work of the mind than of affects
   brought forth from the inner nature

            . . . virtu in internals

Ut animum nostrum purget . . ."

[For the cleansing of the soul.]

Where necessary parts of the design of this volume were not
available in English, Mr. Pound has made tentative translations
"to serve ad interim." The notes and comments interspersed
throughout the text are by him unless otherwise indicated.

M. S.

Confucius to Cummings

There are over three thousand years in the record of poetry but we need a glossary to read Chaucer who died in A.D. 1400. If you pick up this anthology for idle pleasure you had better begin with cummings or Whitman and read what you like. If the book is being used as a classroom text, you can start at the beginning, which may seem like a jumble of fragments. All that one can show in so small a space is the "matter," that is, one can, at best, indicate what feelings and what sorts of fact the poets of earlier time chose to sing.

Homer sang of activity, not limited to warfare, though that topic was popular in his time. He showed interest in practical affairs as well as emotion. Nothing indicates that he attempted to reach Dante's classification of suitable subject matter, or to sort it out as Dante did: love, war, and holiness. He left a sacred book, notwithstanding. Various dimensions of his writing have received inadequate publicity.

Translations of Homer extant at this writing [1958] are inadequate. Most of them have not the merit assigned to Pope by a critic of his time: "Very pretty, not Homer." Most versions cannot be offered as much more than: "Very clumsy, not Homer."

English metrists have been notoriously lazy. Thank God for a few noble exceptions. We have as yet no English idiom developed to capacity for illustrating Homer's melodic and rhythmic force, let alone the subtleties of the Alexandrines. A note on the Egyptian *Conversations in Courtship* (page 278) suggests a new evaluation of Theocritus and Kallimachus as verbal craftsmen. Those who understand only English are faced with similar difficulty in appraisal of French refinement in the decades that followed Gautier's *"Emaux et Camées."*

The Latin record had, definitely, entered the stream of European culture, so that Golding found a natural speech for Ovid's. The matter, tone, quality of other pre-Chaucerian writers entered English paideuma, or our way of thinking in poetry, at various times, but it is simpler to set our specimens in the sequence of their original composition. The active student may enjoy figuring out when and how they got into the minds of later poets, if at all; and with what degree of light or muddle.

As any schoolchild would be insulted if one suggested that it had not intelligence enough to solve a puzzle or pruzzle, we assume that any reader who has been able to get into a junior college will be able to put our mosaic together to her, or to his, satisfaction.

E. P.

June, 1958

Publisher's Note

Ezra Pound has indicated that the brief notes accompanying the selections in this volume contain practically all the *"rettifiche"* that he has wished to make in his published criticism since writing *Guide to Kulchur* and *Carta da Visita* (translated as *The Visiting Card*).

His general outline is condensed, he says, in the statement that he had swallowed the idea that Aeschylus represented the acme of Greek drama, and, neglecting Sophokles, had thought certain qualities found in the best Latin were of Latin origin. Rereading his treatment of the Fenollosa notes and versions of the Japanese Noh, he wished to see how the Greek would measure up under similar or approximately similar treatment. Hence his *Traxiniai*. The emendation of his proportionate estimate of authors in world literature accessible to him can be summarized, then, in his phrase, as "dress (in the military sense) on Sophokles."

The Rachewiltz versions in Italian of Egyptian poetry gave a further jolt to tradition; as his note on page 278 makes clear, the Alexandrines must now be judged in the light of the Egyptian poetry that would have been known to Theocritus and Kallimachus.

Contents

Preface by Marcella Spann   vii

Confucius to Cummings: Preface by Ezra Pound   ix

Publisher's Note   xi

CONFUCIUS [c. 551-479 B.C.]
from THE CLASSIC ANTHOLOGY   3
   Translated by Ezra Pound [1885-   ]

HOMER [c. 950-900 B.C.]
from the ODYSSEY   15
   Translated by George Chapman [?1559-1634]

SAPPHO [630-552 B.C.]
  Achtung   18
   Translated by Thomas Hardy [1840-1928]

AESCHYLUS [525-456 B.C.]
from the AGAMEMNON   19
   Translated by Dallam Simpson [1926-   ]

SOPHOKLES [496-406 B.C.]
from WOMEN OF TRACHIS   22
   Translated by Ezra Pound

THEOCRITUS [fl. 270 B.C.]
from the IDYLLS   25
   Translated by Thomas Creech [1659-1700]

LUCRETIUS [c. 99-55 B.C.]
from DE RERUM NATURA   32
   Translated by John Dryden [1631-1700]

CATULLUS [?84-54? B.C.]
Odi et Amo   33
   Translated by Ezra Pound

VIRGIL [70-19 B.C.]
from the AENEID   34
   Translated by Gavin Douglas [1474-1522]

HORACE [65-8 B.C.]
from the ODES   35
   Translated by Ezra Pound

OVID [43 B.C.-18 A.D.]
from the METAMORPHOSES   37
   Translated by Arthur Golding [1536-c. 1605]

RUTILIUS [fl. 416 A.D.]
Roma   66
   Translated by Ezra Pound

BOETHIUS [c. 475-525]
from DE CONSOLATIONE PHILOSOPHIÆ   68
   Translated by Elizabeth I [1533-1603]

ANONYMOUS [Anglo-Saxon, 8th century]
The Seafarer   69
   Translated by Ezra Pound

RIHAKU [LI PO] [c. 700-762]
Exile's Letter   72
   Translated by Ezra Pound

GODESCHALK [805-869]
Sequaire   75
   Translated by Ezra Pound

ANONYMOUS [12th century?]
Hierusalem   77

THE "OLD CAPTIVE" [?1130 fl.]
from AUCASSIN AND NICOLETTE   79
   Translated by Andrew Lang [1854-1912]

BERTRANS DE BORN [c. 1140-1214]
"A Perigord pres del muralh"   80
A War Song   80
   Translated by Ezra Pound

BERNART DE VENTADORN [1148-1195]
The Lark   81
   Translated by Ezra Pound

WALTHER VON DER VOGELWEIDE [?1170-1230?]
Under the Lindens   82
   Translated by Ford Madox Ford [1873-1939]

ARNAUT DANIEL [c. 1180-1200]
"L'aura amara"   84
"Autet e bas"   85
   Translated by Ezra Pound

ST. FRANCIS OF ASSISI [1182-1226]
Cantico del Sole   86
   Translated by Ezra Pound

GUIDO GUINICELLI [1220-1275]
Canzone: Of the Gentle Heart   88
   Translated by Dante Gabriel Rossetti [1828-1882]

FOLGORE DA SAN GEMIGNANO [fl. 1250]
from OF THE MONTHS   90
   Translated by Dante Gabriel Rossetti

GUIDO CAVALCANTI [1250-1300]
Sonetto VII   91
Sonetto XXXV   92
Ballata V   92
Canzone: Donna mi priegha   93
   Translated by Ezra Pound

DANTE ALIGHIERI [1265-1321]
from LA VITA NUOVA   96
   Translated by Dante Gabriel Rossetti

ANONYMOUS [c. 1300]
Alisoun   100

WILLIAM LANGLAND [?1330-1390?]
from THE VISION OF PIERS PLOWMAN   101

GEOFFREY CHAUCER [?1340-1400]
from THE CANTERBURY TALES   102
Merciles Beaute   105
from THE PARLEMENT OF FOULES   107

ANONYMOUS [c. 1350]
Adam Lay Yboundin   107

CHARLES D'ORLÉANS [1391-1465]
Spring   108
    Translated by Andrew Lang

ANONYMOUS [15th century]
Dear Son, Leave Thy Weeping   109
Ave Maris Stella   110

FRANÇOIS VILLON [1431-1463?]
The Complaint of the Fair Armouress   111
The Epitaph in Form of a Ballad   114
A Fragment on Death   115
    Translated by Algernon C. Swinburne [1837-1909]
His Mother's Service to Our Lady   115
The Ballad of Dead Ladies   117
    Translated by Dante Gabriel Rossetti

LORENZO DE' MEDICI, THE MAGNIFICENT [1449-1492]
from CARNIVAL SONGS   118
    Translated by Richard Aldington [1892-1962]

MICHELANGELO BUONAROTTI [1475-1561]
To the Marchesana of Pescara   119
    Translated by William Wordsworth [1770-1850]

MARTIN LUTHER [1483-1546]
"Ein Feste Burg Ist Unser Gott"   120
    Translated by M. Woolsey Stryker, 1883

HENRY VIII [1491-1547]
Pastime 122
The Holly 123
To His Lady 123

WILLIAM CORNISH [?-1524?]
Gratitude 124

HEATH [temp. Henry VIII]
Women 125

ANONYMOUS [16th century]
Western Wind 126

THOMAS WYATT [?1503-1542]
Epigram 127

SANTA TERESA D'AVILA [1515-1582]
Bookmark 127
    Translated by Henry Wadsworth Longfellow [1807-1882]

JOACHIM DU BELLAY [?1522-1560]
A Sonnet to Heavenly Beauty 128
    Translated by Andrew Lang

PIERRE DE RONSARD [1525-1585]
Of His Lady's Old Age 128
    Translated by Andrew Lang

ELIZABETH I [1533-1603]
The Doubt of Future Foes 129
When I Was Fair and Young 130

GEORGE TURBERVILLE [?1540-1610?]
The Lover to His Lady 131
To His Friend 131

WALTER RALEGH [?1552-1618]
The Nymph's Reply to the Shepherd 132
Epitaph 133
The Lie 133

A.W. [fl. 1585]
Where His Lady Keeps His Heart   136
Upon Visiting His Lady by Moonlight   137
In Praise of the Sun   138

ANTHONY MUNDAY [c. 1553-1633]
Dirge   139

ROBERT GREENE [?1558-1592]
The Palmer's Ode   139
Maesia's Song   141
The Description of Sir Geoffrey Chaucer   141

ANONYMOUS [c. 1600]
Song Set by Nicholas Yonge   142
Song Set by John Farmer   142

ROBERT WILSON [?-1600?]
Simplicity's Song   143

SAMUEL DANIEL [1562-1619]
from THE COMPLAINT OF ROSAMOND   143
from To Delia   145

CHRISTOPHER MARLOWE [1564-1593]
A Fragment   146
The Passionate Shepherd to His Love   147

WILLIAM SHAKESPEARE [1564-1616]
from THE TEMPEST   148
from THE TWO GENTLEMEN OF VERONA   149
from MUCH ADO ABOUT NOTHING   150
from LOVE'S LABOUR'S LOST   151
from A MIDSUMMER NIGHT'S DREAM   152
from AS YOU LIKE IT   158
from THE MERCHANT OF VENICE   162
from TWELFTH NIGHT   163
from CYMBELINE   165
from the SONNETS   166
from KING HENRY V   171

JOHN DAVIES [1569-1626]
from NOSCE TEIPSUM   172

BEN JONSON [1572-1637]
from A CELEBRATION OF CHARIS   173

ROBERT HERRICK [1591-1674]
To His Lovely Mistresses   174

EDMUND WALLER [1606-1687]
Go, Lovely Rose   175
To Mr. Henry Lawes   176

PIETRO METASTASIO [1698-1782]
"Age of Gold"   177
    Translated by Ezra Pound

MARIE-FRANÇOISE-CATHERINE DE BEAUVEAU,
    LA MARQUISE DE BOUFFLERS [1711-1786]
Air: Sentir avec ardeur   178
    Translated by Ezra Pound

CHRISTOPHER SMART [1722-1771]
from JUBILATE AGNO   179

GEORGE CRABBE [1754-1832]
from THE BOROUGH   182

ROBERT BURNS [1759-1796]
The Birks of Aberfeldy   197
Bonnie Lesley   198
Green Grow the Rashes   199

WALTER SAVAGE LANDOR [1775-1864]
Past Ruin'd Ilion Helen Lives   200
Dirce   200

GEORGE GORDON, LORD BYRON [1788-1824]
from DON JUAN   201

FITZ-GREENE HALLECK [1790-1867]
from FANNY   206

FELICIA DOROTHEA HEMANS [1793-1835]
from THE BRERETON OMEN   210

JOHN KEATS [1795-1821]
from ENDYMION   211

THOMAS LOVELL BEDDOES [1803-1849]
from DEATH'S JEST BOOK   213

ELIZABETH BARRETT BROWNING [1806-1861]
from SONNETS FROM THE PORTUGUESE   215

JOHN GREENLEAF WHITTIER [1807-1892]
Barbara Frietchie   218

THÉOPHILE GAUTIER [1811-1872]
from ARS VICTRIX   221
    Translated by H. Austin Dobson [1840-1921]

ROBERT BROWNING [1812-1889]
How It Strikes a Contemporary   221
Pictor Ignotus   225
Garden Fancies   227
Fra Lippo Lippi   231
Andrea del Sarto   242
Youth and Art   250
A Face   252
A Likeness   253
Orpheus and Eurydice   255

HERMAN MELVILLE [1819-1891]
The Ravaged Villa   256

WALT WHITMAN [1819 1892]
I Sing the Body Electric   256
The Centenarian's Story   265
To the States   270

DANTE GABRIEL ROSSETTI [1828-1882]
from THE HOUSE OF LIFE   271

ALGERNON CHARLES SWINBURNE [1837-1909]
from ATALANTA IN CALYDON   272

FRANCIS BRET HARTE [1836-1902]
Plain Language from Truthful James   274

JAMES WHITCOMB RILEY [1849-1916]
Good-by er Howdy-do   276

BENJAMIN FRANKLIN KING, JR. [1857-1894]
from THE SUM OF LIFE   277

ANONYMOUS [Egyptian, c. 1200-1169 B.C.]
from CONVERSATIONS IN COURTSHIP   278
    Translated by Boris de Rachewiltz [1926-   ] and Ezra Pound

THOMAS HARDY [1840-1928]
Heredity   283
Under the Waterfall   284
Faintheart in a Railway Train   286
The Young Glass-Stainer   286

WILLIAM BUTLER YEATS [1865-1939]
Down by the Salley Gardens   287
When You Are Old   287
The Moods   288
He Remembers Forgotten Beauty   288
He Thinks of Those Who Have Spoken Evil of His Beloved   289
The Cold Heaven   289
To a Poet, Who Would Have Me Praise Certain Bad Poets,
    Imitators of His and Mine   289

FORD MADOX FORD [1873-1939]
On Heaven   290
What the Orderly Dog Saw   303
"When the World Was in Building . . ."   304
The Old Houses in Flanders   304

PADRAIC COLUM [1881-   ]
"I Shall Not Die for Thee"   305

WYNDHAM LEWIS [1883-1957]
from ONE-WAY SONG   306

WILLIAM CARLOS WILLIAMS [1883-1963]
The High Bridge above the Tagus River at Toledo   307

EZRA POUND [1885-   ]
Villanelle: The Psychological Hour   308
Envoi [1919]   310

H.D. [HILDA DOOLITTLE] [1886-1961]
"Never More Will the Wind"   311

MARIANNE MOORE [1886-   ]
O To Be a Dragon   311

T. S. ELIOT [1888-   ]
from WHISPERS OF IMMORTALITY   312

BASIL BUNTING [1900-   ]
Gin the Goodwife Stint   313
The Complaint of the Morpethshire Farmer   314

e e cummings [1894-1963]
from ONE TIMES ONE   316

Postscript by Ezra Pound   321

Section for Instructors

    Appendix   I: A Note on Hardy and Ford, by Ezra Pound   325
    Appendix II: Syllabus, by Vincent Miller   329
    Appendix III: Questions for Classroom Use, by Ezra Pound   335
    Appendix IV: Suggestions for Teachers, by Marcella Spann   336
    Appendix V: Selections from the Criticism of Ezra Pound   337

Index of Poets and Translators   343

Index of Titles and First Lines of Poems   345

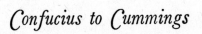

Confucius to Cummings

Confucius

[c. 551–479 B.C.]

from THE CLASSIC ANTHOLOGY

from CHOU AND THE SOUTH

IV

In the South be drooping trees,
long the bough, thick the vine,
Take thy delight,
my prince, in happy ease.

In the South be drooping boughs
the wild vine covers,
that hold delight, delight, good sir,
for eager lovers.

Close as the vine clamps the trees
so complete is happiness,
Good sir, delight delight in ease,
In the South be drooping trees.

from SHAO AND THE SOUTH

III

"Chkk! chkk!" hopper-grass,
nothing but grasshoppers hopping past;
tell me how a lady can
be gay if she sees no gentleman?

But when I've seen a man at rest,
standing still, met at his post,
my heart is no more tempest-toss'd.

2
I climb South Hill to pick the turtle-fern,
seeing no man
such climb's heart-burn

but to see a good man at rest,
standing still, met at his post,
I no more think this trouble lost.

3
To climb South Hill picking the jagged fern
and see no man, who shall not pine and yearn?

But to see good man at rest
standing still there at his post
is the heart's design's utmost.

X

Three stars, five stars rise over the hill
We came at sunset, as was his will.
                    One luck is not for all.

In Orion's hour, Pleiads small
Came with coverlets to the high hall.
Sun's up now,
Time to go.
           One luck is not for all.

from A I R S   O F   P E I

X   *The Efficient Wife's Complaint*

Wind o' the East dark with rain,
a man should not bring his olde wife pain
but should bide concordantly.
Gather *feng* gather *fei,*
man can eat and live thereby,
Now what fault is spoke against me
that I should not wedded die?

Slow road go I, mid-heart in pain,
You scarce came to my domain.
Who saith now the thistle scratches?
Soft as shepherd's-purse that matches
your new leman feasts with you
in full joy as brothers do.

King River's muddied by the Wei
yet pools to clearness presently.
You feast your doxy now she's new
and with me will naught to do.
So come not near my dam and weir,
let my fish-basket be,
In your hate what hold have I,
Indifferent all futurity!

Ready to raft the deep,
wade shallow or dive for gain—
sharing both had and lost—
and help the destitute
whate'er it cost

Not your heart's garden now,
an opponent,

you lower my market price
blocking my good intent.
I worked when we were poor and took no heed,
whom you, now rich, compare to poison weed.

I piled good store to last the winter through
so now you feast, and your new doxy's new.
'Twas I who saved for winter and you who spent,
mine the real work, you now wax violent
forgetting all the past for good or best
when 'twas with me alone that you found rest.

from Y U N G   W I N D

VIII   *Sans Equity and Sans Poise*

Dentes habet.—CATULLUS

A rat too has a skin (to tan)
A rat has a skin at least
But a man who is a mere beast
might as well die,
his death being end of no decency.

A rat also has teeth
but this fellow, for all his size, is beneath
the rat's level,
why delay his demise?

The rat also has feet
but a man without courtesy need not wait
to clutter hell's gate.

Why should a man of no moral worth
clutter the earth?

This fellow's beneath the rat's modus,
why delay his exodus?

A man without courtesy
might quite as well cease to be.

X   *Baroness Mu impeded in her wish*
        to help famine victims in Wei

I wanted to harness and go
share woe in Wei,
I would have made Ts'ao my first halt,
It was never my fault
that a deputy went to my brother
across grass and water,
could he carry my grief?

Without your visa I could not go,
I cannot honour your act
nor retract.
My sympathy was real, your's the offence
if I cannot carry my condolence.
Wrongly you wrought.
I cannot stifle my thought.

(Without your visa, does honour require it so?)

Nor was my thought wrong in this
You would not approve.
I cannot take home my condolence,
If thus wrongly you wrought,
I cannot stifle my thought.
I climb the cornered hill seeking heart's ease,
If sorrow be real, let heart with sorrow's load
go its sole road.

The Hü crowd's vulgar cry
sounds out presumptuously.
I wanted to go to the plains
where the thick grain is.
I would have asked aid of great states,
their kings and great potentates;
some would deny, some do their most,
but I would have had no blame.

All your hundred plans come to naught,
none matched my thought.

❊❊ There is no "progress" from this form. Here the actual author speaks; in Browning's *Personae* the speaker is an imagined character.

from WEI WIND

IV   Pedlar

Hill-billy, hill-billy come to buy
silk in our market, apparently?
toting an armful of calico.

Hill-billy, hill-billy, not at all
but come hither to plot my fall,
offering cloth for raw silk and all,
till I went out over the K'i
to Tun Mount, in fact, quite willingly,
and then I asked for a notary.
I said: It's O.K. with me,
we could be spliced autumnally,
                              be not offended.

Autumn came, was waiting ended?
I climbed the ruin'd wall, looked toward Kuan pass.
On the Kuan frontier no man was.

I wept until you came,
trusted your smiling talk.   One would.
You said the shells were good and the stalks all clear.
You got a cart
and carted off me and my gear.

> *Let doves eat no more mulberries*
> *While yet the leaves be green,*
> *And girls play not with lustful men,*
> *Who can play and then explain,*
>   *for so 'tis usèd,*
>   *and girls be naught excusèd.*

The mulberry tree is bare,
yellow leaves float down thru the air,
Three years we were poor,
now K'i's like a soup of mud,
the carriage curtains wet, I ever straight
and you ambiguous
with never a grip between your word and act.

Three years a wife, to work without a roof,
up with the sun and prompt to go to bed,
never a morning off. I kept my word.
You tyrannize, Brothers unaware,
if told would but grin and swear
(with truth, I must confess):
If I'm in trouble, well, I made the mess.

"Grow old with you," whom old you spite,
K'i has its banks and every swamp an edge.
Happy in pig-tails, laughed to hear your pledge,
sun up, sun up, believing all you said,
who in your acts reverse
(as a matter of course)
all that you ever said
and for the worse,
an end.

from S O N G S   O F   C H E N G

II

Hep-Cat Chung, 'ware my town,
don't break my willows down.
The trees don't matter
but father's tongue, mother's tongue
                    Have a heart, Chung,
                                    it's awful.

Hep-Cat Chung, don't jump my wall
nor strip my mulberry boughs,
The boughs don't matter
But my brothers' clatter!
                    Have a heart, Chung,
                                    it's awful.

Hep-Cat Chung, that is *my* garden wall,
Don't break my sandalwood tree.
The tree don't matter
But the subsequent chatter!
                    Have a heart, Chung,
                                    it's awful.

IX

In chariot like an hibiscus flower at his side
ready to ride and go, with gemmèd belt
Kiang's eldest frail and beauty of the town, our capital;

Like an hibiscus spray to walk with him,
to sway, to hover
as that petal'd flower, with sound of pendants
swinging at her waist, Kiang's eldest loveliness,
say in that sound is her true nature traced,

Nor shall effacèd be,
once known, from memory.

XII

So he won't talk to me when we meet?
Terrible!
        I still can eat.

So clever he won't even come to dinner;
Well, beds are soft,
            and I'm no thinner.

XIII

Be kind, good sir, and I'll lift my sark
and cross the Chen to you,
But don't think you are the only sprig
           in all the younger crew.

Think soft, good sir, and I'll lift my sark
and cross the Wei to you;
But play the pretentious ass again, and
           some other young captain will do.

from SONGS OF T'ANG

XI   *Alba*

Creeper grows over thorn,
bracken wilds over waste, he is gone,
Gone, I am alone.

Creeper overgrows thorn,
bracken spreads over the grave, he is gone,
Gone, I am alone.

The horn pillow is white like rice,
the silk shroud gleams as if with tatters of fire.
In the sunrise I am alone.

A summer's day,
winter's night, a hundred years
and we come to one house together.

Winter's day, summer's night,
each night as winter night,
each day long as of summer,
              but at last to the one same house.

from S O N G S O F C H ' E N

X

Marsh bank, lotus rank
                    and a ladye;
Heart ache and to lie awake
                    and a-fevered.

Marsh edge, valerian in sedge
                    and a ladye;
Hard head she hath.
I lie a-bed
            afflicted.

Marsh bank, lotus rank,
                    a ladye,
straight as an altar stone her loveliness,

I lie in restlessness
                    all the night
                    comfortless.

Aliter

Graceful as acorus or lotus flower
what dame in bower
plagues me to wake from sleep?
I sweat from every vein.

As marsh hath rush or sharp valerian,
Tall formal beauty, and mid-heart my lack!

Marsh bank hath acorus to sway and flare,
Shall lily on lake compare
with a tall woman's loveliness
that though I wake or sleep
                    I turn and toss?

from DEER SING

IV   Fraternitas

Splendour recurrent
in cherry-wood,
in all the world there is
nothing like brotherhood.

Brothers meet
in death and sorrow;
broken line, battle heat,
Brothers stand by;

In a pinch they collaborate
as the ling bird's vertebrae
when friends of either
protractedly just sigh.

Wrangle at home, unite outside
when friends of either are ready of course
to help either with anything
"short of brute force."

And peril past, there be those who
let brothers stew
in their own juice
as unfriends born, of no immediate use.

Set out the dishes
serve the wine,
let brothers dine tonight
with boyhood appetite.

Wife and childer together be
as sound of lutes played concurrently;
there's a deeper tone in fraternity
when elder and younger rise to agree.

Calm over earth, under sky
so be thy hearth and house as they should be;
probe to the utmost plan,
here the sincerity to rest a man.

Translated by Ezra Pound

Homer

[c. 950–900 B.C.]

❊ ❊ The following two lines (from Book I of the *Odyssey*),
quoted by William Webbe in 1586, were ascribed to "Master
Watson, fellow of S. John's," forty years earlier:

> All trauellers doo gladlie report great praise of Vlysses
> For that he knewe manie mens manners, and saw many citties.

Keats delighted in Chapman; for four centuries benevolent men
have been trying to get the Homeric charm into English, one
might almost define it as the retreat from Homer.

Chapman in Book III of the *Iliad* brings the Trojan scene to
the eye with:

> All grave old men, and souldiers they had bene, but for age
> Now left the warres; yet Counsellors they were exceeding sage.
> And as in well-growne woods, on trees, cold spinie Grashoppers
> Sit chirping and send voices out that scarce can pierce our eares
> For softnesse and their weake faint sounds; so (talking on the
>   towre)
> These Seniors of the people sate, who, when they saw the
>   powre
> Of beautie in the Queene ascend, even those cold-spirited
>   Peeres,
> Those wise and almost witherd men, found this heate in their
>   yeares
> That they were forc't (though whispering) to say: . . .

Pope, in impatience, or finding that readers of his time got clogged
in Chapman's magniloquence, hurries along in pentameter:

> There sat the seniors of the Trojan race; . . .
> Chiefs, who no more in bloody fights engage,
> But, wise through time, and narrative with age,
> In summer-days like grasshoppers rejoice,
> A bloodless race, that send a feeble voice.
>   · · · · ·

They cried, 'No wonder, such celestial charms
For nine long years have set the world in arms!
What winning graces! what majestic mien!
She moves a goddess, and she looks a queen.
Yet hence, oh heaven, convey that fatal face,
And from destruction save the Trojan race.'

No wonder that Rouse thought he would get the story into the hearts of his schoolboys by telling it in prose.

from the ODYSSEY

Downe to the King's most bright-kept Baths they went,
Where handmaids did their services present,
Bath'd, balmd them, shirts and well-napt weeds put on,
And by Atrides' side set each his throne.
Then did the handmaid royall water bring,
And to a Laver, rich and glittering,
Of massie gold, powr'd; which she plac't upon
A silver Caldron, into which might runne
The water as they washt. Then set she neare
A polisht table, on which all the cheare
The present could affoord, a reverend Dame
That kept the Larder set. A Cooke then came
And divers dishes, borne thence, serv'd againe,
Furnisht the boord with bolles of gold.

Book IV, lines 58–71

Where neither King nor shepheard want comes neare
Of cheese, or flesh, or sweete milke. All the yeare
They ever milke their Ewes.

Book IV, lines 108–10

From her bed's high and odoriferous roome,
Helen. To whom (of an elaborate loome)
Adresta set a chaire; Alcippe brought
A peece of Tapestrie, of fine wooll wrought;
Phylo a silver Cabinet conferd
(Given by Alcandra, Nuptially endeard
To Lord Polybius, whose abode in Thebes,
Th'Ægyptian citie, was, where wealth in heapes
His famous house held, out of which did go
In gift t'Atrides silver bath-tubs two,
Two Tripods, and of fine gold talents ten).
His wife did likewise send to Helen then
Faire gifts, a Distaffe that of gold was wrought,
And that rich Cabinet that Phylo brought,
Round and with gold ribd, now of fine thred full,
On which extended (crownd with finest wooll
Of violet glosse) the golden Distaffe lay.

Book IV, lines 154–70

'Twelve Herds of Oxen, no lesse Flockes of Sheepe,
As many Herds of Swine, Stals large and steepe,
And equall sort of Goats, which Tenants there
And his owne Sheepherds kept. Then fed he here
Eleven faire stalles of Goats, whose food hath yeilde
In the extreame part of a neighbor Field.
Each Stall his Herdsman hath, an honest Swaine,
Yet every one must every day sustaine
The load of one Beast (the most fat and best
Of all the Stall-fed) to the Woers' Feast.
And I (for my part) of the Swine I keepe
(With foure more Herdsmen) every day help steep
The Wooers' appetites in blood of one,
The most select our choise can fall upon.'

Book XIV, lines 152–65

For my part, I'le not meddle with the cause:
I live a separate life amongst my Swine,
Come at no Towne for any need of mine,
Unlesse the circularly-witted Queene
(When any farre-come guest is to be seene
That brings her newes) commands me bring a Brawn—
About which (all things being in question drawne
That touch the King) they sit, and some are sad
For his long absence, some againe are glad
To waste his goods unwreak't, all talking still.

> *Book XIV, lines 522–31. Translated by
> George Chapman*

Sappho
[630–552 B.C.]

ACHTUNG

Thou shalt be—Nothing.—OMAR KHAYYAM

Tombless, with no remembrance.—SHAKESPEARE

Dead shalt thou lie; and nought
    Be told of thee or thought,
For thou hast plucked not of the Muses' tree:
    And even in Hades' halls
    Amidst thy fellow-thralls
No friendly shade thy shade shall company!

> *Translated by Thomas Hardy, with his references to
> Khayyam and Shakespeare*

Aeschylus

[525–426 B.C.]

from the AGAMEMNON

THE SIGNAL FIRE

WATCHMAN *on roof of palace* [*in Negro dialect*]:

Fo' a yeah or mo' on this roof I'se layed,
Lik a shif'less houn'dog watchin' stars,
Lawd in the morn' an at night I'se prayed,
Fo' mah massa's return frum the Trojun wars.

Look fo' a fire mah massa, he sed,
Look fo' a fire as bright as sun,
Then tell yo' missy ol' Priam's ded,
An' Troytown's down an' yo' massa's won.

So heah Ah is an' heah Ah be,
Lik a shif'less houn'dog waitin' mah king,
Sleepin' an' singin' O! woe am me,
Too scared to sleep an' too sad to sing.

'Coase mah missy am good tho mah missy am weak,
But that cahpetbagger, ain't he a sight
When massa gits back his bone'll creak,
Massa'll skin his hide an' git things right.

[*Sees the signal fire*]
O! Lawdy, O! Glory, an' what am that,
Ashinin' as big an' bright as sun,
O! lemme tell missy to stir her fat,
Fo' Troytown's down an massa's won.

[*Pauses thoughtfully*]
But trouble am comin' an trouble fo' sho,
Trouble as black as th' buzzard bird,
Cat's got mah tongue fo' all I know,
There's nuthin' I'se seen an' nuthin' I'se heard.

CHORUS OF HUMBUGS [*bureaucrats keeping the home fires*]:

1ST BUREAUCRAT:

By Zeus, you know it's been ten years,
Since the old man took the fleet to Troy,
Took a thousand ships (despite my fears)
And the best of our men, you know old boy.

2ND BUREAUCRAT:

Though it was a bit of all right to hear,
How they rallied 'bout him when he called
Screaming like eagles, no eye held a tear,
The whole bloody mess has left me appalled.

3RD BUREAUCRAT:

But let's drink up a toast to Apollo or Pan,
Or offer a prayer to Zeus for the king,
Though I'll miss out the prayer if you like, old man,
As for me, I say, the drink is the thing.

4TH BUREAUCRAT:

So up with your glasses for Atreus' seed,
And down with the nectar that makes spirits soar,
And Godspeed I say to that curious breed,
That would fight ten years for a tu'penny whore.

1st Bureaucrat:

Though infirmed are we and rheumatic with age,
We'll stoutly defend in so far as we're able,
Our pensions, our honour, and while the wars rage,
We'll still do our bit at hearth and at table.

2nd Bureaucrat: [*Clytaemnestra enters*]

Tyndareo's daughter, our most gracious queen,
Our concern is for you, noble woman,
Have you word from the king by sign or by dream,
Do you bring us fair news or ill omen?

1st Bureaucrat:

These dimm'd eyes discern that the altars are lit,
And oil's a bit dear while the war's on,
One dislikes to stint if we've won or we've quit,
But knock up the guard if it's arson.

Shall we hear from your lips dear lady and queen,
The words for which our hearts sorrow,
Have we rightly foretold by what you have seen,
Or do we eat crow on the morrow?

From us came the word that fine fowl of a pair
Resplendent in black and white habit,
Had perched at the right of your pathway out there,
Devouring a poor pregnant rabbit.

Translated by Dallam Simpson

Sophokles

[496–406 B.C.]

from WOMEN OF TRACHIS

KHOROS: *Strophe:*

Kupris bears trophies away.
Kronos' Son, Dis and Poseidon,
There is no one
            shaker unshaken.
Into dust go they all.
Neath Her they must
            give way.

Antistrophe:

Two gods fought for a girl,
Battle and dust!
Might of a River with horns
                crashing.
Four bulls together
            Shall no man tether,
Akheloös neither,
            lashing through Oneudai.

Strophe:

As bow is bent
            The Theban Cub,
Bacchus' own, spiked is his club,
He is God's Son.
                Hurled to one bed,
Might of waters like a charge of bulls crashing.

Get a dowsing rod.
Kupris decides
To whom brides
          fall.

Antistrophe:

Rock and wrack,
Horns into back,
Slug, grunt and groan,
        Grip through to bone.
Crash and thud
Bows against blood
       Grip and grind
       Bull's head and horn.

Strophe:

But the wide-eyed girl on the hill,
Out of it all,
        frail,
Who shall have her?
To stave her and prove her,
Cowless calf lost,
Hurtled away,
       prized for a day?

KHOROS: *Strophe 1:*

Oyez:
Things foretold and forecast:
Toil and moil.
God's Son from turmoil shall
—when twelve seed-crops be past—
be loosed with the last,
       his own.

Twining together, godword found good,
Spoken of old,
   as the wind blew, truth's in the flood.
We and his brood see in swift combine,
   here and at last that:
Amid the dead is no servitude
  nor do they labour.

Antistrophe 1:

Lo, beneath deadly cloud
Fate and the Centaur's curse, black venom spread.
Dank Hydra's blood
Boils now through every vein, goad after goad
from spotted snake to pierce the holy side,
nor shall he last to see a new day's light,
Black shaggy night descends
               as Nessus bade.

Strophe 2:

What mournful case
  who feared great ills to come,
New haste in mating threatening her home,
Who hark'd to reason in a foreign voice
Entangling her in ravage out of choice.
Tears green the cheek with bright dews
                pouring down.
Who mourns apart, alone
Oncoming swiftness in o'erlowering fate
To show what wreck is nested in deceit.

Antistrophe 2:

Let the tears flow.
  Ne'er had bright Herakles in his shining

Need of pity till now
   whom fell disease burns out.
How swift on Oechal's height
   to take a bride.
Black pointed shaft that shielded her in flight,
Attest
That
Kupris stood by and never said a word,
Who now flares here the contriver
manifest . . .
and indifferent.

[*The dea ex machina, hidden behind a grey gauze in her niche, is
lit up strongly so that the gauze is transparent. The apparition
is fairly sudden, the fade-out slightly slower: the audience is al-
most in doubt that she has appeared.*]

Translated by Ezra Pound

Theocritus
[fl. 270 B.C.]

from the IDYLLS

THE ENCHANTMENT

[*Samœtha being forsaken by Delphis resolves to try the force of
Charms to recover his affection; applyes herself to the Moon as a
powerful Goddess in both those matters, and after she hath sent
away her maid, tells the story of her misfortune.*]

Maid, where's my *Lawrel?* Oh my rageing Soul!
Maid, where's the *Potion?* Fill the *Bason* full,
And crown the narrow brim with *Purple* wool:
That I might charm my false, my perjur'd Swain,
And force him back into my arms again:
For *Cruel* he these Twelve long days hath fled,
And knows not whether I'me alive or dead:
He hath not broke my Doors these Twelve long days,
Ah me! perhaps his varying Love decays,
Or else he dotes upon another face.
I'le run to morrow to the *Fencing* house,
And ask him what he means to use me thus:
But now I'le charm him, *Moon,* shine bright and clear,
To thee I will direct my secret prayer;
To *Thee,* and *Hecate,* whom *Dogs* do dread
When stain'd with gore, she stalks amidst the dead:
Hail *frightful Hecate,* assist me still,
Make mine as great as fam'd *Medea's* skill:
   Jynx restore my false, my perjur'd Swain
   And force him back into my Arms again.
First burn the *Flowr,* then strew the *other* on,
Strew it. How? where's your sense and duty gone?
Base *Thestylis!* and am I so forlorn,
And grown so low that I'me become your scorn!
But strew the *Salt,* and say in angry tones
I scatter *Delphid's,* perjur'd *Delphid's* bones.
   Jynx restore my false, my perjur'd Swain
   And force him back into my Arms again.
First *Delphid* injur'd me, he rais'd my flame,
And now I burn this *Bough* in *Delphid's* name:
As this doth blaze, and break away in fume,
How soon it takes! let *Delphid's* Flesh consume.
   Jynx restore my false, my perjur'd Swain,
   And force him back into my Arms again.
As this devoted *Wax* melts o're the Fire
Let *Mindian Delphy* melt in warm desire,

Jynx: "A Bird sacred to *Venus* much used in Love Charms" [*Creech*]

And, *Venus,* as I whirl this *brazen* bowl,
Before my doors let perjur'd *Delphid* rowl:
    Jynx restore my false, my perjur'd Swain,
    And force him back into my Arms again.
Now now I strow the *Flowr, Moon* you can bow
E'en *Rhadamanth,* and all that's fierce below,
Hark *Thestilis,* our Dogs begin to howl,
The *Goddess* comes, go beat the *brazen* bowl.
    Jynx restore my false, my perjur'd Swain,
    And force him back into my Arms again.
The Sea grows smooth, and ease becalms my Wind,
But griefs still rage, and toss my troubled mind:
I burn for *Him,* for *Him* whose Arts betraid
And wrought my shame, for I'me no more a *maid.*
    Jynx restore my false, my perjur'd Swain,
    And force him back into my arms again.
Thrice, thrice I pour, and thrice repeat my charms,
What ever *Boy or Maid* now fills his arms,
Let dark oblivion spread o're *Delphid's* mind,
As dark as that, that once did *Theseus* blind
When he at *Naxos* left his Love behind.
Hippomanes a Plant *Arcadia* bears,
This makes Steeds mad, and this excites the Mares,
And Oh that I could see my *Delphid* come
From th' *Oyly Fencing* House so raveing home.
    Jynx restore my false, my perjur'd Swain,
    And force him back into my Arms again.
This piece from dear false *Delphid's* garment torn
I tear again, and am resolv'd to burn,
Ah cruel *Love!* ah most relentless God,
Why like a Leech still eager on his food,
Dost wound my heart, and suck out all my blood?
    Jynx restore my false, my perjur'd Swain,
    And force him back into my Arms again.
A *Lizzard* squeez'd shall make a powerful bowl
To morrow, strong to tame his stubborn Soul:
Now take these Poysons, I'le procure thee more,

And strew them at the *Threshold* of his door,
That door where violent *Love* hath fixt my mind,
Tho he regards not; *Cruel* and *Unkind!*
Strew them, and spitting say in angry tones,
I scatter *Delphid's*, perjur'd *Delphid's* bones.
  Jynx restore my false, my perjur'd Swain,
  And force him back into my arms again.
Now I'me alone shall I lament my state?
But where shall I begin? what wrought my Fate?
Anaxo Eubul's daughter neatly drest
Begd me to go and see *Diana's* feast,
For fame had told, *Wild beasts* must there be shown
In solem pomp, a *Lioness* was one.
  Tell sacred Moon what first did raise thy flame,
  And whence my Pain, and whence my Passion came.
With Hers my *Nurse,* did all her vows unite,
And bad me go, for 'twould be worth my sight,
So forc't, and finely drest, in Pomp and State
I went, attended by an *evil* Fate.
  Tell sacred Moon what first did raise my flame,
  And whence my Pain, and whence my Passion came.
Near *Lyco's* House break thro the yielding throng,
I saw my Delphis, vigorous, stout, and young,
A Golden Down spread o're his youthful Chin,
His breast, bright *Moon,* was brighter far than thine:
For spread with *glorious* Oyl he lately came
From *noble Fenceing,* and from winning Fame:
  Tell sacred Moon what first did raise my flame
  And whence my Pain, and whence my Passion came.
Oh when I saw, how did the sight surprize!
My *Soul* took Fire, and *sparkeld* thro my eyes,
My *Color* changd, regardless of the show
I hasted home, but came I know not how;
A burning feavour seiz'd my *thoughtful head,*
And *Twelve* long days and nights I kept my bed,
  Tell sacred Moon what first did raise my flame,
  And whence my Pain, and whence my Passion came.

My Rosy *Color* d'yd into a Pale,
My Eyes grew dim, my hair began to fall,
Meer Skin and Bones, I liv'd, I breath'd and prayd,
And sought to every Cunning man for aid:
All *charms* were try'd, and various *Figures* cast,
But ah no help, and time did swiftly wast:
> *Tell sacred Moon what first did raise my flame,*
> *And whence my Pain, and whence my Passion came.*

At last I told my Maid the naked truth,
Go *Thestilis,* have pitty on my youth;
Go find some cure to ease my rageing smart;
Young *Delphid* is the *Tyrant* of my Heart:
Go to the Fenceing House, ther's his delight,
For there he walks, and there he loves to sit.
> *Tell sacred Moon what first did raise my flame,*
> *And whence my Pain, and whence my Passion came.*

And if alone, give him a gentle Nod,
And softly tell him that *Samœtha* wou'd
(Speak, speak, tho modest fear doth strike thee dumb)
Enjoy him here, and beg him he would come.
She went, she found, and told him what I said,
He *Gladly* heard, and eagerly obey'd.
But when he came, how great was the surprize
Chills shook my *Soul,* and I grew *cold* as Ice:
> *Tell sacred Moon what first did raise my flame,*
> *And whence my Pain, and whence my Passion came.*

Cold sweat flow'd down my Cheeks like *driving* rain,
And when I strove to speak, I strove in vain;
No noise would come, not such as lulld in rest
Young *Infants* murmur o're their mothers breast:
No sign of Life did thro my Limbs appear,
But I grew stiff, stiff as this *Gold* I wear:
> *Tell sacred Moon what first did raise my flame,*
> *And whence my Pain, and whence my Passion came.*

Then *cruel* he sate down, he prest my bed,
His eyes were fixt, and as he sate he said,
Samœtha you do me as far surpass,

As I *Philistus* when we ran the race;
Too quick for me in this your kind intent,
You did my hast, tho not my wish prevent.
    Tell sacred Moon what first did raise my flame,
    And whence my Pain, and whence my Passion came.
For I had come at night, by *Love* tis true,
Unsent for I had come to wait on you:
With Apples in my Lap, with Poplar crown'd,
With Ivy twin'd, and Ribbonds neatly bound:
    Tell sacred Moon what first did raise my flame,
    And whence my Pain, and whence my Passion came.
Where if *admitted* t'had been kindly done
For I am thought the *beauty* of the Town;
And tho perhaps I wisht for greater bliss
I would have been contented with a kiss;
But if deny'd, or flam'd with dull delay
Streight fire and force had come, and broke away:
    Tell sacred Moon what first did raise my flame,
    And whence my Pain, and whence my Passion came.
But now to *Venus* my first thanks are due,
The next *Samœtha* must be paid to you,
To you *Samœtha,* you, whose gentle hand
From raging fires secur'd the flaming *brand,*
And saved poor *half-burnt* Me, for *Love* doth raise
Fires fierce as those that in hot *Ætna* blaze;
    Tell sacred Moon what first did raise my flame,
    And whence my Pain, and whence my Passion came.
Young tender *Maids* to unknown Madness drives,
And from warm *Husbands* Arms it forces Wives:
Thus *He,* and *heedless I* believ'd too soon,
He prest *My* hand in *His,* and laid me down
On the soft bed, when streight lock't Arm in Arm
In strickt embraces both grew *gently* warm;
Our *breath* was hot and short, we panting lay,
We look't, we *murmur'd,* and we dy'd away:

Our Cheeks did *glow,* and *fainting* vertue strove,
At last it yielded to the force of Love:
But what need all this talk? bright sacred Moon,
Both were well pleas'd, and some strange thing was done:
And ever since we lov'd, and liv'd at ease,
No *sullen* Minutes broke our *Happiness;*
Till soon this morning e're the Sun could rise,
And drive his Charriot thro the yielding Skies
To fetch the Rosy Morn from waves below,
I heard the fatal news, and knew my woe:
My *Maids* own *Mother,* she that lives hard by,
An Honest Woman, and she scorns to ly;
She came and askt me, is your *Delphid* kind?
And have you firm possession of his Mind?
For I am sure, but whether *Maid* or *Boy*
I cannot tell, he courts *another* joy:
For he drinks *Healths,* and when those Healths are past,
He must be gone, and goes away in hast:
Besides with Garlands all his Rooms are drest,
And he prepares, as for a Marriage Feast;
This as she walkt last night she chanc't to view,
And told it me, and oh, I fear 'tis true!
For *He* was wont to come twice, thrice a day,
He saw me still as he return'd from play;
But now since *he* was here twelve nights are past,
Am I forgotten? am I left at last?
Whilst *perjur'd* he for other Beauty burns,
My Love I'me sure deserv'd more kind returns,
But now I'le Charm, but if he scorns me still
I'le force him down to Hell, by Fate, I will:
Such powerful drugs a *Witch* did once impart
She taught me such strange Charms, such force of Art:
But now farewel bright *Moon,* turn lovely Moon
To Waves below, and drive thy Charriot down,
Go lovely *Moon,* and wake the sleepy Morn:

I'le bear my trouble still, as I have born;
Farewel, and you attending Stars that wheel
Round Nights black Axle-tree, bright Stars, farewel.

Translated by Thomas Creech

❀❀ Forty years ago I found translations from the Latin that
rank with, or surpass, English original verse of their time. I found
no comparable renderings from Greek, nor have we yet in
English any developed prosodic capacity for rendering the Alex-
andrines, or—for the matter of that—the best French techniques
as from Gautier after "Albertus" to 1917. My efforts to indicate
part of the quality of Chinese metric have been sabotaged by the
lethargy, or worse, of American endowments for the suppression
of the life of the soul. The foregoing Theocritus is rendered into,
and given as, a specimen of the style of a period. The text here
follows the edition of 1684, except for a few small concessions to
the modern reader. For Bion, *vide* note on p. 85.

Lucretius

[c. 99–55 B.C.]

from DE RERUM NATURA

"WHAT HAS THIS BUGBEAR DEATH"

What has this bugbear death to frighten man,
If souls can die, as well as bodies can?
For, as before our birth we felt no pain,
When Punic arms infested land and main,
When heav'n and earth were in confusion hurl'd,
For the debated empire of the world,

Which aw'd with dreadful expectation lay,
Sure to be slaves, uncertain who should sway:
So, when our mortal frame shall be disjoin'd,
The lifeless lump uncoupled from the mind,
From sense of grief and pain we shall be free;
We shall not feel, because we shall not *be*.
Tho' earth in seas, and seas in heav'n were lost,
We should not move, we only should be toss'd.
Nay, ev'n suppose when we have suffer'd fate,
The soul could feel in her divided state,
What's that to us? for we are only we
While souls and bodies in one frame agree.
Nay, tho' our atoms should revolve by chance,
And matter leap into the former dance;
Tho' time our life and motion could restore,
And make our bodies what they were before,
What gain to us would all this bustle bring?

Book III, lines 830–853. Translated by John Dryden

Catullus
[?84–54? B.C.]

ODI ET AMO

I hate and love. Why? You may ask but
It beats me. I feel it done to me, and ache.

LXXXV. Translated by Ezra Pound

Virgil
[70–19 B.C.]

❀❀ Virgil's *Aeneid* is available, for those who cannot read Latin, in Gavin Douglas' magnificent Scots version printed in 1553. Its richness and fervor can be judged from the opening lines, but few people can read much of it without need of a glossary, and for that reason we are not including more than this sample.

from the AENEID

"THE BATALIS AND THE MAN"

The batalis and the man I wil discrive
Fra Troyis boundis first that fugitive
By fait to Ytail come and cost Lavyne,
Our land and sey katchit with mekil pyne
By fors of goddis abuse, from euery steid,
Of cruell Iuno throu ald remembrit fede.
Gret pane in batail sufferit he alsso
Or he his goddis brocht in Latio
And belt the cite fra quham, of nobill fame,
The Latyne pepill takyn heth thar name.

Book I, lines 1–10. Translated by Gavin Douglas

Horace

[*65–8 B.C.*]

from the ODES

''BY THE FLAT CUP''

By the flat cup and the splash of new vintage
What, specifically, does the diviner ask of Apollo? Not
Thick Sardinian corn-yield nor pleasant
Ox-herds under the summer sun in Calabria, nor
Ivory nor gold out of India, nor
Land where Liris crumbles her bank in silence
Though the water seems not to move.

Let him to whom Fortune's book
Gives vines in Oporto, ply pruning hook, to the
Profit of some seller that he, the seller,
May drain Syra from gold out-size basins, a
Drink even the Gods must pay for, since he found
It is merchandise, looking back three times,
Four times a year, unwrecked from Atlantic trade-routes.

Olives feed me, and endives and mallow roots.
Delight had I healthily in what lay handy provided.
Grant me now, Latoe:
                    Full wit in my cleanly age,
Nor lyre lack me, to tune the page.

   Book I, 31

✷ ✷ Φρένες ἔμπεδοί. *Odyssey* X, 493.

"ASK NOT UNGAINLY"

Ask not ungainly askings of the end
Gods send us, me and thee, Leucothoë;
Nor juggle with the risks of Babylon,
                    Better to take whatever,
Several, or last, Jove sends us. Winter is winter,
Gnawing the Tyrrhene cliffs with the sea's tooth.

Take note of flavours, and clarity's in the wine's manifest.
Cut loose long hope for a time.
We talk. Time runs in envy of us,
Holding our day more firm in unbelief.

   Book I, 11

"THIS MONUMENT WILL OUTLAST"

This monument will outlast metal and I made it
More durable than the king's seat, higher than pyramids.
Gnaw of the wind and rain?
                    Impotent
The flow of the years to break it, however many.

Bits of me, many bits, will dodge all funeral,
O Libitina-Persephone and, after that,
Sprout new praise. As long as
Pontifex and the quiet girl pace the Capitol
I shall be spoken where the wild flood Aufidus
Lashes, and Daunus ruled the parched farmland:

Power from lowliness: "First brought Aeolic song to Italian
   fashion"—
Wear pride, work's gain! O Muse Melpomene,

By your will bind the laurel.
My hair, Delphic laurel.

Book III, 30. Translated by Ezra Pound

❊❊ The way into Horace is, generally speaking, not via his attempt to contort the Latin tongue into Greek meters, but via the *Satires* where he is using natural language, with more tact than Lucilius, who so irritated his fellow Romans that they have destroyed most of his observations—Roman life being by just that much inferior to Athenian liveliness. It starts with the XII tables, which allow you to beat up the satirists.

Idiom in the *Satires* is sometimes as simple as Ovid's, and Dr. H. R. Fairclough has made an unusual prose translation, easily accessible in the Loeb Classics.

Ovid

[43 B.C.–18 A.D.]

❊❊ Ovid has been luckier than all other writers in the matter of translation. Golding translated the *Metamorphoses* in a volume that has been called "the most beautiful book in our language." Marlowe made a version of the *Amores*. His rendering of Book I, Elegy 13 ["To the Dawn That It Hasten Not"], begins:

Now on the sea from her olde loue comes shee
That drawes the day from heaven's cold axle-tree,
Aurora whither slidest thou down againe,
And brydes from Memnon yeerly shall be slaine,

Now in her tender arms I sweetlie bide,
If euer, now well lies she by my side,
The ayre is colde, and sleep is sweetest now,
And byrdes send foorth shrill notes from every bow.
Whither runst thou, that men and women loue not?

Holde in thy rosie horses that they moue not!
Ere thou rise, stars teach seamen where to saile
But when thou comest, they of their courses faile.
Poore trauilers though tired rise at thy sight,
The painful Hinde by thee to fild is sent,
Slow oxen early in the yoke are pent,
Thou cousenest boys of sleep and dost betray them
To Pedants that with cruel lashes pay them.

❋ ❋ A very brief survey of Elizabethan translators of Latin and
Greek poets is available in Ezra Pound's *Literary Essays*, pub-
lished by New Directions. [M. S.]

from the METAMORPHOSES

ACTEON

Now *Thebes* stood in good estate, now *Cadmus* might thou say
That when thy father banisht thee it was a luckie day.
To joyne aliance both with *Mars* and *Venus* was thy chaunce,
Whose daughter thou hadst tane to wife, who did thee much
        advaunce,
Not only through hir high renowne, but through a noble race
Of sonnes and daughters that she bare: whose children in like
        case
It was thy fortune for to see all men and women growne.
But ay the ende of every thing must marked be and knowne,
For none the name of blessednesse deserveth for to have,
Unlesse the tenor of this life last blessed to his grave.
Among so many prosprous happes that flowde with good suc-
        cesse,
Thine eldest Nephew was a cause of care and sore distresse.
Whose head was armde with palmed hornes, whose own hounds
        in yᵉ wood
Did pull their master to the ground and fill them with his bloud.
But if you sift the matter well, ye shall not finde desart
But cruell fortune to have bene the cause of this his smart.

For who could doe with oversight? Great slaughter had bene made
Of sundrie sortes of savage beastes one morning, and the shade
Of things was waxed verie short. It was the time of day
That mid betweene the East and West the Sunne doth seeme to
       stay;
When as the Thebane stripling thus bespake his companie,
Still raunging in the waylesse woods some further game to spie.
Our weapons and our toyles are moist and staind with bloud of
       Deare:
This day hath done inough as by our quarrie may appeare.
Assoone as with hir scarlet wheeles next morning bringeth light,
We will about our worke againe. But now *Hiperion* bright
Is in the middes of Heaven, and seares the fieldes with firie rayes.
Take up your toyles, and ceasse your worke, and let us go our
       wayes.
They did even so, and ceast their worke. There was a valley thicke
With Pinaple and Cipresse trees that armed be with pricke.
Gargaphie hight this shadie plot, it was a sacred place
To chast *Diana* and the Nymphes that wayted on hir grace.
Within the furthest end thereof there was a pleasant Bowre
So vaulted with the leavie trees, the Sunne had there no powre:
Not made by hand nor mans devise, and yet no man alive,
A trimmer piece of worke than that could for his life contrive.
With flint and Pommy was it wallde by nature halfe about,
And on the right side of the same full freshly flowed out
A lively spring with Christall streame: whereof the upper brim
Was greene with grasse and matted herbes that smelled verie trim.
When *Phebe* felt hir selfe waxe faint, of following of hir game,
It was hir custome for to come and bath hir in the same.
That day she having timely left hir hunting in the chace,
Was entred with hir troupe of Nymphes within this pleasant
       place.
She tooke hir quiver and hir bow the which she had unbent,
And eke hir Javelin to a Nymph that served that intent.
Another Nymph to take hir clothes among hir traine she chose,
Two losde hir buskins from hir legges and pulled of hir hose.
The Thebane Ladie *Crocale* more cunning than the rest,

Did trusse hir tresses handsomly which hung behind undrest.
And yet hir owne hung waving still. Then *Niphe* nete and cleene
With *Hiale* glistring like the grash in beautie fresh and sheene,
And *Rhanis* clearer of hir skin than are the rainie drops,
And little bibling *Phyale,* and *Pseke* that pretie Mops,
Powrde water into vessels large to washe their Ladie with.
Now while she keepes this wont, behold, by wandring in the frith
He wist not whither (having staid his pastime till the morrow)
Comes *Cadmus* Nephew to this thicke: and entring in with sor-
     row
(Such was his cursed cruell fate) saw *Phebe* where she washt.
The Damsels at the sight of man quite out of countnance dasht,
(Bicause they everichone were bare and naked to the quicke)
Did beate their handes against their brests, and cast out such a
     shricke,
That all the wood did ring thereof: and clinging to their dame
Did all they could to hide both hir and eke themselves fro shame.
But *Phebe* was of personage so comly and so tall,
That by the middle of hir necke she overpeerd them all.
Such colour as appeares in Heaven by *Phebus* broken rayes
Directly shining on the Cloudes, or such as is alwayes
The colour of the Morning Cloudes before the Sunne doth show,
Such sanguine colour in the face of *Phœbe* gan to glowe
There standing naked in his sight. Who though she had hir gard
Of Nymphes about hir: yet she turnde hir bodie from him ward.
And casting backe an angrie looke, like as she would have sent
An arrow at him had she had hir bow there readie bent:
So raught the water in hir hande, and for to wreake the spight, ⎫
Besprinckled all the heade and face of the unluckie Knight,   ⎬
And thus forespake the heavie lot that should upon him light. ⎭
Now make thy vaunt among thy Mates, thou sawste *Diana* bare.
Tell if thou can: I give thee leave: tell heardly: doe not spare.
This done, she makes no further threates, but by and by doth
     spread
A payre of lively olde Harts hornes upon his sprinckled head.
She sharpes his eares, she makes his necke both slender, long and
     lanke.

She turnes his fingers into feete, his armes to spindle shanke.
She wrappes him in a hairie hyde beset with speckled spottes,
And planteth in him fearefulnesse. And so away he trottes,
Full greatly wondring to him selfe what made him in that cace
To be so wight and swift of foote. But when he saw his face
And horned temples in the brooke, he would have cryde alas,
But as for then no kinde of speach out of his lippes could passe.
He sight and brayde: for that was then the speach that did re-
    maine,
And downe the eyes that were not his, his bitter teares did raine.
No part remayned (save his minde) of that he earst had beene.
What should he doe? turne home againe to *Cadmus* and the
    Queene?
Or hyde himselfe among the Woods? Of this he was afrayd,
And of the tother ill ashamde. While doubting thus he stayd:
    His houndes espyde him where he was, and Blackfoote first of
    all
    And Stalker speciall good of sent began aloud to call.
This latter was a hound of *Crete,* the other was of *Spart.*
Then all the kenell fell in round, and everie for his part,
Dyd follow freshly in the chase more swifter than the winde,
Spy, Eateal, Scalecliffe, three good houndes comne all of *Arcas*
    kinde.
Strong Kilbucke, currish Savage, Spring, and Hunter fresh of
    smell,
And Lightfoote who to lead a chase did beare away the bell.
Fierce Woodman hurte not long ago in hunting of a Bore
And Shepeheird woont to follow sheepe and neate to fielde afore.
And Laund a fell and eger bitch that had a Wolfe to Syre:
Another brach callde Greedigut with two hir Puppies by hir.
And Ladon gant as any Greewnd a hownd in *Sycion* bred,
Blab, Fleetewood, Patch whose flecked skin w' sundrie spots was
    spred:
Wight, Bowman, Royster, beautie faire and white as winters
    snow,
And Tawnie full of duskie haires that over all did grow,
With lustie Ruffler passing all the resdue there in strength,

And Tempest best of footemanshipe in holding out at length.
And Cole, and Swift, and little Woolfe, as wight as any other,
Accompanide with a *Ciprian* hound that was his native brother,
And Snatch amid whose forehead stoode a starre as white as
    snowe,
The resdue being all as blacke and slicke as any Crowe,
And shaggie Rugge with other twaine that had a Syre of *Crete,*
And dam of *Sparta:* Tone of them callde Jollyboy, a great
And large flewd hound: the tother Chorle who ever gnoorring
    went,
And Ringwood with a shyrle loud mouth the which he freely
    spent,
With divers mo whose names to tell it were but losse of tyme.
This fellowes over hill and dale in hope of pray doe clyme.
Through thick and thin and craggie cliffes where was no way to
    go,
He flyes through groundes where oftentymes he chased had ere
    tho,
Even from his owne folke is he faine (alas) to flee away.
He strayned oftentymes to speake, and was about to say,
I am *Acteon:* know your Lorde and Mayster sirs I pray.
But use of wordes and speach did want to utter forth his minde.
Their crie did ring through all the Wood redoubled with the
    winde.
First Slo did pinch him by the haunch, and next came Kildeere
    in,
And Hylbred fastned on his shoulder, bote him through the
    skinne.
These came forth later than the rest, but coasting thwart a hill,
They did gainecope him as he came, and helde their Master still,
Untill that all the rest came in, and fastned on him to.
No part of him was free from wound. He could none other do
But sigh, and in the shape of Hart with voyce as Hartes are
    woont,
(For voyce of man was none now left to helpe him at the brunt)
By braying show his secret grief among the Mountaynes hie,
And kneeling sadly on his knees with dreerie teares in eye,

As one by humbling of himselfe that mercy seemde to crave,
With piteous looke in stead of handes his head about to wave.
Not knowing that it was their Lord, the huntsmen cheere their
    hounds
With wonted noyse and for *Acteon* looke about the grounds.
They hallow who could lowdest crie still calling him by name
As though he were not there, and much his absence they do
    blame,
In that he came not to the fall, but slackt to see the game.
As often as they named him he sadly shooke his head,
And faine he would have beene away thence in some other stead,
But there he was. And well he could have found in heart to see
His dogges fell deedes, so that to feele in place he had not bee.
They hem him in on everie side, and in the shape of Stagge,
With greedie teeth and griping pawes their Lord in peeces dragge.
So fierce was cruell *Phœbes* wrath, it could not be alayde,
Till of his fault by bitter death the raunsome he had payde.
    Much muttring was upon this fact. Some thought there was ex-
    tended
A great deale more extremitie than neded. Some commended
Dianas doing: saying that it was but worthely
For safegarde of hir womanhod. Eche partie did applie
Good reasons to defende their case. . . .

Book III, lines 150–309

DAEDALUS

Now in this while gan *Dædalus* a wearinesse to take
Of living like a banisht man and prisoner such a time
In *Crete,* and longed in his heart to see his native Clime.
But Seas enclosed him as if he had in prison be.
Then thought he: though both Sea and land King *Minos* stop fro
    me,
I am assurde he cannot stop the Aire and open Skie:
To make my passage that way then my cunning will I trie.

Although that *Minos* like a Lord held all the world beside:
Yet doth the Aire from *Minos* yoke for all men free abide.
This sed: to uncoth Arts he bent the force of all his wits
To alter natures course by craft. And orderly he knits
A rowe of fethers one by one, beginning with the short,
And overmatching still eche quill with one of longer sort,
That on the shoring of a hill a man would thinke them grow.
Even so the countrie Organpipes of Oten reedes in row
Ech higher than another rise. Then fastned he with Flax
The middle quilles, and joyned in the lowest sort with Wax.
And when he thus had finisht them, a little he them bent
In compasse, that the verie Birdes they full might represent.
There stoode ne by him *Icarus* his sonne a pretie Lad:
Who knowing not that he in handes his owne destruction had,
With smiling mouth did one while blow the fethers to and fro
Which in the Aire on wings of Birds did flask not long ago:
And with his thumbes another while he chafes the yelow Wax
And lets his fathers wondrous worke with childish toyes and knax.
Assoone as that the worke was done, the workman by and by
Did peyse his bodie on his wings, and in the Aire on hie
Hung wavering: and did teach his sonne how he should also flie.
I warne thee (quoth he) *Icarus* a middle race to keepe.
For if thou hold to low a gate, the dankenesse of the deepe
Will overlade thy wings with wet. And if thou mount to hie,
The Sunne will sindge them. Therefore see betweene them both
    thou flie.
I bid thee not behold the Starre *Boötes* in the Skie,
Nor looke upon the bigger Beare to make thy course thereby,
Nor yet on *Orions* naked sword. But ever have an eie
To keepe the race that I doe keepe, and I will guide thee right.
In giving counsell to his sonne to order well his flight,
He fastned to his shoulders twaine a paire of uncoth wings.
And as he was in doing it and warning him of things,
His aged cheekes were wet, his handes did quake, in fine he gave
His sonne a kisse the last that he alive should ever have.
And then he mounting up aloft before him tooke his way
Right fearfull for his followers sake: as is the Bird the day

That first she tolleth from hir nest among the braunches hie
Hir tender yong ones in the Aire to teach them for to flie.
So heartens he his little sonne to follow teaching him
A hurtfull Art. His owne two wings he waveth verie trim,
And looketh backward still upon his sonnes. The fishermen
Then standing angling by the Sea, and shepeherdes leaning then
On sheepehookes, and the Ploughmen on the handles of their
  Plough,
Beholding them, amazed were: and thought that they that
  through
The Aire could flie were Gods. And now did on their left side
  stand
The Iles of *Paros* and of *Dele,* and *Samos, Junos* land:
And on their right, *Lebinthos,* and the faire *Calydna* fraught
With store of honie: when the Boy a frolicke courage caught
To flie at randon. Whereupon forsaking quight his guide,
Of fond desire to flie to Heaven, above his boundes he stide.
And there the nerenesse of the Sunne which burnd more hote
  aloft,
Did make the Wax (with which his wings were glewed) lithe and
  soft.
Assoone as that the Wax was molt, his naked armes he shakes,
And wanting wherewithall to wave, no helpe of Aire he takes.
But calling on his father loud he drowned in the wave:
And by this chaunce of his, those Seas his name for ever have.
His wretched Father (but as then no father) cride in feare
O *Icarus* O *Icarus* where art thou? tell me where
That I may finde thee *Icarus.* He saw the fethers swim
Upon the waves, and curst his Art that so had spighted him.
At last he tooke his bodie up and laid it in a grave,
And to the Ile the name of him then buried in it gave.

Book VIII, lines 245–313

MELEAGER

There was the sonne of *Ampycus* of great forecasting wit:
And *Oeclies* sonne who of his wife was unbetrayed yit.
And from the Citie *Tegea* there came the Paragone
Of *Lycey* forrest, *Atalant,* a goodly Ladie, one
Of *Schœnyes* daughters, then a Maide. The garment she did weare
A brayded button fastned at hir gorget. All hir heare
Untrimmed in one only knot was trussed. From hir left
Side hanging on hir shoulder was an Ivorie quiver deft:
Which being full of arrowes, made a clattring as she went.
And in hir right hand shee did beare a Bow already bent.
Hir furniture was such as this. Hir countnance and hir grace
Was such as in a Boy might well be cald a Wenches face,
And in a Wench be cald a Boyes. The Prince of *Calydon*
No sooner cast his eie on hir, but being caught anon
In love, he wisht hir to his wife: but unto this desire
God *Cupid* gave not his consent. The secret flames of fire
He haling inward still did say: O happy man is he
Whom this same Ladie shall vouchsafe hir husband for to be.
The shortnesse of the time and shame would give him leave to
    say
No more: a worke of greater weight did draw him then away.
    A wood thick growen with trees which stoode unfelled to that
        day
        Beginning from a plaine, had thence a large prospect through-
        out
The falling grounds that every way did muster round about.
Assoone as that the men came there, some pitched up the toyles,
Some tooke the couples from the Dogs, and some pursude the
    foyles
In places where the Swine had tract: desiring for to spie
Their owne destruction. Now there was a hollow bottom by,
To which the watershots of raine from all the high grounds drew.
Within the compasse of this pond great store of Oysyers grew:
And Sallowes lithe, and flackring Flags, and moorish Rushes eke,

the sonne of Ampycus: Mopsus   *Oeclies sonne:* Amphiardus

And lazie Reedes on little shankes, and other baggage like.
From hence the Bore was rowzed out, and fiersly forth he flies
Among the thickest of his foes like thunder from the Skies,
When Clouds in meeting force the fire to burst by violence out.
He beares the trees before him downe, and all the wood about
Doth sound of crashing. All the youth with hideous noyse and
    shout
Against him bend their Boarspeare points with hand and courage
    stout.
He rushes forth among the Dogs that held him at a bay,
And now on this side now on that, as any come in way,
He rippes their skinnes and splitteth them, and chaseth them
    away.
Echion first of all the rout a Dart at him did throw,
Which mist, and in a Maple tree did give a little blow.
The next (if he that threw the same had used lesser might,)
The backe at which he aimed it was likely for to smight.
It overflew him. *Jason* was the man that cast the Dart.
With that the sonne of *Ampycus* sayd: *Phœbus* (if with hart
I have and still doe worship thee) now graunt me for to hit
The thing that I doe levell at. *Apollo* graunts him it
As much as lay in him to graunt. He hit the Swine in deede:
But neyther entred he his hide nor caused him to bleede,
For why *Diana* (as the Dart was flying) tooke away
The head of it: and so the Dart could headlesse beare no sway.
But yet the moodie beast thereby was set the more on fire:
And chafing like the lightning swift he uttreth forth his ire.
The fire did sparkle from his eyes: and from his boyling brest
He breathed flaming flakes of fire conceyved in his chest.
And looke with what a violent brunt a mightie Bullet goes
From engines bent against a wall, or bulwarks full of foes:
With even such violence rusht the Swine among the Hunts a
    mayne,
And overthrew *Eupalamon* and *Pelagon* both twaine
That in the right wing placed were. Their fellowes stepping to
And drawing them away, did save their lives with much a do.
But as for poore *Enesimus Hippocoons* sonne had not

The lucke to scape the deadly dint. He would away have got,
And trembling turnde his back for feare. The Swine him over-
tooke,
And cut his hamstrings, so that streight his going him forsooke.
And *Nœstor* to have lost his life was like by fortune ere
The siege of *Troie*, but that he tooke his rist upon his speare:
And leaping quickly up upon a tree that stoode hard by,
Did safely from the place behold his foe whome he did flie.
The Boare then whetting sharpe his tuskes against the Oken
wood,
To mischiefe did prepare himselfe with fierce and cruell mood.
And trusting to his weapons which he sharpened had a new,
In great *Orithyas* thigh a wound with hooked groyne he drew.
The valiant brothers those same twinnes of *Tyndarus* (not yet
Celestiall signes) did both of them on goodly coursers sit ⎫
As white as snow: and ech of them had shaking in his fist ⎬
A lightsome Dart with head of steele to throw it where he lyst: ⎭
And for to wound the bristled Bore they surely had not mist,
But that he still recovered so the coverts of the wood,
That neyther horse could follow him, nor Dart doe any good.
Still after followed *Telamon:* whom taking to his feete
No heede at all for eagernesse, a Maple roote did meete,
Which tripped up his heeles, and flat against the ground him laid.
And while his brother *Peleus* relieved him, the Maid
Of *Tegea* tooke an arrow swift, and shot it from hir bow.
The arrow lighting underneath the havers eare bylow,
And somewhat rasing of the skin, did make the bloud to show.
The Maid hirselfe not gladder was to see that luckie blow,
Than was the Prince *Meleager*. He was the first that saw,
And first that shewed to his Mates the blud that she did draw:
And said, for this thy valiant act due honor shalt thou have.
The men did blush, and chearing up ech other, courage gave
With shouting, and disorderly their Darts by heaps they threw.
The number of them hindred them, not suffring to ensew
That any lighted on the marke at which they all did ame.

the valiant brothers: Castor and Pollux

Behold, enragde against his ende, the hardie Knight that came
From *Arcadie,* rusht rashly with a Pollax in his fist,
And said, you yonglings learne of me what difference is betwist
A wenches weapons and a mans: and all of you give place
To my redoubted force. For though *Diana* in this chase
Should with hir owne shielde him defend, yet should this hand of
    mine,
Even maugre Dame *Dianaas* heart, confound this orped Swine.
Such boasting words as these through pride presumptuously he
    crakes:
And streyning out himselfe upon his tiptoes, streight he takes
His Pollax up with both his hands. But as this bragger ment
To fetch his blow, the cruell beast his malice did prevent:
And in his coddes (the speeding place of death) his tushes puts,
And rippeth up his paunche. Downe falles *Ancæus* and his guts
Come tumbling out besmearde with bloud, and foyled all the
    plot.
Pirithous Ixions sonne at that abashed not:
But shaking in his valiant hand his hunting staffe did goe
Still stoutly forward face to face t'encounter with his foe.
To whome Duke *Theseus* cride a farre. O dearer unto mee
Than is my selfe, my soule I say, stay: lawfull we it see
For valiant men to keepe aloofe. The over hardie hart
In rash adventring of him selfe hath made *Ancæus* smart.
This sed, he threw a weightie Dart of Cornell with a head
Of brasse: which being leveld well was likely to have sped,
But that a bough of Chestnut tree thicke leaved by the way
Did latch it, and by meanes therof the dint of it did stay.
Another Dart that *Jason* threw, by fortune mist the Bore,
And light betwene a Maistifes chaps, and through his guts did
    gore,
And naild him to the earth. The hand of Prince *Meleager*
Plaid hittymissie. Of two Darts his first did flie so far,
And lighted in the ground: the next amid his backe stickt fast.
And while the Bore did play the fiend and turned round agast,
And grunting flang his fome about togither mixt with blood

The giver of the wound (the more to stirre his enmies mood,)
Stept in, and underneath the shield did thrust his Boarspeare
   through.
Then all the Hunters shouting out demeaned joy inough,
And glad was he that first might come to take him by the hand.
About the ugly beast they all with gladnesse gazing stand,
And wondring what a field of ground his carcasse did possesse,
There durst not any be so bolde to touch him. Nerethelesse,
They every of them with his bloud their hunting staves made red.
Then stepped forth *Meleager,* and treading on his hed
Said thus: O Ladie *Atalant,* receive thou here my fee,
And of my glorie vouch thou safe partaker for to bee.
Immediatly the ugly head with both the tusshes brave,
And eke the skin with bristles stur right griesly, he hir gave.
The Ladie for the givers sake, was in hir heart as glad
As for the gift. The rest repinde that she such honor had.
Through all the rout was murmuring: Of whom with roring ⎤
   reare   ⎥
And armes displayd that all the field might easly see and heare, ⎬
The *Thesties* cried, Dame come of, and lay us downe this geare: ⎦
And thou a woman offer not us men so great a shame,
As we to toyle, and thou to take the honor of our game.
Ne let that faire smooth face of thine beguile thee, least that hee
That being doted in thy love did give thee this our fee,
Be over farre to rescow thee. And with that word they tooke
The gift from hir, and right of gift from him. He could not
   brooke
This wrong: but gnashing with his teeth for anger that did boyle
Within, said fiersly: learne ye you that other folkes dispoyle
Of honor given, what diffrence is betweene your threats, and
   deedes.
And therewithall *Plexippus* brest (who no such matter dreedes)
With wicked weapon he did pierce. As *Toxey* doubting stood
What way to take, desiring both t'advenge his brothers blood,
And fearing to be murthered as his brother was before:
Meleager (to dispatch all doubts of musing any more)

Did heate his sword for companie in bloud of him againe,
Before *Plexippus* bloud was cold that did thereon remaine.
  Althæa going toward Church with presents for to yild
    Due thankes and worship to the Gods bycause hir sonne had
    kild
The Boare, beheld hir brothers brought home dead: and by and
    by
She beate hir brest, and filde the towne with shrieking piteously,
And shifting all hir rich aray, did put on mourning weede.
But when she understoode what man was doer of the deede,
She left all mourning, and from teares to vengeance did pro-
    ceede.
There was a certaine firebrand which when *Oenies* wife did lie
In childebed of *Meleagar,* she chaunced to espie
The Destnies putting in the fire: and in the putting in,
She heard them speake these words, as they his fatall threede did
    spin:
O lately borne, like time we give to thee and to this brand.
And when they so had spoken, they departed out of hand.
Immediatly the mother caught the blazing bough away,
And quenched it. This bough she kept full charely many a day:
And in the keeping of the same she kept hir sonne alive.
And now intending of his life him clearely to deprive,
She brought it forth, and causing all the coales and shivers to
Be layëd by, she like a foe did kindle fire thereto.
Fowre times she was about to cast the firebrand in the flame:
Fowre times she pulled backe hir hand from doing of the same.
As moother and as sister both she strove what way to go:
The divers names drew diversly hir stomacke to and fro.
Hir face waxt often pale for feare of mischiefe to ensue:
And often red about the eies through heate of ire she grew.
One while hir looke resembled one that threatned cruelnesse:
Another while ye would have thought she minded pitiousnesse.
And though the cruell burning of hir heart did drie hir teares,
Yet burst out some. And as a Boate which tide contrarie beares
Against the winde, feeles double force, and is compeld to yeelde

To both: So *Thesties* daughter now unable for to weelde
Hir doubtfull passions, diversly is caried of and on:
And chaungeably she waxes calme, and stormes againe anon.
But better sister ginneth she than mother for to be.
And to thintent hir brothers ghostes with bloud to honor, she
In meaning to be one way kinde, doth worke another way
Against kinde. When the plagie fire waxt strong, she thus did say:
Let this same fire my bowels burne. And as in cursed hands
The fatall wood she holding at the Hellish Altar stands,
She said: ye triple Goddesses of wreake, ye Helhounds three,
Beholde ye all this furious fact and sacrifice of mee.
I wreake, and do against all right: with death must death be
     payde:
On mischiefe mischiefe must be heapt: on corse must corse be
     laide:
Confounded let this wicked house with heaped sorrowes bee.
Shall *Oenie* joy his happy sonne in honor for to see,
And *Thestie* mourne bereft of his? Nay: better yet it were,
That eche with other companie in mourning you should beare.
Ye brothers Ghostes and soules new dead, I wish no more, but you
To feele the solemne obsequies which I prepare as now:
And that mine offring you accept, which dearly I have bought,
The yssue of my wretched wombe. Alas, alas what thought
I for to doe? O brothers I besech you beare with me:
I am his mother: so to doe my hands unable be.
His trespasse I confesse deserves the stopping of his breath:
But yet I doe not like that I be Author of his death.
And shall he then with life and limme, and honor to, scape free,
And vaunting in his good successe the King of *Calidon* bee,
And you deare soules lie raked up but in a little dust?
I will not surely suffer it. But let the villaine trust
That he shall die, and draw with him to ruine and decay
His Kingdome, Countrie, and his Sire that doth upon him stay.
Why, where is now the mothers heart and pitie that should raigne
In Parents? and the ten Monthes paines that once I did sustaine?
O would to God thou burned had a babie in this brand,

And that I had not tane it out and quencht it with my hand.
That all this while thou lived hast, my goodnesse is the cause,
And now most justly unto death thine owne desert thee drawes.
Receive the guerdon of thy deede: and render thou agen
Thy twice given life, by bearing first, and secondarly when
I caught this firebrand from the flame: or else come deale with
     me
As with my brothers, and with them let me entumbed be.
I would, and cannot. What then shall I stand to in this case?
One while my brothers corses seeme to prease before my face
With lively Image of their deaths. Another while my minde
Doth yeelde to pitie, and the name of mother doth me blinde.
Now wo is me. To let you have the upper hand is sinne:
But nerethelesse the upper hand O brothers doe you win,
Condicionly that when that I to comfort you withall
Have wrought this feate, my selfe to you resort in person shall.
     This sed, she turnde away hir face, and with a trembling hand
     Did cast the deathfull brand amid the burning fire. The brand
Did eyther sigh, or seeme to sigh in burning in the flame,
Which sorie and unwilling was to fasten on the same.
Meleager being absent and not knowing ought at all,
Was burned with this flame: and felt his bowels to appall
With secret fire. He bare out long the paine with courage stout.
But yet it grieved him to die so cowardly, without
The shedding of his bloud. He thought *Anceus* for to be
A happie man that dide of wound. With sighing called he
Upon his aged father, and his sisters, and his brother,
And lastly on his wife to, and by chaunce upon his mother.
His paine encreased with the fire, and fell therewith againe:
And at the selfe same instant quight extinguisht were both
     twaine.
And as the ashes soft and hore by leysure overgrew
The glowing coales: so leysurly his spirit from him drew.

Book VIII, lines 424–680

PHILEMON AND BAUCIS

Pirithous being over hault of mynde and such a one
As did despyse bothe God and man, did laugh them everychone
Too scorne for giving credit, and sayd thus. The woords thou
    spaakst
Are feyned fancies *Acheloy:* and overstrong thou maakst
The Gods: to say that they can give and take way shapes. This
    scoffe
Did make the heerers all amazde, for none did like thereof.
And *Lelex* of them all the man most rype in yeeres and wit,
Sayd thus. Unmeasurable is the powre of heaven, and it
Can have none end. And looke what God dooth mynd too bring
    about,
Must take effect. And in this case too put yee out of dout.
    Upon the hilles of *Phrygie* neere a Teyle there stands a tree
    Of Oke enclosed with a wall. Myself the place did see.
For *Pithey* untoo *Pelops* feelds did send mee where his father
Did sumtyme reigne. Not farre fro thence there is a poole which
    rather
Had bene dry ground inhabited. But now it is a meare
And Moorecoks, Cootes, and Cormorants doo breede and nestle
    there.
The mightie *Jove* and *Mercurie* his sonne in shape of men
Resorted thither on a tyme. A thousand houses when
For roome too lodge in they had sought, a thousand houses bard
Theyr doores against them. Nerethelesse one Cotage afterward
Receyved them, and that was but a pelting one in deede.
The roofe therof was thatched all with straw and fennish reede.
Howbeet twoo honest auncient folke, (of whom shee *Baucis* hight
And he *Philemon*) in that Cote theyr fayth in youth had plight.
And in that Cote had spent theyr age. And for they paciently
Did beare their simple povertie, they made it light thereby,
And shewed it no thinge to bee repyned at at all.
It skilles not whether there for Hyndes or Maister you doo call,

Teyle: Latin, *tilia,* linden; French, *tilleul*   *pelting:* paltry, worthless, insig-
nificant

For all the houshold were but two: and both of them obeyde,
And both commaunded. When the Gods at this same Cotage
     staid,
And ducking downe their heads, within the low made Wicket
     came,
Philemon bringing ech a stoole, bade rest upon the same
Their limmes: and busie *Baucis* brought them quishons homely
     geere.
Which done, the embers on the harth she gan abrode to steere,
And laid the coales togither that were raakt up overnight,
And with the brands and dried leaves did make them gather
     might,
And with the blowing of hir mouth did make them kindle bright.
Then from an inner house she fetcht seare sticks and clifted
     brands,
And put them broken underneath a Skillet with hir hands.
Hir Husband from their Gardenplot fetcht Coleworts. Of the
     which
She shreaded small the leaves, and with a Forke tooke downe a
     flitche
Of restie Bacon from the Balke made blacke with smoke, and cut
A peece thereof, and in the pan to boyling did it put.
And while this meate a seething was, the time in talke they spent,
By meanes whereof away without much tedousnesse it went.
There hung a Boawle of Beeche upon a spirget by a ring.
The same with warmed water filld the twoo old folke did bring
To bathe their guests foule feete therein. Amid the house there
     stood
A Couch whose bottom sides and feete were all of Sallow wood,
And on the same a Mat of Sedge. They cast upon this bed
A covering which was never wont upon it too be spred
Except it were at solemne feastes: and yet the same was olde
And of the coursest, with a bed of sallow meete to holde.
The Gods sate downe. The aged wife right chare and busie as
A Bee, set out a table, of the which the thirde foote was

---

quishons: cushions   *Coleworts:* specifically cabbage, any green like kale
restie: rancid; old French, *reste*   *spirget:* ear or handle of a cup or pot
chare: careful, cautious

A little shorter than the rest. A tylesherd made it even
And tooke away the shoringnesse: and when they had it driven
To stand up levell, with greene Mintes they by and by it wipte.
Then set they on it *Pallas* fruite with dubble colour stripte,
And Cornels kept in pickle moyst, and Endive, and a roote
Of Radish, and a jolly lump of Butter fresh and soote,
And Egges reare rosted. All these Cates in earthen dishes came.
Then set they downe a graven cup made also of the same
Selfe kinde of Plate, and Mazers made of Beech, whose inner syde
Was rubd with yellow wax. And when they pawsed had a tyde,
Whote meate came pyping from the fyre. And shortly thereupon
A cup of greene hedg wyne was brought. This tane away, anon
Came in the latter course, which was of Nuts, Dates, dryed figges,
Sweete smelling Apples in a Mawnd made flat of Oysyer twigges.
And Prunes and Plums and Purple grapes cut newly from the
    tree,
And in the midst a honnycomb new taken from the Bee.
Besydes all this there did ensew good countnance overmore,
With will not poore nor nigardly. Now all the whyle before,
As often as *Philemon* and Dame *Baucis* did perceyve
The emptie Cup to fill alone, and wyne too still receyve,
Amazed at the straungenesse of the thing, they gan streyght way
With fearfull harts and hands hilld up too frame themselves too
    pray,
Desyring for theyr slender cheere and fare too pardoned bee;
They had but one poore Goose which kept theyr little Tennan-
    tree,
And this too offer too the Gods theyr guestes they did intend.
The Gander wyght of wing did make the slow old folke too spend
Theyr paynes in vayne, and mokt them long. At length he seemd
    too flye
For succor too the Gods themselves, who bade he should not dye,

---

tylesherd: piece of broken tile   *shoringnesse:* Cooper's Thesaurus uses this
passage to illustrate meaning unevenness, get it propped up.   *Pallas fruite:*
olives   *reare:* used only of eggs, slightly cooked   *Cates:* choice viands,
dainties   *Mazers:* originally maple, from which drinking cups without a
foot were made   *Mawnd:* maund, a wicker or woven basket

For wee bee Gods (quoth they) and all this wicked towneship shall
Abye their gylt. On you alone this mischeef shall not fall.
No more but give you up your house, and follow up this hill
Toogither, and upon the top thereof abyde our will.
They bothe obeyd. And as the Gods did lead the way before, ⎤
They lagged slowly after with theyr staves, and labored sore ⎬
Ageinst the rysing of the hill. They were not mickle more ⎦
Than full a flyghtshot from the top, when looking backe they saw
How all the towne was drowned save their lyttle shed of straw.
And as they woondred at the thing and did bewayle the case
Of those that had their neyghbours beene, the old poore Cote so
    base
Whereof they had beene owners erst, became a Church. The
    proppes
Were turned into pillars howge: The straw uppon the toppes
Was yellow, so that all the roof did seeme of burnisht gold:
The floore with Marble paved was: The doores on eyther fold
Were graven. At the sight hereof *Philemon* and his make
Began too pray in feare. Then *Jove* thus gently them bespake.
Declare thou ryghtuowse man, and thou O woman meete too have
A ryghtuowse howsband what yee would most cheefly wish or
    crave.
Philemon taking conference a little with his wyfe,
Declared bothe theyr meenings thus. We covet during lyfe,
Your Chapleynes for too bee too keepe your Temple. And bycause
Our yeeres in concord wee have spent, I pray when death neere
    drawes
Let bothe of us toogither leave our lives: that neyther I
Behold my wyves deceace, nor shee see myne when I doo dye.
Theyr wish had sequele to theyr wyll. As long as lyfe did last,
They kept the Church. And beeing spent with age of yeares fore-
    past,
By chaunce as standing on a tyme without the Temple doore
They told the fortune of the place, *Philemon* old and poore
Saw *Baucis* floorish greene with leaves, and *Baucis* saw likewyse
Philemon braunching out in boughes and twigs before hir eyes.
And as the Bark did overgrow the heades of bothe, eche spake

Too other whyle they myght. At last they eche of them did take
Theyr leave of other bothe at once, and therewithall the bark
Did hyde theyr faces both at once. The *Phrygians* in that park
Doo at this present day still shew the trees that shaped were
Of theyr twoo bodies, growing yit togither joyntly there.
Theis things did aunctent men report of credit verie good.
For why there was no cause why they should lye. As I there stood
I saw the garlands hanging on the boughes, and adding new   ⎤
I sayd let them whom God dooth love be Gods, and honor dew   ⎬
Bee given to such as honor him with feare and reverence trew. ⎦

   Book VIII, lines 785–909

❋ ❋ Similar details of reception of guest by humble hostess were
in the almost wholly lost *Hecale* of Kallimachus.

KING MIDAS

But *Bacchus* was not so content: he quyght forsooke their land,
   And with a better companye removed out of hand
Unto the Vyneyarde of his owne mount *Tmolus,* and the river
Pactolus though as yit no streames of gold it did deliver,
Ne spyghted was for precious sands. His olde accustomd rout
Of woodwards and of franticke froes envyrond him about.
But old *Silenus* was away. The *Phrygian* ploughmen found
Him reeling bothe for droonkennesse and age, and brought him
   bound
With garlands, unto *Midas* king of *Phrygia,* unto whom
The *Thracian* Orphye and the preest *Eumolphus* comming from
The towne of *Athens* erst had taught the Orgies. When he knew
His fellowe and companion of the selfe same badge and crew:
Uppon the comming of this guest, he kept a feast the space
Of twyce fyve dayes and twyce fyve nyghts toogither in that place.
And now theleventh tyme *Lucifer* had mustred in the sky
The heavenly host, when *Midas* commes too *Lydia* jocundly
And yeeldes the old *Silenus* too his fosterchyld. He glad

That he his fosterfather had eftsoones recovered, bad
King *Midas* ask him what he would. Right glad of that was hee,
But not a whit at latter end the better should he bee.
He minding too misuse his giftes, sayd: graunt that all and some
The which my body towcheth bare may yellow gold become.
God *Bacchus* graunting his request, his hurtfull gift performd,
And that he had not better wisht he in his stomacke stormd.
 Rejoycing in his harme away full merye goes the king:
 And for too try his promis true he towcheth every thing.
Scarce giving credit too himself, he pulled yoong greene twiggs
From of an Holmetree: by and by all golden were the spriggs.
He tooke a flintstone from the ground, the stone likewyse became
Pure gold. He towched next a clod of earth, and streight the same
By force of towching did become a wedge of yellow gold.
He gathered eares of rypened corne: immediatly, beholde,
The corne was gold. An Apple then he pulled from a tree:
Yee would have thought the *Hesperids* had given it him. If hee
On Pillars high his fingars layd, they glistred like the sonne.
The water where he washt his hands did from his hands so ronne,
As *Danae* might have beene therwith beguyld. He scarce could
 hold
His passing joyes within his hart, for making all things gold.
Whyle he thus joyd, his officers did spred the boord anon,
And set downe sundry sorts of meate and mancheate theruppon.
Then whither his hand did towch the bread, the bread was massy
 gold:
Or whither he chawde with hungry teeth his meate, yee might be-
 hold
The peece of meate betweene his jawes a plate of gold too bee.
In drinking wine and water mixt, yee myght discerne and see
The liquid gold ronn downe his throte. Amazed at the straunge
Mischaunce, and being both a wretch and rich, he wisht too
 chaunge
His riches for his former state, and now he did abbhorre
The thing which even but late before he cheefly longed for.
No meate his hunger slakes: his throte is shrunken up with
 thurst:

And justly dooth his hatefull gold torment him as accurst.
Then lifting up his sory armes and handes too heaven, he cryde:
O father *Bacchus* pardon mee. My sinne I will not hyde.
Have mercy I beseech thee and vouchsauf too rid mee quyght
From this same harme that seemes so good and glorious untoo
   syght.
The gentle *Bacchus* streight upon confession of his cryme
Restored *Midas* too the state hee had in former tyme.
And having made performance of his promis, hee beereft him
The gift that he had graunted him. And least he should have left
   him
Beedawbed with the dregges of that same gold which wickedly
Hee wisshed had, he willed him too get him by and by
Too that great ryver which dooth ronne by *Sardis* towne, and
   there
Along the chanell up the streame his open armes to beare
Untill he commeth too the spring: and then his head too put
Full underneathe the foming spowt where greatest was the gut,
And so in wasshing of his limbes too wash away his cryme.
The king (as was commaunded him) ageinst the streame did
   clyme.
And streyght the powre of making gold departing quyght from
   him,
Infects the ryver, making it with golden streame too swim.
The force thereof the bankes about so soked in theyr veynes,
That even as yit the yellow gold uppon the cloddes remaynes.
   Then *Midas* hating riches haunts the pasturegrounds and
      groves,
      And up and down with *Pan* among the Lawnds and moun-
      taines roves.
But still a head more fat than wyse, and doltish wit he hath,
The which as erst, yit once againe must woork theyr mayster scath.
The mountayne *Tmole* from loftye toppe too seaward looketh
   downe,
And spreading farre his boorely sydes, extendeth too the towne
Of *Sardis* with the tonesyde and too *Hypep* with the toother.
There *Pan* among the fayrye elves that dawnced round toogither

In setting of his conning out for singing and for play
Uppon his pype of reedes and wax, presuming for too say
Apollos musick was not like too his, did take in hand
A farre unequall match, wherof the *Tmole* for judge should stand.
The auncient judge sitts downe uppon his hill, and ridds his
    eares
From trees: and onely on his head an Oken garlond weares,
Wherof the Acornes dangled downe about his hollow brow.
And looking on the God of neate he sayd: yee neede not now
Too tarry longer for your judge. Then *Pan* blew lowd and strong⎤
His country pype of reedes, and with his rude and homely song ⎬
Delighted *Midas* eares, for he by chaunce was in the throng. ⎦
When *Pan* had doone, the sacred *Tmole* too *Phebus* turnd his
    looke,
And with the turning of his head his busshye heare he shooke.
Then *Phebus* with a crowne of Bay uppon his golden heare
Did sweepe the ground with scarlet robe. In left hand he did
    beare
His viall made of precious stones and Ivorye intermixt,
And in his right hand for too strike, his bowe was reedy fixt:
He was the verrye paterne of a good Musician ryght.   ⎤
Anon he gan with conning hand the tuned strings too smyght,   ⎬
The sweetenesse of the which did so the judge of them delyght,   ⎦
That *Pan* was willed for to put his Reedepype in his cace
And not too fiddle nor too sing where vialls were in place.
    The judgement of the holy hill was lyked well of all,
    Save *Midas,* who found fault therwith and wrongfull did it call.
Apollo could not suffer well his foolish eares too keepe
Theyr humaine shape, but drew them wyde, and made them
    long and deepe,
And filld them full of whytish heares, and made them downe too
    sag,
And through too much unstablenesse continually too wag.
His body keeping in the rest his manly figure still,
Was ponnisht in the part that did offend for want of skill.
And so a slowe paaste Asses eares his heade did after beare.
This shame endevereth he too hyde. And therefore he did weare

A purple nyghtcappe ever since. But yit his Barber who
Was woont too notte him spyëd it: and beeing eager too
Disclose it, when he neyther durst too utter it, nor could
It keepe in secret still, hee went and digged up the mowld,
And whispring softly in the pit, declaard what eares hee spyde
His mayster have, and turning downe the clowre ageine, did hyde
His blabbed woordes within the ground, and closing up the pit
Departed thence and never made mo woordes at all of it.
Soone after, there began a tuft of quivering reedes too growe
Which beeing rype bewrayd theyr seede and him that did them
     sowe:
For when the gentle sowtherne wynd did lyghtly on them blowe,
They uttred foorth the wordes that had been buried in the
     ground,
And so reprovde the Asses eares of *Midas* with theyr sound.

   Book XI, lines 94–216

CYCLOPS

More whyght thou art then Primrose leaf my Lady *Galatee,*
More fresh than meade, more tall and streyght than lofty Al-
     dertree,
More bright than glasse, more wanton than the tender kid for-
     sooth,
Than Cockleshelles continually with water worne, more smoothe,
More cheerefull than the winters Sun, or Sommers shadowe cold,
More seemely and more comly than the Planetree too behold,
Of valew more than Apples bee although they were of gold:
More cleere than frozen yce, more sweete than Grape through
     rype ywis,
More soft than butter newly made, or downe of Cygnet is;
And much more fayre and beawtyfull than gardein too myne eye,
But that thou from my companye continually doost flye.
And thou the selfsame *Galate,* art more tettish for too frame
Than Oxen of the wildernesse whom never wyght did tame:

More fleeting than the waves, more hard than warryed Oke too
    twyne,
More tough than willow twiggs, more lyth than is the wyld
    whyght vyne:
More than this rocke unmovable, more violent than a streame,
More prowd than Peacocke praysd, more feerce than fyre and
    more extreeme:
More rough than Breers, more cruell than the new delivered
    Beare,
More mercilesse than troden snake, than sea more deafe of eare:
And which (and if it lay in mee I cheefly would restrayne)
Not only swifter paced than the stag in chace on playne,
But also swifter than the wynd and flyghtful ayre. But if
Thou knew me well, it would thee irke to flye and bee a greef
Too tarrye from mee. Yea thou wouldst endevor all thy powre
Too keepe mee wholly too thy self. The Quarry is my bowre
Heawen out of whole mayne stone. No Sun in sommer there can
    swelt,
No nipping cold in wintertyme within the same is felt.
Gay Apples weying downe the boughes have I, and Grapes like
    gold,
And purple Grapes on spreaded Vynes as many as can hold,
Bothe which I doo reserve for thee. Thyself shalt with thy hand
The soft sweete strawbryes gather, which in wooddy shadowe
    stand.
The Cornell berryes also from the tree thy self shalt pull,
And pleasant plommes, sum yellow lyke new wax, sum blew, sum
    full
Of ruddy jewce. Of Chestnutts eeke (if my wyfe thou wilt bee)
Thou shalt have store: and frutes all sortes: All trees shall serve
    for thee.
This Cattell heere is all myne owne. And many mo besyde ⎤
Doo eyther in the bottoms feede, or in the woodes them hyde, ⎬
And many standing at theyr stalles doo in my Cave abyde. ⎦
The number of them (if a man should ask) I cannot showe.
Tush, beggars of theyr Cattell use the number for too knowe.
And for the goodnesse of the same, no whit beleeve thou mee,

But come thyself (and if thou wilt) the truth therof too see.
See how theyr udders full doo make them straddle. Lesser ware
Shet up at home in cloce warme peends, are Lambes. There also
    are
In other pinfolds Kidds of selfsame yeaning tyme. Thus have
I alwayes mylke as whyte as snow, whereof I sum doo save
Too drink, and of the rest is made good cheese. And furthermore
Not only stale and common gifts and pleasures wherof store
Is too bee had at eche mannes hand, (as Leverets, Kidds, and Does,
A payre of pigeons, or a nest of birds new found, or Roes),
Shall untoo thee presented bee. I found this toother day
A payre of Bearewhelpes, eche so lyke the other as they lay
Uppon a hill, that scarce yee eche discerne from other may.
And when that I did fynd them I did take them up, and say
Theis will I for my Lady keepe for her therwith too play.
Now put thou up thy fayre bryght head good *Galat* I thee pray
Above the greenish waves: now come my *Galat,* come away,
And of my present take no scorne. I know my selfe too bee
A jollye fellow. For even now I did behold and see
Myne image in the water sheere, and sure mee thought I tooke
Delyght too see my goodly shape and favor, in the brooke.
Behold how big I am, not *Jove* in heaven (for so you men
Report one *Jove* too reigne, of whom I passe not for too ken)
Is howger than this doughty corce of myne. A bush of heare
Dooth overdreepe my visage grim, and shadowes as it were
A grove uppon my shoulders twayne. And think it not too bee ⎤
A shame for that with bristled heare my body rough yee see.   ⎬
A fowle ilfavored syght it is too see a leavelesse tree,   ⎦
A lothely thing it is, a horse without a mane too keepe.
As fethers doo become the birdes, and wooll becommeth sheepe,
Even so a beard and bristled skin becommeth also men.
I have but one eye, which dooth stand amid my frunt: what then?
This one round eye of myne is lyke a myghty target. Why?
Vewes not the Sun all things from heaven? Yit but one only eye
Hath hee: moreover in your Seas my father beares the sway.
Him will I make thy fathrinlaw. Have mercy I the pray,
And harken too myne humble sute. For only untoo thee

Yeeld I. Even I of whom bothe heaven and *Jove* despysed bee
And eeke the percing thunderbolt, doo stand in awe and feare
Of thee O *Nerye*. Thyne ill will is greevouser too beare
Than is the deadly Thunderclappe. Yit could I better fynd
In hart too suffer this contempt of thyne with pacient mynd,
If thou didst shonne all other folk as well as mee. But why
Rejecting *Cyclops* doost thou love dwarf *Acis?* why say I
Preferst thou *Acis* unto mee? well let him liked bee
Both of himself, and also (which I would be lothe) of thee.
And if I catch him he shall feele that in my body is
The force that should bee. I shall paunch him quicke. Those
    limbes of his
I will in peeces teare, and strew them in the feeldes, and in
Thy waters, if he doo thee haunt. For I doo swelt within,
And being chaafte the flame dooth burne more feerce too my un-
    rest.
Mee thinks mount *Aetna* with his force is closed in my brest.
And yit it nothing moveth thee. . . .

Book XIII, lines 929–1021

CONCLUSION

Now have I brought a woork too end which neither *Joves* fierce
    wrath,
Nor swoord, nor fyre, nor freating age with all the force it hath
Are able too abolish quyght. Let comme that fatall howre
Which (saving of this brittle flesh) hath over mee no powre,
And at his pleasure make an end of myne uncerteyne tyme.
Yit shall the better part of mee assured bee too clyme
Aloft above the starry skye. And all the world shall never
Be able for too quench my name. For looke how farre so ever
The Romane Empyre by the ryght of conquest shall extend,
So farre shall all folke reade this woorke. And tyme without all
    end

(If Poets as by prophesie about the truth may ame)
My lyfe shall everlastingly bee lengthened still by fame.

> Book XV, lines 984–995. Translated by
> Arthur Golding

❊ ❊ Compare the passages from the *Metamorphoses,* given here
in Golding's translation, with Horace on the same themes.

W. H. D. Rouse notes that Golding's version was one of the
six great books which Shakespeare had read, as perhaps no other
man ever will. Cf. Yeats:

> I made it out of a mouthful of air,
> Their children's children shall say they have lied.

Alexander Moring, a London publisher, issued, at the start of
this century, six folios which can be taken as the fruit of, and/or
the basis for a lot more, humanism; intended to show what
Shakespeare had read: Golding's Ovid; North's Plutarch; and
Holinshed. The instructor can find themes for abundant lectures
in the Meleager story, reaching backward into Sophokles and *his*
backgrounds, and forward into Shakespeare's stage plays. Shake-
speare's histories are not dead record, they also reach forward.

The King's Library (title given the series) demonstrated the
civilization that inheres in, and can be transmitted by, a small
number of opulent authors enjoyed rather than analyzed.

Rutilius

[fl. 416 A.D.]

❊ ❊ The great break with older civilization came with the fall of
Alexander. The fall of Rome was a lesser calamity. We are indi-
cating in briefest line that fall.

Rutilius Claudius Namantianus, in A.D. 416, leaves Rome

when estates in Gaul are endangered by the Gothic invasions.
The devotion to Rome and the Empire occasions his valediction.

R O M A

Again and again I kiss thy gates at departing
And against our will leave thy holy door-stone,
Praying in tears and with praises
                such words as can pierce our tears.

Hear us, Queen, Fairest in all the earth, *Roma,*
Taking post twixt the sky's poles,
Nurse of men! Mother of gods,
                        do thou hear us.
Ever we hymn thee and will, while the Fates can have power.
No guest can forget thee.
                It were worse crime than forgetting the sun
If we ceased holding thy honour in heart,
Thou impartial as sunlight to the splash of all outer sea-bords.
All that Apollo over-rides in his quadriga
Hast thou combined into equity:
Many strange folk in one fatherland,
To their good, not seeking to dominate;
Gavest law to the conquered as consorts;
Made city what had been world.

They say that Venus was thy mother, that is by Aeneas,
Mars for father hadst'ou through Romulus,
Making mild armed strength, she in conquest:
One god in two natures;
                        Joy out of strife by sparing
O'ercamest the sources of terror
        In love with all that remains.

   Translated by Ezra Pound

Boethius

[c. 475–525]

from DE CONSOLATIONE PHILOSOPHIÆ

"HAPPY TOO MUCH"

Happy too much, the former age
    With faithful field content,
Not lost by sluggish lust,
    That wonts the long fasts
To loose by sun-begotten acorn;
    That knew not Bacchus' gifts
With molten honey mixed,
    Nor silken shining fleece
With Tyrian venom dyed.
    Sound sleeps gave the grass;
Their drink the running stream;
    Shades gave the highest pine.
The depth of sea they fathomed not,
    Nor wares, chosen from far,
Made strangers find new shores.
    Then were the navies still;
Nor bloodshed, by cruel hate
    Had fearful weapons stained.
What first fury to foes, should
    Any arms raise,
When cruel wounds he saw,
    And no reward for blood?
Would God [that] again our former time
    To wonted manners [let] fall!
But greedy-getting love burns
    Sorer than Aetna with her flames.

navies: The Queen had read *classis,* navy, for *classicum,* trumpet

O who the first man was
  Of hidden gold the weight,
Or gems that willing lurked
  The dear danger dig'd.

Book II, Metre V. Translated by Elizabeth I

❀ ❀ Boethius was a Roman senator and consul imprisoned under Theodoric the Ostrogoth, finally murdered. Modification of the Queen's spelling has seemed advisable, to make it more easily understandable. The version is not given as a model of style, but to indicate Boethius' position in the history of occidental mind. If he had few readers, as Dante says, he had a number of translators famous in their own right: King Alfred, Chaucer, among them. All rather unreadable. But one way to gauge the culture of an age is to note the interests of those highly placed. The gamut runs from Boethius, shall we say, "downward"?

Boethius says that Philosophy appeared to him "of stately face, with flaming eyes, of fresh colour, and insight above the common worth of men." The figure was sometimes the size of a woman, "sometimes towering into heaven." Familiarity with this form of perception would have saved several barrels of speculation re Dante's visions.

Anonymous

[Anglo-Saxon, 8th century]

THE SEAFARER

May I for my own self song's truth reckon,
Journey's jargon, how I in harsh days
Hardship endured oft.

Bitter breast-cares have I abided,
Known on my keel many a care's hold,
And dire sea-surge, and there I oft spent
Narrow nightwatch nigh the ship's head
While she tossed close to cliffs. Coldly afflicted,
My feet were by frost benumbed.
Chill its chains are; chafing sighs
Hew my heart round and hunger begot
Mere-weary mood. Lest man know not
That he on dry land loveliest liveth,
List how I, care-wretched, on ice-cold sea,
Weathered the winter, wretched outcast
Deprived of my kinsmen;
Hung with hard ice-flakes, where hail-scur flew,
There I heard naught save the harsh sea
And ice-cold wave, at whiles the swan cries,
Did for my games the gannet's clamour,
Sea-fowls' loudness was for me laughter,
The mews' singing all my mead-drink.
Storms, on the stone-cliffs beaten, fell on the stern
In icy feathers; full oft the eagle screamed
With spray on his pinion.
                              Not any protector
May make merry man faring needy.
This he little believes, who aye in winsome life
Abides 'mid burghers some heavy business,
Wealthy and wine-flushed, how I weary oft
Must bide above brine.
Neareth nightshade, snoweth from north,
Frost froze the land, hail fell on earth then,
Corn of the coldest. Nathless there knocketh now
The heart's thought that I on high streams
The salt-wavy tumult traverse alone.
Moaneth alway my mind's lust
That I fare forth, that I afar hence
Seek out a foreign fastness.
For this there's no mood-lofty man over earth's midst,
Not though he be given his good, but will have in his youth greed;

Nor his deed to the daring, nor his king to the faithful
But shall have his sorrow for sea-fare
Whatever his lord will.
He hath not heart for harping, nor in ring-having
Nor winsomeness to wife, nor world's delight
Nor any whit else save the wave's slash,
Yet longing comes upon him to fare forth on the water.
Bosque taketh blossom, cometh beauty of berries,
Fields to fairness, land fares brisker,
All this admonisheth man eager of mood,
The heart turns to travel so that he then thinks
On flood-ways to be far departing.
Cuckoo calleth with gloomy crying,
He singeth summerward, bodeth sorrow,
The bitter heart's blood. Burgher knows not—
He the prosperous man—what some perform
Where wandering them widest draweth.
So that but now my heart burst from my breastlock,
My mood 'mid the mere-flood,
Over the whale's acre, would wander wide.
On earth's shelter cometh oft to me,
Eager and ready, the crying lone-flyer,
Whets for the whale-path the heart irresistibly,
O'er tracks of ocean; seeing that anyhow
My lord deems to me this dead life
On loan and on land, I believe not
That any earth-weal eternal standeth
Save there be somewhat calamitous
That, ere a man's tide go, turn it to twain.
Disease or oldness or sword-hate
Beats out the breath from doom-gripped body.
And for this, every earl whatever, for those speaking after—
Laud of the living, boasteth some last word,
That he will work ere he pass onward,
Frame on the fair earth 'gainst foes his malice,
Daring ado, . . .
So that all men shall honour him after
And his laud beyond them remain 'mid the English,

Aye, for ever, a lasting life's-blast,
Delight 'mid the doughty.
                    Days little durable,
And all arrogance of earthen riches,
There come now no kings nor Cæsars
Nor gold-giving lords like those gone.
Howe'er in mirth most magnified,
Whoe'er lived in life most lordliest,
Drear all this excellence, delights undurable!
Waneth the watch, but the world holdeth.
Tomb hideth trouble. The blade is layed low.
Earthly glory ageth and seareth.
No man at all going the earth's gait,
But age fares against him, his face paleth,
Grey-haired he groaneth, knows gone companions,
Lordly men, are to earth o'ergiven,
Nor may he then the flesh-cover, whose life ceaseth,
Nor eat the sweet nor feel the sorry,
Nor stir hand nor think in mid heart,
And though he strew the grave with gold,
His born brothers, their buried bodies
Be an unlikely treasure hoard.

Translated by Ezra Pound

Rihaku (Li Po)

[c. 700–762]

EXILE'S LETTER

To So-Kin of Rakuyo, ancient friend, Chancellor of Gen.
Now I remember that you built me a special tavern

By the south side of the bridge at Ten-Shin.
With yellow gold and white jewels, we paid for songs and laughter
And we were drunk for month on month, forgetting the kings and
     princes.
Intelligent men came drifting in from the sea and from the west
     border,
And with them, and with you especially
There was nothing at cross purpose,
And they made nothing of sea-crossing or of mountain-crossing,
If only they could be of that fellowship,
And we all spoke out our hearts and minds, and without regret.
And then I was sent off to South Wei,
     smothered in laurel groves,
And you to the north of Raku-hoku,
Till we had nothing but thoughts and memories in common.
And then, when separation had come to its worst,
We met, and travelled into Sen-Go,
Through all the thirty-six folds of the turning and twisting waters,
Into a valley of the thousand bright flowers,
That was the first valley;
And into ten thousand valleys full of voices and pine-winds.
And with silver harness and reins of gold,
Out came the East of Kan foreman and his company.
And there came also the "True man" of Shi-yo to meet me,
Playing on a jewelled mouth-organ.
In the storied houses of San-Ko they gave us more Sennin music,
Many instruments, like the sound of young phœnix broods.
The foreman of Kan Chu, drunk, danced
     because his long sleeves wouldn't keep still
With that music playing,
And I, wrapped in brocade, went to sleep with my head on his lap,
And my spirit so high it was all over the heavens,
And before the end of the day we were scattered like stars, or rain.
I had to be off to So, far away over the waters,
You back to your river-bridge.

And your father, who was brave as a leopard,
Was governor in Hei Shu, and put down the barbarian rabble.
And one May he had you send for me,
  despite the long distance.
And what with broken wheels and so on, I won't say it wasn't
  hard going,
Over roads twisted like sheep's guts.
And I was still going, late in the year,
  in the cutting wind from the North,
And thinking how little you cared for the cost,
  and you caring enough to pay it.
And what a reception:
Red jade cups, food well set on a blue jewelled table,
And I was drunk, and had no thought of returning.
And you would walk out with me to the western corner of the
  castle,
To the dynastic temple, with water about it clear as blue jade,
With boats floating, and the sound of mouth-organs and drums,
With ripples like dragon-scales, going grass green on the water,
Pleasure lasting, with courtezans, going and coming without hin-
  drance,
With the willow flakes falling like snow,
And the vermilioned girls getting drunk about sunset,
And the water, a hundred feet deep, reflecting green eyebrows
—Eyebrows painted green are a fine sight in young moonlight,
Gracefully painted—
And the girls singing back at each other,
Dancing in transparent brocade,
And the wind lifting the song, and interrupting it,
Tossing it up under the clouds.
   And all this comes to an end.
   And is not again to be met with.
I went up to the court for examination,
Tried Layu's luck, offered the Choyo song,
And got no promotion,
   and went back to the East Mountains
   White-headed.

And once again, later, we met at the South bridge-head.
And then the crowd broke up, you went north to San palace,
And if you ask how I regret that parting:
It is like the flowers falling at Spring's end
          Confused, whirled in a tangle.
What is the use of talking, and there is no end of talking,
There is no end of things in the heart.
I call in the boy,
Have him sit on his knees here
          To seal this,
And send it a thousand miles, thinking.

Translated by Ezra Pound

Godeschalk

[805–869]

SEQUAIRE

The Pharisee murmurs when the woman weeps, conscious of guilt.

Sinner, he despises a fellow-in-sin. Thou, unacquainted with sin, hast regard for the penitent, cleansest the soiled one, loved her to make her most fair.

She embraces the feet of the master, washes them with tears, dries them with her hair; washing and drying them she anointed them with unguent, covered them with kisses.

These are the feasts which please thee, O Wisdom of the Father!

Born of the Virgin, who disdained not the touch of a sinner.

Chaste virgins, they immaculately offer unto the Lord the sacrifice of their pure bodies, choosing Christ for their deathless bridegroom.

O happy bridals, whereto there are no stains, no heavy dolors of childbirth, no rival mistress to be feared, no nurse molestful!

Their couches, kept for Christ alone, are walled about by angels of the guard, who, with drawn swords, ward off the unclean lest any paramour defile them.

Therein Christ sleepeth with them: happy is this sleep, sweet the rest there, wherein true maid is fondled in the embraces of her heavenly spouse.

Adorned are they with fine linen, and with a robe of purple; their left hands hold lilies, their right hands roses.

On these the lamb feedeth, and with these is he refreshed; these flowers are his chosen food.

He leapeth, and boundeth and gamboleth among them.

With them doth he rest through the noon-heat.

It is upon their bosoms that he sleepeth at mid-day, placing his head between their virgin breasts.

Virgin Himself, born of a virgin mother, virginal retreats above all he seeketh and loveth.

Quiet is his sleep upon their bosoms, that no spot by any chance should soil His snowy fleece.

Give ear unto this canticle, most noble company of virgin devotees, that by it our devotion may with greater zeal prepare a temple for the Lord.

Translated by Ezra Pound

Anonymous
[12th century?]

HIERUSALEM

Hierusalem, my happy home,
    When shall I come to thee?
When shall my sorrows have an end,
    Thy joys when shall I see?

O happy harbour of the saints,
    O sweet and pleasant soil,
In thee no sorrow may be found,
    No grief, no care, no toil.

There lust and lucre cannot dwell,
    There envy bears no sway;
There is no hunger, heat, nor cold,
    But pleasure every way.

Thy walls are made of precious stones,
    Thy bulwarks diamonds square;
Thy gates are of right orient pearl,
    Exceeding rich and rare.

Thy turrets and thy pinnacles
    With carbuncles do shine;
Thy very streets are paved with gold,
    Surpassing clear and fine.

Ah, my sweet home, Hierusalem,
    Would God I were in thee!
Would God my woes were at an end,
    Thy joys that I might see!

Thy gardens and thy gallant walks
   Continually are green;
There grows such sweet and pleasant flowers
   As nowhere else are seen.

Quite through the streets, with silver sound,
   The flood of life doth flow;
Upon whose banks on every side
   The wood of life doth grow.

There trees for evermore bear fruit,
   And evermore do spring;
There evermore the angels sit,
   And evermore do sing.

Our Lady sings *Magnificat*
   With tune surpassing sweet;
And all the virgins bear their part,
   Sitting about her feet.

Hierusalem, my happy home,
   Would God I were in thee!
Would God my woes were at an end,
   Thy joys that I might see!

> *Translated from the Latin anonymously,*
> *perhaps 16th century*

The "Old Captive"

[?1130 fl.]

❊ ❊ The "Old Captive" wrote the story of Aucassin and Nicolette partly in verse but mostly in prose. The distinguished scholar G. Paris dates it as early as 1130.

from AUCASSIN AND NICOLETTE

"WHO WOULD LIST"

Who would list to the good lay
Gladness of the captive grey?
'Tis how two young lovers met,
Aucassin and Nicolette,
Of the pains the lover bore
And the sorrows he outwore,
For the goodness and the grace,
Of his love, so fair of face.

Sweet the song, the story sweet,
There is no man hearkens it,
No man living 'neath the sun,
So outwearied, so foredone,
Sick and woful, worn and sad,
But is healèd, but is glad,
　　'Tis so sweet.

Translated by Andrew Lang

Bertrans de Born

[c. 1140–1214]

"A PERIGORD PRES DEL MURALH"

At Perigord near to the wall,
Aye, within a mace throw of it,
I will come armed upon Baiart, and if I find there
    that fat-bellied Poitevin,
He shall see how my steel cuts.

For upon the field I will make a bran-mash of his brains, mixed
with the *maille* of his armor.

❋ ❋ Earlier in the same *sirvente* Bertrans says:

Every day I am resoling and sewing up the barons and remelt-
ing them and warming them over, for I thought to get them
started (loosen them up), but I am indeed a fool to bother with
the business, for they are of worse workmanship than the iron
(statue of) St. Lunart, wherefore a man's an ass who troubles about
them.

Every day I contend and contest and skirmish, and defend and
carry backward and forward the battle; and they destroy and burn
my land, and make wreck of my trees, and scatter the corn through
the straw, and I have no enemy, bold or coward, who does not
attack me.

A WAR SONG

Well pleaseth me the sweet time of Easter
That maketh the leaf and the flower come out.
And it pleaseth me when I hear the clamor
Of the birds, their song through the wood;

And it pleaseth me when I see through the meadows
The tents and pavilions set up, and great joy have I
When I see o'er the campagna knights armed and horses arrayed.

And it pleaseth me when the scouts set in flight the folk with their
    goods;
And it pleaseth me when I see coming together after
    them an host of armed men.
And it pleaseth me to the heart when I see strong
    castles beseiged,
And barriers broken and riven, and I see the host on
    the shore all about shut in with ditches,
And closed in with lisses of strong piles.

    Translated by Ezra Pound

Bernart de Ventadorn
    [1148–1195]

THE LARK

                    Quant ieu vey la' lauzeta mover
                    De joi sas alas contral ray.

When I see the lark a-moving
For joy his wings against the sunlight,
Who forgets himself and lets himself fall
For the sweetness which goes into his heart;
Ai! what great envy comes unto me for him whom I see so
    rejoicing!

I marvel that my heart melts not for desiring.
Alas! I thought I knew so much
Of Love, and I know so little of it, for I cannot
Hold myself from loving
Her from whom I shall never have anything toward.
She hath all my heart from me, and she hath from me all my wit
And myself and all that is mine.
And when she took it from me she left me naught
Save desiring and a yearning heart.

Translated by Ezra Pound

Walther von der Vogelweide
[?1170–1230?]

UNDER THE LINDENS

Under the lindens on the heather,
There was our double resting-place,
Side by side and close together
Garnered blossoms, crushed, and grass
Nigh a shaw in such a vale:
Tandaradei,
Sweetly sang the nightingale.

I came a-walking through the grasses;
Lo! my dear was come before.
Ah! what befell then—listen, listen, lasses—
Makes me glad for evermore.
Kisses?—thousands in good sooth:
Tandaradei,
See how red they've left my mouth.

There had he made ready—featly, fairly—
All of flow'ring herbs a yielding bed,
And that place in secret still smiles rarely.
If by chance your foot that path should tread,
You might see the roses pressed,
Tandaradei,
Where e'enow my head did rest.

How he lay beside me, did a soul discover
(Now may God forfend such shame from me):
Not a soul shall know it save my lover;
Not a soul could see save I and he,
And a certain small brown bird:
Tandaradei,
Trust him not to breathe a word.

Translated by Ford Madox Ford, 1907

❀❀ Inclusion of Vogelweide signifies no pretense to being spe-
cialists in German poetry. Will Vesper's book seems sympathetic,
notably alive in *Du bist schwarz und doch bin schön, ihr Tochter
von Hierusalem*, Vogelweide, von Morungen, and very little pro-
sodic progress thereafter. Heine is the easiest German poetry for
foreigners to understand before they have more than a smatter-
ing of the language, and probably "gets in first" before they be-
come competent judges of his confrères.

Arnaut Daniel

[c. 1180–1200]

"L'AURA AMARA"

L'aura amara
Fals bruoills brancutz
Clarzir
Quel doutz espeissa ab fuoills,
Els letz
Becs
Dels auzels ramencs
Ten balps e mutz,
Pars
E non-pars;
Per qu'eu m'esfortz
De far e dir
Plazers
A mains per liei
Que m'a virat bas d'aut,
Don tem morir
Sils afans no m'asoma.

❄❄ This is the model given in the first strophe of the IXth canzone. The seventeen rhymes are repeated in the same order in the five subsequent strophes. The English translation matches this so far as the externals are concerned.

The bitter air
Strips panoply
From trees
Where softer winds set leaves,
And glad
Beaks

Now in brakes are coy,
Scarce peep the wee
Mates
And un-mates.
     What gaud's the work?
     What good the glees?
What curse
I strive to shake!
Me hath she cast from high,
In fell disease
I lie, and deathly fearing.

✳✳ Note on Provençal strophic forms: Pound printed English diagrams of these canzoni not to show that they ought to be used in our time but to illustrate what had been done in Provence and was not impossible to copy in English. The reason for the strophes being the same shape is that the tune was only as long as one strophe and had to be repeated. The prosodic triumph of Bion's "Adonis" is in a different category and no English diagram of its music has yet been even approximately adequate to convey it to readers ignorant of the original language.

The birds' noise is imitated in the VIIIth canzone. One *can* do it in English, but more as stunt than as expression of feeling.

[M. S.]

"AUTET E BAS"

Autet e bas entrels prims fuoills
Son nou de flors li ram eil renc
E noi ten mut bec ni gola
Nuills auzels, anz braia e chanta
Cadahus
En son us;
Per joi qu'ai d'els e del tems
Chant, mas amors mi asauta
Quels motz ab lo son acorda.

Now high and low, where leaves renew,
Come buds on bough and spalliard pleach
And no beak nor throat is muted;
Auzel each in tune contrasted
Letteth loose
Wriblis spruce,
Joy for them and spring would set
Song on me, but Love assaileth
Me and sets my words t' his dancing.

Translated by Ezra Pound

❊ ❊ *Wriblis,* in the above, is an archaic word meaning "war-blings." *They reduce/Pains, and noose;* or, *Burns profuse,/Held recluse.* The rhymes exist in English, *abuse, traduce, Christus, pro-duce,* etc. Hunting for such curios can conceivably be useful to a very determined writer who wants to know his language better than he would by mere day-dreaming. Pound frequently quotes Richter: "These are the laws of harmony and counterpoint. They have *nothing* to do with musical composition, which is a totally different activity." [M. S.]

Saint Francis of Assisi
[1182–1226]

CANTICO DEL SOLE

Most high Lord,
Yours are the praises,
The glory and the honors,
And to you alone must be accorded
All graciousness; and no man there is

Who is worthy to name you.
Be praisèd, O God, and be exalted,
My Lord, of all creatures,
And in especial of the most high Sun
Which is your creature, O Lord, that makes clear
The day and illumines it,
Whence by its fairness and its splendor
It is become thy face;
And of the white moon (be praisèd, O Lord)
And of the wandering stars,
Created by you in the heaven
So brilliant and so fair.
Praisèd be my Lord, by the flame
Whereby night groweth illumined
In the midst of its darkness,
For it is resplendent,
Is joyous, fair, eager; is mighty.
Praisèd be my Lord, of the air,
Of the winds, of the clear sky,
And of the cloudy, praisèd
Of all seasons whereby
Live all these creatures
Of lower order.
Praisèd be my Lord
By our sister the water,
Element meetest for man,
Humble and chaste in its clearness.
Praisèd be the Lord by our mother
The Earth that sustaineth,
That feeds, that produceth
Multitudinous grasses
And flowers and fruitage.
Praisèd be my Lord, by those
Who grant pardons through his love,
Enduring their travail in patience
And their infirmity with joy of the spirit.
Praisèd be my Lord by death corporal

Whence escapes no one living.
Woe to those that die in mutual transgression
And blessed are they who shall
Find in death's hour thy grace that comes
From obedience to thy holy will,
Wherethrough they shall never see
The pain of the death eternal.
Praise and give grace to my Lord,
Be grateful and serve him
In humbleness e'en as ye owe.
Praise him all creatures!

Translated by Ezra Pound

Guido Guinicelli

[1220–1275]

CANZONE: OF THE GENTLE HEART

Within the gentle heart Love shelters him
As birds within the green shade of the grove.
Before the gentle heart, in Nature's scheme,
Love was not, nor the gentle heart ere Love.
For with the sun, at once,
So sprang the light immediately; nor was
Its birth before the sun's.
And Love hath his effect in gentleness
Of very self; even as
Within the middle fire the heat's excess.

The fire of Love comes to the gentle heart
Like as its virtue to a precious stone;

To which no star its influence can impart
Till it is made a pure thing by the sun;
For when the sun hath smit
From out its essence that which there was vile,
The star endoweth it.
And so the heart created by God's breath
Pure, true, and clean from guile,
A woman, like a star, enamoureth.

In gentle heart Love for like reason is
For which the lamp's high flame is fann'd and bow'd:
Clear, piercing bright, it shines for its own bliss;
Nor would it burn there else, it is so proud.
For evil natures meet
With love as it were water met with fire,
As cold abhorring heat.
Through gentle heart Love doth a track divine,—
Like knowing like; the same
As diamond runs through iron in the mine.

The sun strikes full upon the mud all day;
It remains vile, nor the sun's worth is less.
"By race I am gentle," the proud man doth say:
He is the mud, the sun is gentleness.
Let no man predicate
That aught the name of gentleness should have,
Even in a king's estate,
Except the heart there be a gentle man's.
The star-beam lights the wave,—
Heaven holds the star and the star's radiance.

God, in the understanding of high Heaven,
Burns more than in our sight the living sun;
There to behold His Face unveil'd is given;
And Heaven, whose will is homage paid to One,
Fulfils the things which live
In God, from the beginning excellent.

So should my lady give
That truth which in her eyes is glorified,
On which her heart is bent,
To me whose service waiteth at her side.

My lady, God shall ask, "What dared'st thou?"
(When my soul stands with all her acts review'd);
"Thou passed'st Heaven, into My sight, as now,
To make Me of vain love similitude.
To Me doth praise belong,
And to the Queen of all the realm of grace
Who endeth fraud and wrong."
Then may I plead: "As though from Thee he came,
Love wore an angel's face:
Lord, if I loved her, count it not my shame."

Translated by Dante Gabriel Rossetti

Folgore da San Gemignano
[fl. 1250]

from OF THE MONTHS: TWELVE SONNETS
Addressed to a Fellowship of Sienese Nobles

AUGUST

For August, be your dwelling thirty towers
    Within an Alpine valley mountainous,
    Where never the sea-wind may vex your house,
    But clear life separate, like a star, be yours.

There horses shall wait saddled at all hours,
    That ye may mount at morning or at eve:
    On each hand either ridge ye shall perceive,
    A mile apart, which soon a good beast scours.
So alway, drawing homewards, ye shall tread
    Your valley parted by a rivulet
    Which day and night shall flow sedate and smooth.
There all through noon ye may possess the shade,
    And there your open purses shall entreat
    The best of Tuscan cheer to feed your youth.

Translated by Dante Gabriel Rossetti

Guido Cavalcanti
[1250–1300]

SONETTO VII

Who is she that comes, makyng turn every man's eye
And makyng the air to tremble with a bright clearnesse
That leadeth with her Love, in such nearnesse
No man may proffer of speech more than a sigh?

Ah God, what she is like when her owne eye turneth, is
Fit for Amor to speake, for I cannot at all;
Such is her modesty, I would call
Every woman else but an useless uneasiness.

No one could ever tell all of her pleasauntness
In that every high noble vertu leaneth to herward,
So Beauty sheweth her forth as her Godhede;

Never before was our mind so high led,
Nor have we so much of heal as will afford
That our thought may take her immediate in its embrace.

SONETTO XXXV
To Guido Orlando

(He explains the miracles of the Madonna of Or San Michele,
by telling whose image it is.)

My Lady's face it is they worship there
At San Michele in Orto, Guido mine,
Near her fair semblance that is clear and holy
Sinners take refuge and get consolation,

Whoso before her kneeleth reverently
No longer wasteth but is comforted;
The sick are healed and devils driven forth,
And those with crooked eyes see straightway straight.

Great ills she cureth in an open place,
With reverence the folk all kneel unto her,
And two lamps shed the glow about her form.

Her voice is borne out through far-lying ways
'Till brothers minor cry: "Idolatry!"
For envy of her precious neighborhood.

BALLATA V

Light do I see within my Lady's eyes
And loving spirits in its plenisphere
Which bear in strange delight on my heart's care
Till Joy's awakened from that sepulchre.

That which befalls me in my Lady's presence
Bars explanation intellectual,
I seem to see a lady wonderful
Spring forth between her lips, one whom no sense
Can fully tell the mind of, and one whence
Another, in beauty, springeth marvellous,
From whom a star goes forth and speaketh thus:
"Now thy salvation is gone forth from thee."

There where this Lady's loveliness appeareth,
Is heard a voice which goes before her ways
And seems to sing her name with such sweet praise
That my mouth fears to speak what name she beareth,
And my heart trembles for the grace she weareth,
While far in my soul's deep the sighs astir
Speak thus: "Look well! For if thou look on her,
Then shalt thou see her virtue risen in heaven."

✷✷ This ballata seems to contain the seed of Dante's *Paradiso*.
An ideogram of Italian poetry in the "Primi Secoli" can be com-
posed from St. Francis' "Cantico del Sole," Guinicelli's canzone
given above, and a very few other poems by the major writers of
the time.

The careful student of Dante will want to correlate his thought
with Cavalcanti's canzoni to Love, Poverty, and Fortune.

CANZONE: DONNA MI PRIEGHA

A lady asks me
        I speak in season
    She seeks reason for an affect, wild often
    That is so proud he hath Love for a name
Who denys it can hear the truth now
Wherefore I speak to the present knowers
Having no hope that low-hearted
        Can bring sight to such reason

Be there not natural demonstration
       I have no will to try proof-bringing
Or say where it hath birth
What is its virtu and power
Its being and every moving
Or delight whereby 'tis called "to love"
Or if man can show it to sight.

Where memory liveth,
       it takes its state
Formed like a diafan from light on shade
Which shadow cometh of Mars and remaineth
Created, having a name sensate,
Custom of the soul,
       will from the heart;
Cometh from a seen form which being understood
Taketh locus and remaining in the intellect possible
Wherein hath he neither weight nor still-standing,
Descendeth not by quality but shineth out
Himself his own effect unendingly
Not in delight but in the being aware
Nor can he leave his true likeness otherwhere.

He is not vertu but cometh of that perfection
Which is so postulate not by the reason
But 'tis felt, I say.
Beyond salvation, holdeth his judging force
Deeming intention to be reason's peer and mate,
Poor in discernment, being thus weakness' friend
Often his power cometh on death in the end,
Be it withstayed
       and so swinging counterweight.
Not that it were natural opposite, but only
Wry'd a bit from the perfect,
Let no man say love cometh from chance
Or hath not established lordship

Holding his power even though
      Memory hath him no more.

Cometh he to be
      when the will
From overplus
Twisteth out of natural measure,
Never adorned with rest Moveth he changing colour
Either to laugh or weep
Contorting the face with fear
      resteth but a little
Yet shall ye see of him That he is most often
With folk who deserve him
And his strange quality sets sighs to move
Willing man look into that forméd trace in his mind
And with such uneasiness as rouseth the flame.
Unskilled can not form his image.
He himself moveth not, drawing all to his stillness,
Neither turneth about to seek his delight
Nor yet to seek out proving
Be it so great or so small.

He draweth likeness and hue from like nature
So making pleasure more certain in seeming
Nor can stand hid in such nearness,
Beautys be darts tho' not savage
Skilled from such fear a man follows
Deserving spirit, that pierceth.
Nor is he known from his face
But taken in the white light that is allness
Toucheth his aim
Who heareth, seeth not form
But is led by its emanation.
Being divided, set out from colour,
Disjunct in mid darkness
Grazeth the light, one moving by other,

Being divided, divided from all falsity
Worthy of trust
From him alone mercy proceedeth.

Go, song, surely thou mayest
Whither it please thee
For so art thou ornate that thy reasons
Shall be praised from thy understanders,
With others hast thou no will to make company.

Translated by Ezra Pound

❋❋ The text of the above canzone follows Pound's translation
in his Canto XXXVI; variant readings may be found in his trans-
lations of and essays on Cavalcanti. [M. S.]

Dante Alighieri
[1265–1321]

from LA VITA NUOVA

from CANZONE II

A very pitiful lady, very young,
Exceedingly rich in human sympathies,
Stood by what time I clamored upon death,
And at the wild words wandering on my tongue,
And at the piteous look within mine eyes,
She was affrighted, . . .

❊ ❊ Of the visions in that troubled sleep of his, the later stanza:

Then saw I many broken hinted sights,
In the uncertain state I stepped into
Me seemed to be I know not in what place,
Where ladies through the streets, like mournful lights,
Ran with loose hair, and eyes that frighten'd you
By their own terror, and a pale amaze:
The while, little by little, as I thought,
The sun ceased, and the stars began to gather,
And each wept at the other;
And birds dropp'd in mid-flight out of the sky;
And earth shook suddenly;
And I was 'ware of one, hoarse and tired out,
Who ask'd of me: "Hast thou not heard it said? . . .
Thy lady, she that was so fair, is dead."

from CANZONE III

That she hath gone to Heaven suddenly,
And hath left love below to mourn with me.

Beatrice is gone up into high Heaven,
The kingdom where the angels are at peace:
And lives with them; and to her friends is dead.
Not by the frost of winter was she driven
Away, like others; nor by summer heats;
But through a perfect gentleness, instead.
For from the lamp of her meek lowlihead
Such an exceeding glory went up hence
That it woke wonder in the Eternal Sire,
Until a sweet desire
Enter'd Him for that lovely excellence,
So that He bade her to Himself aspire;
Counting this weary and most evil place
Unworthy of a thing so full of grace.

THE CONCLUSION

About this time, it happened that a great number of persons undertook a pilgrimage, to the end that they might behold that blessed portraiture bequeathed unto us by our Lord Jesus Christ as the image of his beautiful countenance (upon which countenance my dear lady now looked continually). And certain among these pilgrims, who seemed very thoughtful, passed by a path which is well-nigh in the midst of the city where my most gracious lady was born, and abode, and at last died.

Then I, beholding them, said within myself: These pilgrims seem to be come from very far; and I think they can not have heard speak of this lady, or known anything concerning her. Their thoughts are not of her, but of other things; it may be, of their friends who are far distant, and whom we, in our turn, know not. . . . And when the last of them had gone by me, I bethought me to write a sonnet, showing forth mine inward speech. . . . And I wrote this sonnet:

Ye pilgrim folk advancing pensively
As if in thought of distant things, I pray,
Is your own land indeed so far away
As by your aspect it would seem to be,—
That nothing of our grief comes over ye
Though passing through the mournful town midway;
Like unto men that understand today
Nothing at all of her great misery?

Yet if ye will but stay, whom I accost,
And listen to my words a little space,
At going ye shall mourn with a loud voice.
It is her Beatrice that she hath lost;
Of whom the least word spoken holds such grace
That men weep hearing it, and have no choice.

And I . . . resolved that I would write also a new thing, . . .

therefore I made this sonnet, which narrates my condition, . . .

Beyond the sphere which spreads to widest space
Now soars the sigh that my heart sends above:
A new perception born of grieving love
Guideth it upward through the untrodden ways.
When it hath reach'd the end, and stays,
It sees a lady round whom splendors move
In homage; till, by the great light thereof
Abash'd, the pilgrim spirit stands at gaze.
It sees her such, that when it tells me this
Which it hath seen, I understand it not,
It hath a speech so subtle and so fine,
And yet I know its voice within my thought
Often remembereth me of Beatrice:
So that I understand it, ladies mine.

After writing this sonnet, it was given unto me to behold a very
wonderful vision; wherein I saw things which determined me
that I would say nothing further of this most blessed one, until
such time as I could discourse more worthily concerning her. And
to this end I labor all I can, as she well knoweth. Wherefore if it
be His pleasure through whom is the life of all things, that my
life continue with me a few years, it is my hope that I shall yet
write concerning her what hath not before been written of any
woman. After the which, may it seem good unto Him who is the
Master of Grace, that my spirit should go hence to behold the
glory of its lady, to wit, of that blessed Beatrice who now gazeth
continually on His countenance *qui est per omnia sæcula bene-
dictus.* Laus Deo.

Translated by Dante Gabriel Rossetti

❋ ❋ In this wise Dante prepared for the *Commedia,* the comple-
tion of which is generally thought to have occurred nine years
later.

Anonymous

[c. 1300]

ALISOUN

Bitwene Mersh and Averil,
    When spray biginneth to springe,
The lutel fowl hath hire wil
    On hire lud to singe.
    Ich libbe in love-longinge
For semlokest of alle thinge;
He may me blisse bringe:
    Ich am in hire baundoun.
An hendy hap ichabbe yhent;
Ichot from hevene it is me sent;
From alle wimmen my love is lent,
    And light on Alisoun.

On heu hire her is fair ynogh,
    Hire browe browne, hire eye blake;
With lossum chere he on me logh,
    With middel smal and wel ymake.
    Bote he me wolle to hire take,
    For te buen hire owen make,
    Longe to liven ichulle forsake,
        And feye fallen adown.

Nightes when I wende and wake,
    Forthy min wonges waxeth won;
Levedy, al for thine sake
    Longinge is ylent me on.
    In world nis non so witer mon
    That al hire bounte telle con;
    Hire swire is whittore then the swon,
        And feirest may in towne.

Ich am for wowing al forwake,
  Wery so water in wore,
Lest eny reve me my make;
  Ichabbe y-yirned yore:
  Betere is tholien while sore
  Then mournen evermore.
  Geinest under gore,
    Herkne to my roun:
  An hendy hap ichabbe yhent;
  Ichot from hevene it is me sent;
  From alle wimmen my love is lent,
    And light on Alisoun.

❋ ❋ The anonymous "Alisoun" is too beautiful to omit, and it must carry a glossary (following Auden and Pearson in their five-volume *Poets of the English Language*):

on hire lud: ? in her language	*semlokest:* fairest	*baundoun:* control
hendy: lucky *lent:* taken away	*lossum chere:* lovely face	*logh:* smiled
feye: dead *wonges:* cheeks *witer:* clever	*swire:* neck	*tholien:* pain
geinest under gore: most gracious under gown	*roun:* voice	

William Langland
[?1330–1390?]

from THE VISION OF PIERS PLOWMAN

❋ ❋ *Piers Plowman* is commonly taken as the start of English poetry as it emerges from Anglo-Saxon, a tongue more difficult for the average American than is French or German. There is an admirable selection of passages from this poem in Volume I of the Auden-Pearson *Poets of the English Language,* to which the reader is cheerfully referred. But the *Plowman* needs to be translated, or so loaded with glossary that anyone but a student probably gives it up. The quality may be guessed from this modification:

And I bowed my body and beheld all about
And saw the sun and the sea and the sand after,
And where the birds and beasts walked by their mates,
Wild wormes in woods and wonderful fowls
With flecked feathers and many colors.

❀ ❀ *Wormes* refers to any dragon or saurian; *yeden,* given here as "walked," can be approached through an obsolete form of "go"; *briddes* might be guessed to be "birds"; and the original of "many" is *fele.*

Geoffrey Chaucer
[?1340–1400]

❀ ❀ As Chaucer cannot be read by most of us without a glossary, only enough of him is given to show that he carried the French lyric beauty into English and portrayed characters in a way French medieval poets had not.

from THE CANTERBURY TALES

from THE PROLOGUE

Whan that Aprille with his shoures soote
The droghte of Marche hath perced to the roote,
And bathed every veyne in swich licour

Of which vertu engendred is the flour;
Whan Zephirus eek with his sweete breeth
Inspired hath in every holt and heeth
The tendre croppes, and the yonge sonne
Hath in the Ram his halve cours yronne,
And smale foweles maken melodye,
That slepen al the nyght with open ye
(So priketh hem nature in hir corages);
Thanne longen folk to goon on pilgrimages,
And palmeres for to seken straunge strondes,
To ferne halwes, kowthe in sondry londes;
And specially from every shires ende
Of Engelond to Caunterbury they wende,
The hooly blisful martir for to seke,
That hem hath holpen whan that they were seeke.
    Bifil that in that seson on a day,
In Southwerk at the Tabard as I lay
Redy to wenden on my pilgrymage
To Caunterbury with ful devout corage,
At nyght was come into that hostelrye
Wel nyne and twenty in a compaignye,
Of sondry folk, by aventure yfalle
In felaweshipe, and pilgrimes were they alle,
That toward Caunterbury wolden ryde. . . .

    Ther was also a Nonne, a PRIORESSE,
That of hir smylyng was ful symple and coy;
Hire gretteste ooth was but by Seinte Loy;
And she was cleped madame Eglentyne.
Ful weel she soong the service dyvyne
Entuned in hir nose ful semely,
And Frenssh she spake ful faire and fetisly,
After the scole of Stratford atte Bowe,
For Frenssh of Parys was to hire unknowe.

        . . . . .

And al was conscience and tendre herte.
Ful semyly hir wympul pynched was;
Hir nose tretys; hir eyen greye as glas,
Hir mouth ful smal, and therto softe and reed;
But sikerly she hadde a fair forheed;
It was almoost a spanne brood, I trowe;
For, hardily, she was nat undergrowe,
Ful fetys was hir cloke, as I was war.
Of smal coral aboute hire arm she bar
A peire of bedes, gauded al with grene,
And theron heng a brooch of gold ful sheene,
On which ther was first write a crowned A,
And after *Amor vincit omnia.* . . .

A MONK ther was, a fair for the maistrie,
An outridere, that lovede venerie,
       . . . . .
He yaf nat of that text a pulled hen,
That seith that hunters ben nat hooly men,
Ne that a monk, whan he is recchelees,
Is likned til a fissh that is waterlees,—
This is to seyn, a monk out of his cloystre.
But thilke text heeld he nat worth an oystre;
And I seyde his opinion was good.
What sholde he studie and make hymselven wood,
Upon a book in cloystre alwey to poure,
Or swynken with his handes, and laboure,
As Austyn bit? How shal the world be served?

A MARCHANT was ther with a forked berd,
In mottelee, and hye on horse he sat;
Upon his heed a Flaundryssh bever hat,
His bootes clasped faire and fetisly.
His resons he spak ful solempnely,
Sownynge alwey th' encrees of his wynnyng. . . .

A SERGEANT OF THE LAWE, war and wys,
That often hadde been at the Parvys,
Ther was also, ful riche of excellence.
Discreet he was and of greet reverence—
He semed swich, his wordes weren so wise.
Justice he was ful often in assise,
By patente and by pleyn commissioun.
For his science and for his heigh renoun,
Of fees and robes hadde he many oon.
So greet a purchasour was nowher noon:
Al was fee symple to hym in effect;
His purchasyng myghte nat been infect.
Nowher so bisy a man as he ther nas,
And yet he semed bisier than he was. . . .

MERCILES BEAUTE
A Triple Roundel

I   Captivity

Your yën two wol slee me sodenly,
I may the beautè of hem not sustene,
So woundeth hit through-out my herte kene.

And but your word wol helen hastily
My hertes wounde, whyl that hit is grene,
    Your yën two wol slee me sodenly,
    I may the beautè of hem not sustene.

Upon my trouthe I sey yow feithfully,
That ye ben of my lyf and deeth the quene;
For with my deeth the trouthe shal be sene.
    Your yën two wol slee me sodenly,
    I may the beautè of hem not sustene,
    So woundeth hit through-out my herte kene.

II   Rejection

So hath your beautè fro your herte chaced
Pitee, that me ne availeth not to pleyne;
For Daunger halt your mercy in his cheyne.

Giltles my deeth thus han ye me purchaced;
I sey yow sooth, me nedeth not to feyne;
    So hath your beautè fro your herte chaced
    Pitee, that me ne availeth not to pleyne.

Allas! that nature hath in yow compassed
So greet beautè, that no man may atteyne
To mercy, though he sterve for the peyne.
    So hath your beautè fro your herte chaced
    Pitee, that me ne availeth not to pleyne;
    For Daunger halt your mercy in his cheyne.

III   Escape

Sin I fro Love escaped am so fat,
I never thenk to ben in his prison lene;
Sin I am free, I counte him not a bene.

He may answere, and seye this or that;
I do no fors, I speke right as I mene.
    Sin I fro Love escaped am so fat,
    I never thenk to ben in his prison lene.

Love hath my name y-strike out of his sclat,
And he is strike out of my bokes clene
For ever-mo; ther is non other mene.
    Sin I fro Love escaped am so fat,
    I never thenk to ben in his prison lene;
    Sin I am free, I counte him not a bene.

from THE PARLEMENT OF FOULES

ROUNDEL

"Now welcom somer, with thy sonne softe,
That hast this wintres weders over-shake,
And driven awey the longe nightes blake!"

"Seynt Valentyn, that art ful hy on-lofte;—
Thus singen smale foules for thy sake—
   Now welcom somer, with thy sonne softe,
   That hast this wintres weders over-shake.

"Wel han they cause for to gladen ofte,
Sith ech of hem recovered hath his make;
Ful blisful may they singen when they wake;
   Now welcom somer, with thy sonne softe,
   That hast this wintres weders over-shake,
   And driven awey the longe nightes blake."

Anonymous
   [c. 1350]

ADAM LAY YBOUNDIN

         O felix culpa!
Adam lay yboundin, boundin in a bond,
Foure thousand winter thought he not to long.
And al was for an appil, an appil that he took,
As clerkes findin wretin in here book.
Ne hadde the appil take ben, the appil taken ben,
Ne hadde never our Lady a ben hevene quen.

Blissed be the time that appil take was,
Therfore we mown singin *Deo Gratias.*

Charles d'Orléans
[1391–1465]

SPRING

> The new-liveried year.—SIR HENRY WOTTON

The year has changed his mantle cold
   Of wind, of rain, of bitter air;
And he goes clad in cloth of gold,
   Of laughing suns and season fair;
No bird or beast of wood or wold
   But doth with cry or song declare
The year lays down his mantle cold.
All founts, all rivers, seaward rolled,
   The pleasant summer livery wear,
   With silver studs on broidered vair;
The world puts off its raiment old,
The year lays down his mantle cold.

Translated by Andrew Lang

Anonymous
[15th century]

✻ ✻ In 1939 the Clarendon Press of Oxford issued a collection
of *Religious Lyrics of the Fifteenth Century,* chosen by Carleton

Brown, many of which were unknown to average scholars. Only advanced students can read them without a glossary, and it would be perfectly useless to present them here as they stand in the manuscripts, anonymous and mixed with Latin.

DEAR SON, LEAVE THY WEEPING

A Baby is born, us bliss to bring;
A maiden I heard loudly sing:
"Dear son, now leave thy weeping,
Thy fader is the king of bliss."

"Nay, dear mother, for you weep I not,
But for things that shall be wrought
Before that I have mankind i-bought,
Was never pain like it, I wis."

"Peace, dear son, say thou me not so!
Thou art my child, I have no mo.
Alas that I should see this woe,
It were to me great heaviness."

"My hands, modere, that ye now see,
They shall be nailed on a tree;
My feet also fastened shall be—
Full many shall weep that it shall see."

"Alas! dear son, sorrow now is my hap
To see my child that sucks my pap
So rwthfully taken out of my lap,
It were to me great heaviness."

"Also, modere, there shall a spear
My tender heart all to-tear,
The blood shall keuyre my body there,
Great rwthe it shall be to see."

modere: mother   *hap:* fortune   *rwthfully:* pitifully   *keuyre:* run over

Deo patri sit gloria . . .

"Ah, dear son, that is a heavy case;
When Gabriel knelt before my face
And say: 'Hail Lady full of grace,'
He never told me nothing of this."

Gloria tibi domine . . .

"Dear modere, peace, now I you pray,
And take no sorrow for what I say;
But sing this song: 'bye, bye, lowlay,'
To drive away all heaviness."

AVE MARIS STELLA

Ave maris stella, the star of the sea,
Dei mater alma, blessed mot Ye be,
Atque semper virgo, pray thy son for me,
Felix coeli porta, that I may come to thee.
Gabriel that archangel he was messenger,
So fair he greeted our Lady with an AVE so clear.
Hail be thou, Mary! be thou, Mary,
Full of God's grace and queen of mercy.
All that arn to greet without deadly sin,
Forty days of pardon God grant him.

arn: earn, manage

❋ ❋ These songs can be set against the Temple Odes in the Con-
fucian Anthology when we come to answer Mr. Cookson's chal-
lenge, *vide* the Preface, p. vii.

The Latin interpolations here have been shortened. Poems in
mixed language were not uncommon during the Middle Ages,
when the language of teaching was Latin.

François Villon
[1431–1463?]

THE COMPLAINT OF
THE FAIR ARMOURESS

1

Meseemeth I heard cry and groan
    That sweet who was the armourer's maid;
For her young years she made sore moan,
    And right upon this wise she said;
    "Ah fierce old age with foul bald head,
To spoil fair things thou art over fain;
    Who holdeth me? who? would God I were dead!
Would God I were well dead and slain!

2

"Lo, thou hast broken the sweet yoke
    That my high beauty held above
All priests and clerks and merchant-folk;
    There was not one but for my love
    Would give me gold and gold enough,
Though sorrow his very heart had riven,
    To win from me such wage thereof
As now no thief would take if given.

3

"I was right chary of the same,
    God wot it was my great folly,
For love of one sly knave of them,
    Good store of that same sweet had he;
    For all my subtle wiles, perdie,
God wot I loved him well enow;
    Right evilly he handled me,
But he loved well my gold, I trow.

4

"Though I gat bruises green and black,
    I loved him never the less a jot;
Though he bound burdens on my back,
    If he said 'Kiss me, and heed it not,'
    Right little pain I felt, God wot,
When that foul thief's mouth, found so sweet,
    Kissed me—Much good thereof I got!
I keep the sin and the shame of it.

5

"And he died thirty year agone.
    I am old now, no sweet thing to see;
By God, though, when I think thereon,
    And of that good glad time, woe's me,
    And stare upon my changed body
Stark naked, that has been so sweet,
    Lean, wizen, like a small dry tree,
I am nigh mad with the pain of it.

6

"Where is my faultless forehead's white,
    The lifted eyebrows, soft gold hair,
Eyes wide apart and keen of sight,
    With subtle skill in the amorous air;
    The straight nose, great nor small, but fair,
The small carved ears of shapeliest growth,
    Chin dimpling, color good to wear,
And sweet red splendid kissing mouth?

7

"The shapely slender shoulders small,
    Long arms, hands wrought in glorious wise,
Round little breasts, the hips withal
    High, full of flesh, not scant of size,

Fit for all amorous masteries;
*** ***** *****, *** *** ****** **** ***
   ******* ******, ***** ******
** * ***** ****** ** **** *****?

8

"A writhled forehead, hair gone grey,
   Fallen eyebrows, eyes gone blind and red,
Their laughs and looks all fled away,
   Yea, all that smote men's hearts are fled;
   The bowed nose, fallen from goodlihead;
Foul flapping ears like water-flags;
   Peaked chin, and cheeks all waste and dead,
And lips that are two skinny rags:

9

"Thus endeth all the beauty of us.
   The arms made short, the hands made lean,
The shoulders bowed and ruinous,
   The breasts, alack! all fallen in;
   The flanks too, like the breasts, grown thin
** *** *** ***** *****, *** ** **!
   *** *** **** ******, ** ****** *** ****,
**** *** **** ****** ****** ** *******-****.

10

"So we make moan for the old sweet days,
   Poor old light women, two or three
Squatting about the straw-fire's blaze,
   The bosom crushed against the knee,
   Like fagots on a heap we be,
Round fires soon lit, soon quenched and done;
   And we were once so sweet, even we!
Thus fareth many and many an one."

THE EPITAPH IN FORM OF A BALLAD
Which Villon Made for Himself and His Comrades,
Expecting to Be Hanged Along with Them

Men, brother men, that after us yet live,
Let not your hearts too hard against us be;
For if some pity of us poor men ye give,
The sooner God shall take of you pity.
Here we are five or six strung up, you see,
And here the flesh that all too well we fed
Bit by bit eaten and rotten, rent and shred,
And we the bones grow dust and ash withal;
Let no man laugh at us discomforted,
But pray to God that he forgive us all.

If we call on you, brothers, to forgive,
Ye should not hold our prayer in scorn, though we
Were slain by law; ye know that all alive
Have not wit alway to walk righteously;
Make therefore intercession heartily
With him that of a virgin's womb was bred,
That his grace be not as a dry well-head
For us, nor let hell's thunder on us fall;
We are dead, let no man harry or vex us dead,
But pray to God that he forgive us all.

The rain has washed and laundered us all five,
And the sun dried and blackened; yea, perdie,
Ravens and pies with beaks that rend and rive
Have dug our eyes out, and plucked off for fee
Our beards and eyebrows; never are we free,
Not once, to rest; but here and there still sped,
Drive at its wild will by the wind's change led,
More pecked of birds than fruits on garden-wall;
Men, for God's love, let no gibe here be said,
But pray to God that he forgive us all.

Prince Jesus, that of all art lord and head,
Keep us, that hell be not our bitter bed;
We have nought to do in such a master's hall.
Be not ye therefore of our fellowhead,
But pray to God that he forgive us all.

A FRAGMENT ON DEATH

And Paris be it or Helen dying,
   Who dies soever, dies with pain.
He that lacks breath and wind for sighing,
    His gall bursts on his heart; and then
    He sweats, God knows what sweat! again,
No man may ease him of his grief;
   Child, brother, sister, none were fain
To bail him thence for his relief.

Death makes him shudder, swoon, wax pale,
   Nose bend, veins stretch, and breath surrender,
Neck swell, flesh soften, joints that fail
    Crack their strained nerves and arteries slender.
    O woman's body found so tender,
Smooth, sweet, so precious in men's eyes,
   Must thou too bear such count to render?
Yes; or pass quick into the skies.

Translated by Algernon Charles Swinburne

HIS MOTHER'S SERVICE TO OUR LADY

Lady of Heaven and earth, and therewithal
   Crowned Empress of the nether clefts of Hell,—
I, thy poor Christian, on thy name do call,
   Commending me to thee, with thee to dwell,
   Albeit in nought I be commendable.

But all mine undeserving may not mar
Such mercies as thy sovereign mercies are;
    Without the which (as true words testify)
No soul can reach thy Heaven so fair and far.
    Even in this faith I choose to live and die.

Unto thy Son say thou that I am His,
    And to me graceless make Him gracious.
Sad Mary of Egypt lacked not of that bliss,
    Nor yet the sorrowful clerk Theophilus,
    Whose bitter sins were set aside even thus
Though to the Fiend his bounden service was.
Oh help me, lest in vain for me should pass
    (Sweet Virgin that shalt have no loss thereby!)
The blessed Host and sacring of the Mass.
    Even in this faith I choose to live and die.

A pitiful poor woman, shrunk and old,
    I am, and nothing learn'd in letter-lore.
Within my parish-cloister I behold
    A painted Heaven where harps and lutes adore,
    And eke an Hell whose damned folk seethe full sore:
One bringeth fear, the other joy to me.
That joy, great Goddess, make thou mine to be,—
    Thou of whom all must ask it even as I;
And that which faith desires, that let it see.
    For in this faith I choose to live and die.

O excellent Virgin Princess! thou didst bear
King Jesus, the most excellent comforter,
Who even of this our weakness craved a share
    And for our sake stooped to us from on high,
Offering to death His young life sweet and fair.
Such as He is, Our Lord, I Him declare,
    And in this faith I choose to live and die.

THE BALLAD OF DEAD LADIES

Tell me now in what hidden way is
   Lady Flora the lovely Roman?
Where's Hipparchia, and where is Thais,
   Neither of them the fairer woman?
   Where is Echo, beheld of no man,
Only heard on river and mere,—
   She whose beauty was more than human? . . .
But where are the snows of yester-year?

Where's Héloise, the learned nun,
   For whose sake Abeillard, I ween,
Lost manhood and put priesthood on?
   (From Love he won such dule and teen!)
   And where, I pray you, is the Queen
Who willed that Buridan should steer
   Sewed in a sack's mouth down the Seine? . . .
But where are the snows of yester-year?

White Queen Blanche, like a queen of lilies,
   With a voice like any mermaiden,—
Bertha Broadfoot, Beatrice, Alice,
   And Ermengarde the lady of Maine,—
   And that good Joan whom Englishmen
At Rouen doomed and burned her there,—
   Mother of God, where are they then? . . .
But where are the snows of yester-year?

Nay, never ask this week, fair lord,
   Where they are gone, nor yet this year,
Save with thus much for an overword,—
   But where are the snows of yester-year?

Translated by Dante Gabriel Rossetti

Lorenzo de' Medici, the Magnificent
[1449–1492]

from CARNIVAL SONGS

TRIUMPH OF BACCHUS AND ARIADNE

How fair is youth that flies so fast! Then be happy, ye who may;
what's to come is still unsure.

Here are Bacchus and his lady, both so fair and both in love; and,
since time is swift and cheating, in delight they dwell together.
Joyous are these Nymphs and others! Then be happy, ye who
may; what's to come is still unsure.

These laughing youthful Satyrs, in the woodlands and mountains,
spy upon the lurking-places of the Nymphs whom they adore!
Warm with Bacchus now they dance and leap! Then be happy,
ye who may; what's to come is still unsure.

These Nymphs delight to yield to them, and none give Love de-
nial save coarse and graceless folk; mingled now together, ever
they make merry. Then be happy, ye who may; what's to come
is still unsure.

This Ass's burden coming up behind is old Silenus, drunk and
happy, full of flesh and years. He cannot stand upright, yet he
laughs and ever rejoices. Then be happy, ye who may; what's
to come is still unsure.

After them comes Midas; all he touches turns to gold; whom then
does his wealth make merry, since the man is not content?

How can one that thirsts for ever taste any pleasure? Then be
happy, ye who may; what's to come is still unsure.

Open wide your ears, there's no delight in tomorrow; old and
young and men and women, let us all be gay to-day; every sad
thought fall away; let us ever feast together. Then be happy,
ye who may; what's to come is still unsure.

Ladies and ye youthful lovers, long live Bacchus, long live Love!
Let each make music, dance and sing, let every heart be fired
with pleasure! Not with labor, not with grief! Whoever lives,
let him rejoice with us; then be happy, ye who may; what's to
come is still unsure. How fair is youth that flies so fast!

Translated by Richard Aldington

Michelangelo Buonarotti
[1475–1564]

TO THE MARCHESANA OF PESCARA

Yes! hope may with my strong desire keep pace,
And I be undeluded, unbetrayed;
For if of our affections none find grace
In sight of Heaven, then, wherefore hath God made
The world which we inhabit? Better plea
Love cannot have, than that in loving thee
Glory to that eternal Peace is paid,
Who such divinity to thee imparts
As hallows and makes pure all gentle hearts.

His hope is treacherous only whose love dies
With beauty, which is varying every hour;
But, in chaste hearts uninfluenced by the power
Of outward change, there blooms a deathless flower,
That breathes on earth the air of paradise.

Translated by William Wordsworth

❋❋ The great sculptor's sonnets have a place of their own in Italian poetry, after the early, less rhetorical poetry of the "First Centuries." He died, as you see, in the year of Shakespeare's birth.

Martin Luther
[1483–1546]

"EIN FESTE BURG IST UNSER GOTT"

A Tower of Refuge is our God!
  A goodly ward and weapon.
He'll help us free, tho force or fraud
  To us may now mishappen.
     That old Arch-enemy
      Would our undoing be;
    Gross might and vast device
    His dreadful armor is.
On Earth can none withstand him.

By our might could we do no more
  Than vainly to have striven:
But for us the right Man will war,
  Whom God Himself hath given.

Dost ask, who this can be?
Christ Jesus! It is HE!
The Lord of Sabaoth,
None other God, in troth.
The field He holds forever.

For tho the world with demons swarmed,
All minded to devour us,
Not greatly were our souls alarmed;
They cannot overpower us.
This world's dark Prince may still
Lour sullen as he will;
For he can harm us naught.
'Tis past. His doom is wrought.
One word can bring his downfall!

That Word, for all they do, shall stand,
No thank to them that jeer it!
Yea, on the plain He's at our hand,
By His own Gift and Spirit.
And should they take our life,
Fame, fortune, child and wife,—
Let them all this begin:
But nothing can they win,
And God gives us the kingdom.

Translated by M. Woolsey Stryker, 1883

Henry VIII
[1491–1547]

PASTIME

Pastime with good company
I love and shall, until I die.
Grudge who list, but none deny!
So God be pleased, thus live will I.
   For my pastance,
   Hunt, sing and dance,
   My heart is set.
     All goodly sport
     For my comfort
   Who shall me let?

Youth must have some dalliance,
Of good or ill some pastance.
Company me thinks the best,
All thoughts and fancies to digest;
   For idleness
   Is chief mistress
   Of vices all.
     Then who can say
     But mirth and play
   Is best of all?

Company with honesty
Is virtue, vices to flee;
Company is good and ill,
But every man has his free will.
   The best ensue,
   The worst eschew!
   My mind shall be,

pastance: pastime

Virtue to use,
Vice to refuse;
Thus shall I use me.

THE HOLLY

Green groweth the holly; so doth the ivy.
Though winter blastés blow never so high,
Green groweth the holly.

As the holly groweth green,
And never changeth hue,
So I am, ever hath been
Unto my lady true;

As the holly groweth green
With ivy all alone,
When flowerés cannot be seen
And green wood leaves be gone.

Now unto my lady
Promise to her I make,
From all other only
To her I me betake.

Adieu, mine own lady,
Adieu, my special,
Who hath my heart truly,
Be sure, and ever shall!

TO HIS LADY

Whereto should I express
My inward heaviness?
No mirth can make me fain,
Till that we meet again.

Do way, dear heart! Not so!
   Let no thought you dismay.
Though ye now part me fro,
   We shall meet when we may.

When I remember me
   Of your most gentle mind,
It may in no wise agree
   That I should be unkind.

The daisy delectable,
   The violet wan and blo,
Ye are not variable.
   I love you and no mo.

I make you fast and sure.
   It is to me great pain
Thus long to endure
   Till that we meet again.

do way: have done   *blo:* pale

William Cornish
[?–1524?]

GRATITUDE

   Pleasure it is
      To hear, iwis,
   The birdès sing.

iwis: truly

The deer in the dale,
The sheep in the vale,
    The corn springing.
God's purveyance
For sustenance
        It is for man.
Then we always
To him give praise,
        And thank him than,
        And thank him than.

Heath

[temp. Henry VIII]

WOMEN

These women all
Both great and small
    Are wavering to and fro,
Now here, now there,
Now everywhere;
    But I will not say so.

So they love to range,
Their minds doth change
    And make their friend their foe;
As lovers true
Each day they choose new;
    But I will not say so.

They laugh, they smile,
They do beguile,
   As dice that men doth throw.
Who useth them much
Never shall be rich;
   But I will not say so.

Some hot, some cold,
There is no hold
   But as the wind doth blow;
When all is done,
They change like the moon;
   But I will not say so.

So thus one and other
Taketh after their mother,
   As cock by kind doth crow.
My song is ended,
The best may be amended;
   But I will not say so.

Anonymous

[16th century]

WESTERN WIND

Western wind, when will thou blow,
   The small rain down can rain?
Christ, if my love were in my arms
   And I in my bed again!

Thomas Wyatt
[?1503–1542]

EPIGRAM

A face that should content me wonders well,
    Should not be fair but lovely to behold,
With gladsome cheer all grief for to expel;
    With sober looks so would I that it should
Speak without words such words as none can tell;
    The tress also should be of crispèd gold.
        With wit and these, might chance I might be tied
        And knit again the knot that should not slide.

Santa Teresa d'Avila
[1515–1582]

BOOKMARK

Let nothing disturb thee,
Nothing affright thee;
All things are passing;
God never changeth;
Patient endurance
Attaineth to all things;
Who God possesseth
In nothing is wanting;
Alone God sufficeth.

Translated by Henry Wadsworth Longfellow

Joachim du Bellay

[?1522–1560]

A SONNET TO HEAVENLY BEAUTY

If this our little life is but a day
   In the Eternal,—if the years in vain
   Toil after hours that never come again,—
If everything that hath been must decay,
Why dreamest thou of joys that pass away,
   My soul, that my sad body doth restrain?
   Why of the moment's pleasure art thou fain?
Nay, thou has wings,—nay, seek another stay.

There is the joy whereto each soul aspires,
And there the rest that all the world desires,
   And there is love, and peace, and gracious mirth;
And there in the most highest heavens shalt thou
Behold the Very Beauty, whereof now
   Thou worshippest the shadow upon earth.

Translated by Andrew Lang

Pierre de Ronsard

[1525–1585]

OF HIS LADY'S OLD AGE

When you are very old, at evening
You'll sit and spin beside the fire, and say,

Humming my songs, "Ah well, ah well-a-day!
When I was young, of me did Ronsard sing."
None of your maidens that doth hear the thing,
   Albeit with her weary task foredone,
   But wakens at my name, and calls you one
Blest, to be held in long remembering.

I shall be low beneath the earth, and laid
On sleep, a phantom in the myrtle shade,
   While you beside the fire, a grandame grey,
My love, your pride, remember and regret;
Ah, love me, love! we may be happy yet,
   And gather roses, while 'tis called to-day.

Translated by Andrew Lang

Elizabeth I

[1533–1603]

THE DOUBT OF FUTURE FOES

The doubt of future foes exiles my present joy,
And wit me warns to shun such snares as threaten mine annoy.
For falsehood now doth flow and subject faith doth ebb,
Which would not be if reason ruled or wisdom weaved the web.
But clouds of toys untried do cloak aspiring minds,
Which turn to rain of late repent by course of changèd winds.
The top of hope supposed, the root of ruth will be,
And fruitless all their grassèd guiles, as shortly ye shall see.
The dazzled eyes with pride, which great ambition blinds,
Shall be unsealed by worthy wights whose foresight falsehood
   finds.

The daughter of debate that eke discord doth sow,
Shall reap no gain where former rule hath taught still peace to
    grow.
No foreign banished wight shall anchor in this port;
Our realm it brooks no stranger's force, let them elsewhere resort.
Our rusty sword with rest shall first his edge employ
To poll the tops that seek such change and gape for joy.

※ ※ From Puttenham's *Arte of English Poesie* (1589); ascribed
uncertainly to Elizabeth. [M. S.]

WHEN I WAS FAIR AND YOUNG

When I was fair and young, and favor gracèd me,
    Of many was I sought, their mistress for to be;
But I did scorn them all, and answered them therefore,
      Go, go, go, seek some otherwhere,
        Impórtune me no more!

How many weeping eyes I made to pine with woe,
    How many sighing hearts, I have no skill to show;
Yet I the prouder grew, and answered them therefore,
      Go, go, go, seek some otherwhere,
        Impórtune me no more!

Then spake fair Venus' son, that proud victorious boy,
    And said: Fine dame, since that you be so coy,
I will so pluck your plumes that you shall say no more,
      Go, go, go, seek some otherwhere,
        Impórtune me no more!

When he had spake these words, such change grew in my breast
    That neither night nor day since that, I could take any rest.
Then lo! I did repent that I had said before,
      Go, go, go, seek some otherwhere,
        Impórtune me no more!

George Turberville

[?1540–1610?]

THE LOVER TO HIS LADY
That gazed much up to the skies

My girl, thou gazest much
   Upon the golden skies:
Would I were heaven! I would behold
   Thee then with all mine eyes.

TO HIS FRIEND
Promising that though her beauty fade, yet his love shall last

I wot full well that beauty cannot last;
   No rose that springs but lightly doth decay,
And feature like a lily leaf doth waste,
   Or as the cowslip in the midst of May;
     I know that tract of time doth conquer all,
     And beauty's buds like fading flowers do fall.

That famous dame, fair Helen, lost her hue
   When withered age with wrinkles changed her cheeks,
Her lovely looks did loathsomeness ensue,
   That was the *A per se* of all the Greeks.
     And sundry more that were as fair as she,
     Yet Helen was as fresh as fresh might be.

No force for that, I price your beauty light
   If so I find you steadfast in good will.
Though few there are that do in age delight,
   I was your friend, and so do purpose still;
     No change of looks shall breed my change of love,
     Nor beauty's want my first good will remove.

Walter Ralegh
[?1552–1618]

THE NYMPH'S REPLY TO
THE SHEPHERD

If all the world and love were young,
And truth in every shepherd's tongue,
These pretty pleasures might me move
To live with thee and be thy love.

Time drives the flocks from field to fold,
When rivers rage and rocks grow cold,
And Philomel becometh dumb;
The rest complains of cares to come.

The flowers do fade, and wanton fields
To wayward winter reckoning yields;
A honey tongue, a heart of gall,
Is fancy's spring, but sorrow's fall.

Thy gowns, thy shoes, thy beds of roses,
Thy cap, thy kirtle, and thy posies
Soon break, soon wither, soon forgotten,—
In folly ripe, in reason rotten.

Thy belt of straw and ivy buds,
Thy coral clasps and amber studs,
All these in me no means can move
To come to thee and be thy love.

But could youth last and love still breed,
Had joys no date nor age no need,

Then these delights my mind might move
To live with thee and be thy love.

✵ ✵ An answer to Marlowe's "Passionate Shepherd to His Love"
(see below, p. 147); both poems appeared in the collection *England's Helicon* (1600), Ralegh's over the signature "Ignoto."
[M. S.]

EPITAPH

Even such is Time, which takes in trust
Our youth, our joys, and all we have,
And pays us but with age and dust;
Who in the dark and silent grave,
When we have wandered all our ways,
Shuts up the story of our days:
And from which earth, and grave, and dust,
The Lord shall raise me up, I trust.

THE LIE

Go, soul, the body's guest,
    Upon a thankless arrant;
Fear not to touch the best,
    The truth shall be thy warrant:
        Go, since I needs must die,
        And give the world the lie.

Say to the Court, it glows,
    And shines like rotten wood;
Say to the Church, it shows
    What's good, and doth no good:
        If Church and Court reply,
        Then give them both the lie.

Tell Potentates they live
    Acting by others' action;
Not loved unless they give,
    Not strong but by a faction:
      If Potentates reply,
      Give Potentates the lie.

Tell men of high condition,
    That manage the estate,
Their purpose is ambition,
    Their practice only hate:
      And if they once reply,
      Then give them all the lie.

Tell them that brave it most,
    They beg for more by spending,
Who, in their greatest cost,
    Seek nothing but commending:
      And if they make reply,
      Then tell them all they lie.

Tell zeal it wants devotion;
    Tell love it is but lust;
Tell time it metes but motion;
    Tell flesh it is but dust:
      And wish them not reply,
      For thou must give the lie.

Tell age it daily wasteth;
    Tell honour how it alters;
Tell beauty how she blasteth;
    Tell favour how it falters:
      And as they shall reply,
      Give every one the lie.

Tell wit how much it wrangles
    In tickle points of niceness:
Tell wisdom she entangles
    Herself in over-wiseness:
        And when they do reply,
        Straight give them both the lie.

Tell physic of her boldness;
    Tell skill it is prevention;
Tell charity of coldness;
    Tell law it is contention:
        And as they do reply,
        So give them still the lie.

Tell fortune of her blindness;
    Tell nature of decay;
Tell friendship of unkindness;
    Tell justice of delay:
        And if they will reply,
        Then give them all the lie.

Tell arts they have no soundness,
    But vary by esteeming;
Tell schools they want profoundness,
    And stand too much on seeming:
        If arts and schools reply,
        Give arts and schools the lie.

Tell faith it's fled the city;
    Tell how the country erreth;
Tell, manhood shakes off pity,
    Tell, virtue least preferreth:
        And if they do reply,
        Spare not to give the lie.

So when thou hast, as I
   Commanded thee, done blabbing;
Although to give the lie
   Deserves no less than stabbing:
      Stab at thee he that will,
      No stab the soul can kill.

A. W.

[fl. 1585]

WHERE HIS LADY KEEPS HIS HEART

Sweet Love, mine only treasure,
For service long unfeigned,
Wherein I nought have gained,
Vouchsafe this little pleasure,
   To tell me in what part
   My Lady keeps my heart.

If in her hair so slender,
Like golden nets entwined,
Which fire and art have fined;
Her thrall my heart I render,
   For ever to abide
   With locks so dainty tied.

If in her eyes she bind it,
Wherein that fire was framed,
By which it is inflamed,
I dare not look to find it;
   I only wish it sight,
   To see that pleasant light.

But if her breast have deigned
With kindness to receive it,
I am content to leave it,
Though death thereby were gained:
    Then, Lady, take your own,
    That lives for you alone.

UPON VISITING HIS LADY BY MOONLIGHT

The night, say all, was made for rest;
And so say I, but not for all:
To them the darkest nights are best,
Which give them leave asleep to fall;
    But I that seek my rest by light
    Hate sleep, and praise the clearest night.

Bright was the Moon, as bright as day,
And Venus glistered in the west,
Whose light did lead the ready way,
That brought me to my wishèd rest:
    Then each of them increased their light
    While I enjoyed her heavenly sight.

Say, gentle Dames, what moved your mind
To shine so bright above your wont?
Would Phœbe fair Endymion find?
Would Venus see Adonis hunt?
    No, no, you fearèd by her sight
    To lose the praise of beauty bright.

At last, for shame you shrunk away,
And thought to 'reave the world of light;
Then shone my Dame with brighter ray,
Than that which comes from Phœbus' sight:
    None other light but hers I praise
    Whose nights are clearer than the days.

IN PRAISE OF THE SUN

Ubi amor, ibi oculus

The golden sun that brings the day,
And lends men light to see withal,
In vain doth cast his beams away,
Where they are blind on whom they fall:
  There is no force in all his light
  To give the mole a perfect sight.

But thou, my sun, more bright than he
That shines at noon in summer tide,
Hast given me light and power to see;
With perfect skill my sight to guide.
  Till now I lived as blind as mole,
  That hides her head in earthly hole.

I heard the praise of beauty's grace,
Yet deemed it nought but Poet's skill;
I gazed on many a lovely face,
Yet found I none to bind my will:
  Which made me think, that beauty bright
  Was nothing else but red and white.

But now thy beams have cleared my sight,
I blush to think I was so blind:
Thy flaming eyes afford me light,
That beauty's blaze each where I find:
  And yet these Dames, that shine so bright,
  Are but the shadow of thy light.

❋ ❋ Three poems from Francis Davison's *A Poetical Rhapsody* (1602), one of the popular miscellanies of the Elizabethan era; the author being unidentified, except by his initials. [M. S.]

Anthony Munday
[c. 1553–1633]

DIRGE

Weep, weep, ye woodmen, wail;
    Your hands with sorrow wring!
Your master Robin Hood lies dead,
    Therefore sigh as you sing.

Here lies his primer and his beads,
    His bent bow and his arrows keen,
His good sword and his holy cross.
    Now cast on flowers fresh and green;

And, as they fall, shed tears and say
    Well-a, well-a-day! well-a, well-a-day!
Thus cast ye flowers, and sing,
    And on to Wakefield take your way.

Robert Greene
[?1558–1592]

THE PALMER'S ODE

Old Menalcas on a day,
As in field this shepherd lay,
Tuning of his oaten pipe,
Which he hit with many a stripe,

Said to Coridon that he
Once was young and full of glee:
'Blithe and wanton was I then;
Such desires follow men.
As I lay and kept my sheep,
Came the God that hateth sleep,
Clad in armour all of fire,
Hand in hand with Queen Desire;
And with a dart that wounded nigh,
Pierced my heart as I did lie;
That when I woke I 'gan swear,
Phillis' beauty palm did bear.
Up I start, forth went I,
With her face to feed mine eye:
There I saw Desire sit,
That my heart with love had hit,
Laying forth bright beauty's hooks
To entrap my grazing looks.
Love I did and 'gan to woo,
Pray and sigh; all would not do:
Women, when they take the toy,
Covet to be counted coy.
Coy she was, and I 'gan court,
She thought love was but a sport.
Profound hell was in my thought,
Such a pain Desire had wrought,
That I sued with sighs and tears.
Still ingrate she stopped her ears,
Till my youth I had spent.
Last a passion of Repent
Told me flat that Desire
Was a brand of love's fire,
Which consumeth men in thrall,
Virtue, youth, wit, and all.
At this saw back I start,
Beat Desire from my heart,
Shook off love and made an oath,

To be enemy to both.
Old I was when thus I fled
Such fond toys as cloyed my head.
But this I learned at Virtue's gate,
The way to good is never late.'

MAESIA'S SONG

Sweet are the thoughts that savour of content,
    The quiet mind is richer than a crown;
Sweet are the nights in careless slumber spent,
    The poor estate scorns Fortune's angry frown.
Such sweet content, such minds, such sleep, such bliss,
    Beggars enjoy, when princes oft do miss.

The homely house that harbours quiet rest,
    The cottage that affords no pride nor care,
The mean that 'grees with country music best,
    The sweet consort of mirth and music's fare,
Obscured life sets down a type of bliss;
    A mind content both crown and kingdom is.

THE DESCRIPTION OF SIR GEOFFREY CHAUCER

His stature was not very tall,
Lean he was, his legs were small,
Hosed within a stock of red,
A buttoned bonnet on his head,
From under which did hang, I ween,
Silver hairs both bright and sheen.
His beard was white, trimmed round,
His countenance blithe and merry found.
A sleeveless jacket large and wide,
With many plights and skirts side,

Of water camlet did he wear;
A whittle by his belt he bare,
His shoes were corned, broad before,
His inkhorn at his side he wore,
And in his hand he bore a book.
Thus did this ancient poet look.

Anonymous

[c. 1600]

SONG SET BY NICHOLAS YONGE

Brown is my Love, but graceful;
And each renowned whiteness
Matched with thy lovely brown loseth its brightness.

Fair is my Love, but scornful;
Yet have I seen despised
Dainty white lilies, and sad flowers well prized.

SONG SET BY JOHN FARMER

Take Time while Time doth last,
Mark how Fair fadeth fast,
Beware if Envy reign,
Take heed of proud Disdain.
Hold fast now in thy youth,
Regard thy vowed Truth,
Lest when thou waxeth old
Friends fail and Love grow cold.

Robert Wilson

[?–1600?]

SIMPLICITY'S SONG

Simplicity sings it and 'sperience doth prove,
  No biding in London for Conscience and Love.
        The country hath no peer,
        Where Conscience comes not once a year;
        And Love so welcome to every town,
        As wind that blows the houses down.
                Sing down, adown, down, down, down.
Simplicity sings it and 'sperience doth prove,
No dwelling in London, no biding in London, for Conscience and
                Love.

Samuel Daniel

[1562–1619]

from THE COMPLAINT OF ROSAMOND

LONELY BEAUTY

What greater torment ever could have been,
Than to enforce the fair to live retired?
For what is beauty if it be not seen?
Or what is 't to be seen if not admired,
And though admired, unless in love desired?
  Never were cheeks of roses, locks of amber,
  Ordained to live imprisoned in a chamber.

Nature created beauty for the view,
Like as the fire for heat, the sun for light;
The fair do hold this privilege as due
By ancient charter, to live most in sight,
And she that is debarred it, hath not right.
    In vain our friends from this do us dehort,
    For beauty will be where is most resort.

Witness the fairest streets that Thames doth visit,
The wondrous concourse of the glitt'ring fair;
For what rare woman decked with beauty is it
That thither covets not to make repair?
The solitary country may not stay her;
    Here is the center of all beauties best,
    Excepting Delia, left t' adorn the west.

Here doth the curious with judicial eyes
Contemplate beauty gloriously attired;
And herein all our chiefest glory lies,
To live where we are praised and most desired.
O! how we joy to see ourselves admired,
    Whilst niggardly our favours we discover;
    We love to be beloved, yet scorn the lover.

Yet would to God my foot had never moved
From country safety, from the fields of rest,
To know the danger to be highly loved,
And live in pomp to brave among the best;
Happy for me, better had I been blest,
    If I unluckily had never strayed,
    But lived at home a happy country maid,

Whose unaffected innocency thinks
No guileful fraud, as doth the courtly liver;
She's decked with truth; the river where she drinks
Doth serve her for her glass, her counsel-giver;
She loves sincerely, and is lovèd ever;

Her days are peace, and so she ends her breath—
True life, that knows not what's to die till death.

So should I never have been regist'red
In the black book of the unfortunate,
Nor had my name enrolled with maids misled,
Which brought their pleasures at so high a rate;
Nor had I taught, through my unhappy fate,
    This lesson, which myself learnt with expense,
    How most it hurts that most delights the sense.

from TO DELIA

VI

When winter snows upon thy sable hairs,
    And frost of age hath nipped thy beauties near;
    When dark shall seem thy day that never clears,
    And all lies withered that was held so dear,
    Then take this picture which I here present thee,
    Limned with a pencil not all unworthy;
    Here see the gifts that God and nature lent thee,
    Here read thyself, and what I suffered for thee.
    This may remain thy lasting monument,
    Which happily posterity may cherish;
    These colours with thy fading are not spent,
    These may remain when thou and I shall perish.
    If they remain, then thou shalt live thereby;
    They will remain, and so thou canst not die.

Christopher Marlowe
[1564–1593]

A FRAGMENT

I walked along a stream for pureness rare,
   Brighter than sunshine, for it did acquaint
      The dullest sight with all the glorious prey,
      That in the pebble-paved channel lay.

No molten crystal, but a richer mine,
   Even Nature's rarest alchemy ran there,
Diamonds resolved, and substance more divine,
   Through whose bright gliding current might appear
A thousand naked nymphs, whose ivory shine,
   Enamelling the banks, made them more dear
      Than ever was that glorious palace gate,
      Where the day-shining sun in triumph sat.

Upon this brim the eglantine and rose,
   The tamarisk, olive, and the almond tree,
As kind companions in one union grows,
   Folding their twining arms, as oft we see
Turtle-taught lovers either other close,
   Lending to dullness feeling sympathy.
      And as a costly valance o'er a bed,
      So did their garland tops the brook o'erspread.

Their leaves that differed both in shape and show,
   (Though all were green) yet difference such in green,
Like to the checkered bent of Iris' bow,
   Prided the running main as it had been—

THE PASSIONATE SHEPHERD
TO HIS LOVE

Come live with me and be my love,
    And we will all the pleasures prove
That valleys, groves, hills and fields,
Woods, or steepie mountains yields.

And we will sit upon the rocks,
Seeing the shepherds feed their flocks,
By shallow rivers to whose falls
Melodious birds sing madrigals.

And I will make thee beds of roses
And a thousand fragrant posies,
A cap of flowers, and a kirtle
Embroidered all with leaves of myrtle;

A gown made of the finest wool
Which from our pretty lambs we pull;
Fair linèd slippers for the cold,
With buckles of the purest gold;

A belt of straw and ivy buds,
With coral clasps and amber studs:
And if these pleasures may thee move,
Come live with me and be my love.

The shepherds' swains shall dance and sing
For thy delight each May morning:
If these delights thy mind may move,
Then live with me and be my love.

✳✳ From *England's Helicon* (1600), as is Ralegh's answer, given
above, p. 132. [M. S.]

William Shakespeare
[1564–1616]

from THE TEMPEST

ARIEL'S SONG

Come unto these yellow sands,
    And then take hands.
Curtsied when you have and kiss'd,
    The wild waves whist,
Foot it featly here and there;
And, sweet sprites, the burthen bear.
    Hark, hark!
        Burthen, dispersedly: Bowgh, wawgh!
    The watchdogs bark.
        Burthen, dispersedly: Bowgh, wawgh!
Hark, hark! I hear
    The strain of strutting chanticleer
        Cry, cock-a-diddle-dowe.

    Act I, Scene 2

"WHERE THE BEE SUCKS"

    Where the bee sucks, there suck I.
    In a cowslip's bell I lie;
    There I couch when owls do cry.
    On the bat's back I do fly
    After summer merrily.
Merrily, merrily shall I live now
Under the blossom that hangs on the bough.

    Act V, Scene 1

EPILOGUE
spoken by PROSPERO

Now my charms are all o'erthrown,
And what strength I have's mine own,
Which is most faint. Now 'tis true
I must be here confin'd by you,
Or sent to Naples. Let me not
Since I have my dukedom got
And pardon'd the deceiver, dwell
In this bare island by your spell;
But release me from my bands
With the help of your good hands.
Gentle breath of yours my sails
Must fill, or else my project fails,
Which was to please. Now I want
Spirits to enforce, art to enchant;
And my ending is despair,
Unless I be reliev'd by prayer,
Which pierces so that it assaults
Mercy itself and frees all faults.
As you from crimes would pardon'd be,
Let your indulgence set me free.

Act V, Scene 1

from THE TWO GENTLEMEN OF VERONA

"MY THOUGHTS DO HARBOUR"

'My thoughts do harbour with my Silvia nightly,
    And slaves they are to me, that send them flying.
O, could their master come and go as lightly,
    Himself would lodge where (senseless) they are lying!
My herald thoughts in thy pure bosom rest them,
    While I, their king, that thither them importune,

Do curse the grace that with such grace hath blest them,
  Because myself do want my servants' fortune;
I curse myself, for they are sent by me,
That they should harbour where their lord would be.'

  Act III, Scene 1

❈ ❈ The song "Who Is Silvia?" is omitted on the grounds it
should never be seen apart from its musical setting. [M. S.]

  from MUCH ADO ABOUT NOTHING

"SIGH NO MORE, LADIES"

Sigh no more, ladies, sigh no more!
  Men were deceivers ever,
One foot in sea, and one on shore;
  To one thing constant never.
    Then sigh not so,
    But let them go,
  And be you blithe and bonny,
Converting all your sounds of woe
  Into Hey nonny, nonny.

Sing no more ditties, sing no moe,
  Of dumps so dull and heavy!
The fraud of men was ever so,
  Since summer first was leavy.
    Then sigh not so, &c.

  Act II, Scene 3

EPITAPH

  Done to death by slanderous tongues
    Was the Hero that here lies.

Death, in guerdon of her wrongs,
   Gives her fame which never dies.
So the life that died with shame
Lives in death with glorious fame.

Hang thou there upon the tomb,
Praising her when I am dumb.

   Act V, Scene 3

SONG

Pardon, goddess of the night,
Those that slew thy virgin knight;
For the which, with songs of woe,
Round about her tomb they go.
   Midnight, assist our moan,
   Help us to sigh and groan
      Heavily, heavily.
   Graves, yawn and yield your dead,
   Till death be uttered
      Heavily, heavily.

   Act V, Scene 3

❋❋ Shakespeare's lyrics if not the absolute fountainhead are at any rate the channel from which almost all later melodic and rhythmic variety in song-strophe has flowed into English and American verse.

from LOVE'S LABOUR'S LOST

"IF SHE BE MADE OF WHITE AND RED"

MOTH: If she be made of white and red,
   Her faults will ne'er be known;

For blushing cheeks by faults are bred
    And fears by pale white shown.
Then if she fear, or be to blame,
    By this you shall not know;
For still her cheeks possess the same
    Which native she doth owe.

A dangerous rhyme, master, against the reason of white and red.

    Act I, Scene 2

from A MIDSUMMER NIGHT'S DREAM

"THROUGH THE FOREST HAVE I GONE"

PUCK: Through the forest have I gone,
But Athenian found I none
On whose eyes I might approve
This flower's force in stirring love.
Night and silence! Who is here?
Weeds of Athens he doth wear.
This is he (my master said)
Despised the Athenian maid;
And here the maiden, sleeping sound
On the dank and dirty ground.
Pretty soul! she durst not lie
Near this lack-love, this kill-courtesy.
Churl, upon thy eyes I throw
All the power this charm doth owe.
When thou wak'st, let love forbid
Sleep his seat on thy eyelid.
So awake when I am gone;
For I must now to Oberon.

    Act II, Scene 2

BOTTOM'S SONG

BOTTOM: The woosel cock so black of hue,
　　　With orange-tawny bill,
　The throstle with his note so true,
　　　The wren with little quill—

TITANIA: What angel wakes me from my flowery bed?

BOTTOM: The finch, the sparrow, and the lark,
　　　The plain-song cuckoo gray,
　Whose note full many a man doth mark,
　　　And dares not answer nay.

　　Act III, Scene 1

"FLOWER OF THIS PURPLE DYE"

OBERON: Flower of this purple dye,
Hit with Cupid's archery,
Sink in apple of his eye!
When his love he doth espy,
Let her shine as gloriously
As the Venus of the sky.
When thou wak'st, if she be by,
Beg of her for remedy.

PUCK: Captain of our fairy band,
Helena is here at hand,
And the youth, mistook by me,
Pleading for a lover's fee.
Shall we their fond pageant see?
Lord, what fools these mortals be!

OBERON: Stand aside. The noise they make
Will cause Demetrius to awake.

PUCK: Then will two at once woo one.
That must needs be sport alone;
And those things do best please me
That befall prepost'rously.

Act III, Scene 2

"UP AND DOWN"

PUCK: Up and down, up and down,
I will lead them up and down.
I am fear'd in field and town.
Goblin, lead them up and down.

Act III, Scene 2

"YET BUT THREE?"

ROBIN: Yet but three? Come one more.
Two of both kinds makes up four.
Here she comes, curst and sad.
Cupid is a knavish lad
Thus to make poor females mad.

Act III, Scene 2

"ASLEEP, MY LOVE?"

THISBE: Asleep, my love?
    What, dead, my dove?
O Pyramus, arise!
    Speak, speak! Quite dumb?
    Dead, dead? A tomb
Must cover thy sweet eyes.

These lily lips,
This cherry nose,
These yellow cowslip cheeks,
    Are gone, are gone.
    Lovers, make moan!
His eyes were green as leeks.
    O Sisters Three,
    Come, come to me,
With hands as pale as milk;
    Lay them in gore,
    Since you have shore
With shears his thread of silk.
    Tongue, not a word!
    Come, trusty sword;
Come, blade, my breast imbrue!
                    [*Stabs herself.*]
    And farewell, friends.
    Thus Thisby ends.
Adieu, adieu, adieu.
                    [*Dies.*]

Act V, Scene 1

"NOW THE HUNGRY LION ROARS"

PUCK: Now the hungry lion roars,
    And the wolf behowls the moon;
Whilst the heavy ploughman snores,
    All with weary task fordone.
Now the wasted brands do glow,
    Whilst the screech owl, screeching loud,
Puts the wretch that lies in woe
    In remembrance of a shroud.
Now it is the time of night
    That the graves, all gaping wide,
Every one lets forth his sprite,

In the churchway paths to glide;
And we fairies, that do run
    By the triple Hecate's team,
From the presence of the sun,
    Following darkness like a dream,
Now are frolic. Not a mouse
Shall disturb this hallow'd house.
I am sent, with broom, before,
To sweep the dust behind the door.

Act V, Scene 2

"THROUGH THE HOUSE"

OBERON: Through the house give glimmering light
    By the dead and drowsy fire;
Every elf and fairy sprite
    Hop as light as bird from brier;
And this ditty, after me,
Sing and dance it trippingly.

TITANIA: First, rehearse your song by rote,
To each word a warbling note.
Hand in hand, with fairy grace,
Will we sing, and bless this place.

                              [*Song and dance.*]

OBERON: Now, until the break of day,
Through this house each fairy stray.
To the best bride-bed will we,
Which by us shall blessed be;
And the issue there create
Ever shall be fortunate.
So shall all the couples three
Ever true in loving be;

And the blots of Nature's hand
Shall not in their issue stand;
Never mole, harelip, nor scar,
Nor mark prodigious, such as are
Despised in nativity,
Shall upon their children be.
With this field-dew consecrate,
Every fairy take his gait,
And each several chamber bless,
Through this palace, with sweet peace.
And the owner of it blest
Ever shall in safety rest.
Trip away; make no stay;
Meet me all by break of day.

Exeunt [all but ROBIN GOODFELLOW].

ROBIN: If we shadows have offended,
Think but this, and all is mended—
That you have but slumber'd here
While these visions did appear.
And this weak and idle theme,
No more yielding but a dream,
Gentles, do not reprehend.
If you pardon, we will mend.
And, as I am an honest Puck,
If we have unearned luck
Now to scape the serpent's tongue,
We will make amends ere long;
Else the Puck a liar call.
So, good night unto you all.
Give me your hands, if we be friends,
And Robin shall restore amends.

Act V, Scene 2

from AS YOU LIKE IT

SONG

AMIENS: Under the greenwood tree
   Who loves to lie with me,
   And turn his merry note
   Unto the sweet bird's throat,
Come hither, come hither, come hither!
     Here shall he see
     No enemy
But winter and rough weather.

ALL: Who doth ambition shun,
   And loves to live i' th' sun,
   Seeking the food he eats,
   And pleas'd with what he gets,
Come hither, come hither, come hither!
     Here shall he see
     No enemy
But winter and rough weather.

JAQUES: If it do come to pass
   That any man turn ass,
   Leaving his wealth and ease
   A stubborn will to please,
Ducdame, ducdame, ducdame!
     Here shall he see
     Gross fools as he,
An if he will come to me.

   Act II, Scene 5

ducdame: presumably *"duc et dames,"* duke and ladies

SONG

AMIENS: Blow, blow, thou winter wind,
   Thou art not so unkind
     As man's ingratitude;
   Thy tooth is not so keen,
   Because thou art not seen,
     Although thy breath be rude.
Heigh-ho! sing heigh-ho! unto the green holly.
Most friendship is feigning, most loving mere **folly**:
       Then heigh-ho, the holly!
       This life is most jolly.

   Freeze, freeze, thou bitter sky,
   That dost not bite so nigh
     As benefits forgot.
   Though thou the waters warp,
   Thy sting is not so sharp
     As friend rememb'red not.
Heigh-ho! sing, &c.

   Act II, Scene 7

"WHY SHOULD THIS A DESERT BE"

CELIA (*reading*): 'Why should this a desert be,
   For it is unpeopled? No!
Tongues I'll hang on every tree
   That shall civil sayings show:
Some, how brief the life of man
   Runs his erring pilgrimage,
That the stretching of a span
   Buckles in his sum of age;
Some, of violated vows
   'Twixt the souls of friend and friend;
But upon the fairest boughs,

Or at every sentence end,
Will I "Rosalinda" write,
   Teaching all that read to know
The quintessence of every sprite
   Heaven would in little show.
Therefore heaven Nature charg'd
   That one body should be fill'd
With all graces wide-enlarg'd.
   Nature presently distill'd
Helen's cheek, but not her heart,
   Cleopatra's majesty,
Atalanta's better part,
   Sad Lucretia's modesty.
Thus Rosalinde of many parts
   By heavenly synod was devis'd,
Of many faces, eyes, and hearts,
   To have the touches dearest priz'd.
Heaven would that she these gifts should have,
And I to live and die her slave.'

Act III, Scene 2

SONG

JAQUES: What shall he have that kill'd the deer?
His leather skin and horns to wear.
   Then sing him home.
        [*The rest shall bear this burthen.*]
Take thou no scorn to wear the horn;
It was a crest ere thou wast born:
   Thy father's father wore it,
   And thy father bore it.
The horn, the horn, the lusty horn,
Is not a thing to laugh to scorn.

Act IV, Scene 2

SONG

ROSALIND: 'If the scorn of your bright eyne
Have power to raise such love in mine,
Alack, in me what strange effect
Would they work in mild aspect!
Whiles you chid me, I did love;
How then might your prayers move!
He that brings this love to thee
Little knows this love in me;
And by him seal up thy mind,
Whether that thy youth and kind
Will the faithful offer take
Of me and all that I can make,
Or else by him my love deny,
And then I'll study how to die.'

Act IV, Scene 3

SONG

It was a lover and his lass—
    With a hey, and a ho, and a hey nonino—
That o'er the green cornfield did pass
    In springtime, the only pretty ring-time,
When birds do sing, hey ding a ding, ding;
Sweet lovers love the spring.

Between the acres of the rye—
    With a hey, and a ho, and a hey nonino—
These pretty country folks would lie,
    In springtime, &c.

This carol they began that hour—
    With a hey, and a ho, and a hey nonino—

How that a life was but a flower
   In springtime, &c.

And therefore take the present time—
   With a hey, and a ho, and a hey nonino—
For love is crowned with the prime
   In springtime, &c.

    Act V, Scene 3

from THE MERCHANT OF VENICE

"ALL THAT GLISTERS IS NOT GOLD"

MOROCCO: 'All that glisters is not gold—
Often have you heard that told.
Many a man his life hath sold
But my outside to behold.
Gilded tombs do worms infold.
Had you been as wise as bold,
Young in limbs, in judgment old,
Your answer had not been inscroll'd.
Fare you well; your suit is cold.'

    Act II, Scene 7

"THE FIRE SEVEN TIMES TRIED THIS"

ARRAGON: 'The fire seven times tried this.
Seven times tried that judgment is
That did never choose amiss.
Some there be that shadows kiss;
Such have but a shadow's bliss.
There be fools alive iwis,
Silver'd o'er, and so was this.

Take what wife you will to bed,
I will ever be your head.
So be gone; you are sped.'

   Act II, Scene 9

A SONG
the whilst BASSANIO *comments on the caskets to himself.*

Tell me, where is fancy bred,
Or in the heart, or in the head?
How begot, how nourished?
   Reply, reply.
It is engend'red in the eyes,
With gazing fed; and fancy dies
In the cradle where it lies.
   Let us all ring fancy's knell.
   I'll begin it—Ding, dong, bell.

ALL: Ding, dong, bell.

   Act III, Scene 2

   from TWELFTH NIGHT

"O MISTRESS MINE"

CLOWN: O mistress mine, where are you roaming?
O, stay and hear! your true-love's coming,
   That can sing both high and low.
Trip no further, pretty sweeting;
Journeys end in lovers meeting,
   Every wise man's son doth know.

What is love? 'Tis not hereafter;
Present mirth hath present laughter;
    What's to come is still unsure:
In delay there lies no plenty;
Then come kiss me, sweet and twenty!
    Youth's a stuff will not endure.

Act II, Scene 3

THE [CLOWN'S] SONG

Come away, come away, death,
    And in sad cypress let me be laid.
Fly away, fly away, breath;
    I am slain by a fair cruel maid.
My shroud of white, stuck all with yew,
        O, prepare it!
My part of death, no one so true
        Did share it.

Not a flower, not a flower sweet,
    On my black coffin let there be strown;
Not a friend, not a friend greet
    My poor corpse, where my bones shall be thrown.
A thousand thousand sighs to save,
        Lay me, O, where
Sad true lover never find my grave,
        To weep there!

Act II, Scene 4

from CYMBELINE

SONG

GUIDERIUS: Fear no more the heat o' th' sun
 Nor the furious winter's rages;
Thou thy worldly task hast done,
 Home art gone, and ta'en thy wages.
Golden lads and girls all must,
As chimney-sweepers, come to dust.

AVIRAGUS: Fear no more the frown o' th' great;
 Thou art past the tyrant's stroke.
Care no more to clothe and eat;
 To thee the reed is as the oak.
The sceptre, learning, physic, must
All follow this and come to dust.

G.: Fear no more the lightning-flash—
A.:   Nor the all-dreaded thunder-stone;
G.: Fear not slander, censure rash;
A.:   Thou hast finish'd joy and moan.
BOTH: All lovers young, all lovers must
    Consign to thee and come to dust.

G.: No exorciser harm thee!
A.: Nor no witchcraft charm thee!
G.: Ghost unlaid forbear thee!
A.: Nothing ill come near thee!
BOTH: Quiet consummation have,
    And renowned be thy grave.

  Act IV, Scene 2

from the SONNETS

I

From fairest creatures we desire increase,
That thereby beauty's rose might never die,
But as the riper should by time decease,
His tender heir might bear his memory;
But thou, contracted to thine own bright eyes,
Feed'st thy light's flame with self-substantial fuel,
Making a famine where abundance lies,
Thyself thy foe, to thy sweet self too cruel.
Thou that art now the world's fresh ornament
And only herald to the gaudy spring,
Within thine own bud buriest thy content
And, tender churl, mak'st waste in niggarding.
    Pity the world, or else this glutton be,
    To eat the world's due, by the grave and thee.

XVIII

Shall I compare thee to a summer's day?
Thou are more lovely and more temperate.
Rough winds do shake the darling buds of May,
And summer's lease hath all too short a date.
Sometime too hot the eye of heaven shines,
And often is his gold complexion dimm'd;
And every fair from fair sometime declines,
By chance, or nature's changing course, untrimm'd;
But thy eternal summer shall not fade
Nor lose possession of that fair thou ow'st,
Nor shall Death brag thou wand'rest in his shade
When in eternal lines to time thou grow'st.
    So long as men can breathe or eyes can see,
    So long lives this, and this gives life to thee.

XXIX

When, in disgrace with Fortune and men's eyes,
I all alone beweep my outcast state,
And trouble deaf heaven with my bootless cries,
And look upon myself and curse my fate,
Wishing me like to one more rich in hope,
Featur'd like him, like him with friends possess'd,
Desiring this man's art, and that man's scope,
With what I most enjoy contented least;
Yet in these thoughts myself almost despising,
Haply I think on thee, and then my state,
Like to the lark at break of day arising
From sullen earth, sings hymns at heaven's gate;
    For thy sweet love rememb'red such wealth brings
    That then I scorn to change my state with kings.

XXX

When to the sessions of sweet silent thought
I summon up remembrance of things past,
I sigh the lack of many a thing I sought
And with old woes new wail my dear time's waste.
Then can I drown an eye (unus'd to flow)
For precious friends hid in death's dateless night,
And weep afresh love's long since cancell'd woe,
And moan th' expense of many a vanish'd sight.
Then can I grieve at grievances foregone,
And heavily from woe to woe tell o'er
The sad account of fore-bemoaned moan,
Which I new pay as if not paid before.
    But if the while I think on thee, dear friend,
    All losses are restor'd and sorrows end.

L I I I

What is your substance, whereof are you made,
That millions of strange shadows on you tend?
Since every one hath, every one, one shade,
And you, but one, can every shadow lend.
Describe Adonis, and the counterfeit
Is poorly imitated after you.
On Helen's cheek all art of beauty set,
And you in Grecian tires are painted new.
Speak of the spring, and foison of the year:
The one doth shadow of your beauty show,
The other as your bounty doth appear,
And you in every blessed shape we know.
 In all external grace you have some part,
  But you like none, none you, for constant heart.

L V

Not marble nor the gilded monuments
Of princes shall outlive this pow'rful rhyme;
But you shall shine more bright in these contents
Than unswept stone, besmear'd with sluttish time.
When wasteful war shall statues overturn,
And broils root out the work of masonry,
Nor Mars his sword nor war's quick fire shall burn
The living record of your memory.
'Gainst death and all-oblivious enmity
Shall you pace forth; your praise shall still find room
Even in the eyes of all posterity
That wear this world out to the ending doom.
 So, till the judgment that yourself arise,
  You live in this, and dwell in lovers' eyes.

LXVI

Tir'd with all these, for restful death I cry:
As, to behold desert a beggar born,
And needy nothing trimm'd in jollity,
And purest faith unhappily forsworn,
And gilded honour shamefully misplac'd,
And maiden virtue rudely strumpeted,
And right perfection wrongfully disgrac'd,
And strength by limping sway disabled,
And art made tongue-tied by authority,
And folly (doctor-like) controlling skill,
And simple truth miscall'd simplicity,
And captive good attending captain ill.
    Tir'd with all these, from these would I be gone,
    Save that, to die, I leave my love alone.

LXXIII

That time of year thou mayst in me behold
When yellow leaves, or none, or few, do hang
Upon those boughs which shake against the cold,
Bare ruin'd choirs where late the sweet birds sang.
In me thou see'st the twilight of such day
As after sunset fadeth in the West,
Which by-and-by black night doth take away,
Death's second self, that seals up all in rest.
In me thou see'st the glowing of such fire
That on the ashes of his youth doth lie,
As the deathbed whereon it must expire,
Consum'd with that which it was nourish'd by.
    This thou perceiv'st, which makes thy love more strong,
    To love that well which thou must leave ere long.

CVI

When in the chronicle of wasted time
I see descriptions of the fairest wights,
And beauty making beautiful old rhyme
In praise of ladies dead and lovely knights,
Then, in the blazon of sweet beauty's best,
Of hand, of foot, of lip, of eye, of brow,
I see their antique pen would have express'd
Even such a beauty as you master now.
So all their praises are but prophecies
Of this our time, all you prefiguring;
And, for they look'd but with divining eyes,
They had not skill enough your worth to sing;
    For we, which now behold these present days,
    Have eyes to wonder, but lack tongues to praise.

CVII

Not mine own fears, nor the prophetic soul
Of the wide world, dreaming on things to come,
Can yet the lease of my true love control,
Suppos'd as forfeit to a confin'd doom.
The mortal moon hath her eclipse endur'd,
And the sad augurs mock their own presage;
Incertainties now crown themselves assur'd,
And peace proclaims olives of endless age.
Now with the drops of this most balmy time
My love looks fresh, and Death to me subscribes,
Since, spite of him, I'll live in this poor rhyme,
While he insults o'er dull and speechless tribes;
    And thou in this shalt find thy monument
    When tyrants' crests and tombs of brass are spent.

※ ※ The pupil who has by now attained a taste for poetry will
find her or his minimum library, or the minimum in easily obtain-
able editions, *viz.:*

Dent's Dante, the *Divine Comedy* and *Vita Nuova* bilingual; or Binyon's translation without the Italian text.

Shakespeare's Sonnets and lyrics.

Dent's translations from Ovid, there being no currently available edition of the complete *Metamorphoses* in Golding's version.

Gavin Douglas' *Aeneid;* hard to get hold of, but it can be found in some university libraries by students who want to learn the Scots tongue.

As to public relations, Mr. Yeats has stated rather firmly: They do NOT like poetry. They like something else, but they like to *think* they like poetry.

Edward FitzGerald's subversive translation of the *Rubaiyat* has, or had, great charm for several generations not in search of moral uplift.

from KING HENRY V

EPILOGUE

Thus far, with rough and all-unable pen,
   Our bending author hath pursu'd the story,
In little room confining mighty men,
   Mangling by starts the full course of their glory.
Small time; but in that small, most greatly lived
   This Star of England. Fortune made his sword;
By which the world's best garden he achieved,
   And of it left his son imperial lord.
Henry the Sixth, in infant bands crown'd King
   Of France and England, did this king succeed;
Whose state so many had the managing
   That they lost France and made his England bleed;
Which oft our stage hath shown; and for their sake
In your fair minds let this acceptance take.

❀❀ England's great, true, uneven epic is in the series of Shakespeare's "Histories," as distinct from literary imitations. Both the active Tudors and the degenerate Stuarts were literate.

John Davies
[1569–1626]

from NOSCE TEIPSUM

THE SOUL AND THE BODY

But how shall we this union well express?
 Nought ties the soul; her subtlety is such,
She moves the body, which she doth possess,
 Yet no part toucheth, but by virtue's touch.

Then dwells she not therein as in a tent;
 Nor as a pilot in his ship doth sit;
Nor as the spider in his web is pent;
 Nor as the wax retains the print in it;

Nor as a vessel water doth contain;
 Nor as one liquor in another shed;
Nor as the heat doth in the fire remain;
 Nor as a voice throughout the air is spread.

But as the fair and cheerful morning light
 Doth here and there her silver beams impart,
And in an instant doth herself unite
 To the transparent air, in all and part;

Still resting whole, when blows the air divide,
 Abiding pure, when th' air is most corrupted,
Throughout the air her beams dispersing wide,
 And when the air is tossed, not interrupted:

So doth the piercing soul the body fill,
 Being all in all in part diffused,

Indivisible, incorruptible still,
    Not forced, encountered, troubled or confused.

And as the sun above the light doth bring,
    Though we behold it in the air below,
So from th' eternal Light the soul doth spring,
    Though in the body she her powers do show.

❊❊ The gentler reader, exacerbated by the crudities of most
current poetic practice, might find considerable solace in those
parts of Coleridge's *Biographia Literaria* dealing specifically with
poetry, and in other sections of Davies' *Soule of Man and the
Immortalitie Thereof.*

Ben Jonson
[1572–1637]

from A CELEBRATION OF CHARIS

HER TRIUMPH

See the chariot at hand here of love,
    Wherein my lady rideth!
Each that draws is a swan or a dove,
    And well the car love guideth.
As she goes, all hearts do duty
        Unto her beauty;
And enamoured do wish so they might
        But enjoy such a sight,
That they still were to run by her side,
Through swords, through seas, whither she would ride.

Do but look on her eyes; they do light
    All that love's world compriseth!
Do but look on her hair; it is bright
    As love's star when it riseth!
Do but mark, her forehead's smoother
      Than words that soothe her;
And from her arched brows, such a grace
      Sheds itself through the face,
As alone there triumphs to the life
All the gain, all the good of the elements' strife.

Have you seen but a bright lily grow
    Before rude hands have touched it?
Ha' you marked but the fall o' the snow
    Before the soil hath smutched it?
Have you felt the wool of beaver,
      Or swan's down ever?
Or have smelt o' the bud o' the briar?
      Or the nard in the fire?
Or have tasted the bag of the bee?
O so white! O so soft! O so sweet is she!

Robert Herrick

[1591–1674]

TO HIS LOVELY MISTRESSES

One night i' th' year, my dearest Beauties, come
And bring those dew-drink-offerings to my tomb.
When thence ye see my reverend ghost to rise,
And there to lick th' effusèd sacrifice:

Though paleness be the Livery that I wear,
Look ye not wan, or colourless for fear.
Trust me, I will not hurt ye; or once shew
The least grim look, or cast a frown on you:
Nor shall the tapers when I'm there, burn blue.
This I may do (perhaps) as I glide by,
Cast on my Girls a glance, and loving eye:
Or fold mine arms and sigh, because I've lost
The world so soon, and in it, you the most.
Than these, no fears more on your fancies fall,
Though then I smile, and speak no words at all.

Edmund Waller

[1606–1687]

GO, LOVELY ROSE!

Go, lovely Rose!
    Tell her that wastes her time and me,
That now she knows,
    When I resemble her to thee,
    How sweet and fair she seems to be.

Tell her that's young,
    And shuns to have her graces spied,
That hadst thou sprung
    In deserts where no men abide,
    Thou must have uncommended died.

Small is the worth
    Of beauty from the light retired;

Bid her come forth,
    Suffer herself to be desired,
    And not blush so to be admired.

Then die! that she
    The common fate of all things rare
May read in thee;
    How small a part of time they share
    That are so wondrous sweet and fair!

TO MR. HENRY LAWES
Who had then newly set a song of mine in the year 1635

Verse makes heroic virtue live;
But you can life to verses give.
As when in open air we blow,
And breath, though strain'd, sounds flat and low;
But if a trumpet take the blast,
It lifts it high, and makes it last:
So in your airs our numbers dress'd,
Make a shrill sally from the breast
Of nymphs, who, singing what we penn'd,
Our passions to themselves commend;
While love, victorious with thy art,
Governs at once their voice and heart.
    You by the help of tune and time,
Can make that song that was but rhyme.
Not pleading, no man doubts the cause;
Or questions verses set by Lawes.
    As a church window, thick with paint,
Lets in a light but dim and faint;
So others, with division, hide
The light of sense, the poet's pride:
But you alone may proudly boast
That not a syllable is lost;

The writer's, and the setter's skill
At once the ravish'd ears do fill.
Let those which only warble long,
And gargle in their throats a song,
Content themselves with Ut, Re, Mi:
Let words, and sense, be set by thee.

Pietro Metastasio

[1698–1782]

"AGE OF GOLD"

Age of Gold, I bid thee come
To this Earth, was erst thy home!
Age of Gold, if e'er thou wast
And art not mere dream laid waste!

Thou art not fled; ne'er wast mere dreaming;
Art not now mere feignèd seeming.
Every simple heart knows this:
Candour still thy substance is.

Translated by Ezra Pound

❋ ❋ The modes and the tunes remain; from Arnaut Daniel to
Jannequin's music; from simple troubadour songs to Irish popu-
lar ditties; from Lorenzo de'Medici (page 118) to Shakespeare's
"Mistress Mine," to Metastasio in 1750.

Marie-Françoise-Catherine de Beauveau, la Marquise de Boufflers

[1711–1786]

AIR: SENTIR AVEC ARDEUR

Say what you will in two
Words and get through.
Long, frilly
Palaver is silly.

Know how to read? you *must*
Before you can write. An idiot
Will always
Talk a lot.

You need not always narrate;
    cite; date,
But listen a while and not say: "I! I!"
Want to know why?

The *me* is tyrannical;
        academical.
Early, late
Boredom's cognate mate
    in step at his side
And I with a *me*, I fear,

                yet again!

Say what you will in two
Words and get through!

Long, frilly
Palaver is silly.

Translated by Ezra Pound

❉❉ Approximate; *vide* Marianne Moore's commendation in
Like a Bulwark.

Christopher Smart
[1722–1771]

from JUBILATE AGNO

"FOR I WILL CONSIDER MY CAT JEOFFRY"

For I will consider my Cat Jeoffry.
For he is the servant of the Living God, duly and daily serving
  him.
For at the first glance of the glory of God in the East he worships
  in his way.
For is this done by wreathing his body seven times round with
  elegant quickness.
For then he leaps up to catch the musk, which is the blessing of
  God upon his prayer.
For he rolls upon prank to work it in.
For having done duty and received blessing he begins to consider
  himself.
For this he performs in ten degrees.
For first he looks upon his fore-paws to see if they are clean.

For secondly he kicks up behind to clear away there.

For thirdly he works it upon stretch with the fore paws extended.

For fourthly he sharpens his paws by wood.

For fifthly he washes himself.

For sixthly he rolls upon wash.

For seventhly he fleas himself, that he may not be interrupted upon the beat.

For eighthly he rubs himself against a post.

For ninthly he looks up for his instructions.

For tenthly he goes in quest of food.

For having consider'd God and himself he will consider his neighbour.

For if he meets another cat he will kiss her in kindness.

For when he takes his prey he plays with it to give it chance.

For one mouse in seven escapes by his dallying.

For when his day's work is done his business more properly begins.

For [he] keeps the Lord's watch in the night against the adversary.

For he counteracts the powers of darkness by his electrical skin & glaring eyes.

For he counteracts the Devil, who is death, by brisking about the life.

For in his morning orisons he loves the sun and the sun loves him.

For he is of the tribe of Tiger.

For the Cherub Cat is a term of the Angel Tiger.

For he has the subtlety and hissing of a serpent, which in goodness he suppresses.

For he will not do destruction, if he is well-fed, neither will he spit without provocation.

For he purrs in thankfulness, when God tells him he's a good Cat.

For he is an instrument for the children to learn benevolence upon.

For every house is incompleat without him & a blessing is lacking in the spirit.

For the Lord commanded Moses concerning the cats at the departure of the Children of Israel from Egypt.

For every family had one cat at least in the bag.

For the English Cats are the best in Europe.

For he is the cleanest in the use of his fore-paws of any quadrupede.

For the dexterity of his defence is an instance of the love of God to him exceedingly.

For he is the quickest to his mark of any creature.

For he is tenacious of his point.

For he is a mixture of gravity and waggery.

For he knows that God is his Saviour.

For there is nothing sweeter than his peace when at rest.

For there is nothing brisker than his life when in motion.

For he is of the Lord's poor and so indeed is he called by benevolence perpetually—Poor Jeoffry! poor Jeoffry! the rat has bit thy throat.

For I bless the name of the Lord Jesus that Jeoffry is better.

For the divine spirit comes about his body to sustain it in compleat cat.

For his tongue is exceeding pure so that it has in purity what it wants in musick.

For he is docile and can learn certain things.

For he can set up with gravity which is patience upon approbation.

For he can fetch and carry, which is patience in employment.

For he can jump over a stick which is patience upon proof positive.

For he can spraggle upon waggle at the word of command.

For he can jump from an eminence into his master's bosom.

For he can catch the cork and toss it again.

For he is hated by the hypocrite and miser.

For the former is affraid of detection.

For the latter refuses the charge.

For he camels his back to bear the first notion of business.

For he is good to think on, if a man would express himself neatly.

For he made a great figure in Egypt for his signal services.

For he killed the Icneumon-rat very pernicious by land.

For his ears are so acute that they sting again.

For from this proceeds the passing quickness of his attention.

For by stroaking of him I have found out electricity.

For I perceived God's light about him both wax and fire.

For the Electrical fire is the spiritual substance, which God sends
   from heaven to sustain the bodies both of man and beast.

For God has blessed him in the variety of his movements.

For, tho he cannot fly, he is an excellent clamberer.

For his motions upon the face of the earth are more than any
   other quadrupede.

For he can tread to all the measures upon the musick.

For he can swim for life.

For he can creep.

George Crabbe

[1754–1832]

from THE BOROUGH

LETTER XXIV: SCHOOLS

To every Class we have a School assign'd,
Rules for all Ranks and Food for every Mind:
Yet one there is, that small regard to Rule
Or Study pays, and still is deem'd a School;
That, where a deaf, poor, patient Widow sits,
And awes some thirty Infants as she knits;
Infants of humble, busy Wives, who pay
Some trifling Price for Freedom through the day.
At this good Matron's Hut the Children meet,
Who thus becomes the Mother of the Street;
Her Room is small, they cannot widely stray,—
Her Threshold high, they cannot run away:
Though deaf, she sees the Rebel-heroes shout,—

Though lame, her white Rod nimbly walks about;
With Band of Yarn she keeps Offenders in,
And to her Gown the sturdiest Rogue can pin:
Aided by these, and Spells and tell-tale Birds,
Her Power they dread and reverence her Words.

To Learning's second Seats we now proceed,
Where humming Students gilded Primers read;
Or Books with Letters large and Pictures gay,
To make their Reading but a kind of Play—
"Reading made Easy," so the Titles tell,
But they who read must first begin to spell:
There may be Profit in these Arts, but still
Learning is Labour, call it what you will;
Upon the youthful Mind an heavy Load,
Nor must we hope to find the Royal Road.
Some will their easy steps to Science show,
And some to Heaven itself their By-way know;
Ah! trust them not,—who Fame or Bliss would share,
Must learn by Labour, and must live by Care.

Another Matron of superior kind,
For Higher Schools prepares the rising Mind;
Preparatory she her Learning calls,
The step first made to Colleges and Halls.

She early sees to what the Mind will grow,
Nor abler Judge of Infant-Powers I know;
She sees what soon the lively will impede,
And how the steadier will in turn succeed;
Observes the dawn of Wisdom, Fancy, Taste,
And knows what Parts will wear and what will waste:
She marks the Mind too lively, and at once
Sees the gay Coxcomb and the rattling Dunce.

Long has she liv'd, and much she loves to trace
Her former Pupils, now a lordly Race;

Whom when she sees rich Robes and Furs bedeck,
She marks the Pride which once she strove to check:—
A Burgess comes, and she remembers well
How hard her task to make his Worship spell;
Cold, selfish, dull, inanimate, unkind,
'Twas but by Anger he display'd a Mind:
Now civil, smiling, complaisant, and gay,
The World has worn th' unsocial Crust away;
That sullen Spirit now a softness wears,
And, save by fits, e'en Dulness disappears:
But still the Matron can the Man behold,
Dull, selfish, hard, inanimate and cold.
A Merchant passes;—"Probity and Truth,
Prudence and Patience, mark'd thee from thy Youth."
Thus she observes, but oft retains her Fears
For him, who now with Name unstain'd appears;
Nor hope relinquishes, for one who yet
Is lost in Error and involv'd in Debt;
For latent Evil in that Heart she found,
More open here, but here the Core was sound.

　　Various our Day-schools: here behold we one
Empty and still;—the Morning Duties done,
Soil'd, tatter'd, worn, and thrown in various heaps,
Appear their Books, and there Confusion sleeps;
The Workmen all are from the Babel fled,
And lost their Tools, till the return they dread:
Meantime the Master, with his wig awry,
Prepares his Books for business by-and-by:
Now all th' Insignia of the Monarch laid
Beside him rest, and none stand by afraid;
He, while his Troop light-hearted leap and play,
Is all intent on Duties of the Day;
No more the Tyrant stern or Judge severe,
He feels the Father's and the Husband's Fear.

Ah! little think the timid trembling Crowd,
That one so wise, so pow'rful, and so proud,
Should feel himself, and dread the humble ills
Of Rent-day Charges and of Coalman's Bills;
That while they Mercy from their Judge implore,
He fears himself—a knocking at the Door;
And feels the Burthen as his Neighbour states
His humble Portion to the Parish-rates.

They sit th' allotted Hours, then eager run,
Rushing to Pleasure when the Duty's done:
His Hour of Leisure is of different kind,
Then Cares domestic rush upon his Mind,
And half the Ease and Comfort he enjoys,
Is when surrounded by Slates, Books, and Boys.

Poor *Reuben Dixon* has the noisiest School
Of ragged Lads, who ever bow'd to Rule;
Low in his Price—the Men who heave our Coals,
And clean our Causeways, send him Boys in shoals:
To see poor *Reuben*, with his Fry beside,—
Their half-check'd Rudeness and his half-scorn'd Pride,—
Their Room, the Sty in which th' Assembly meet,
In the close Lane behind the *Northgate Street;*
T' observe his vain Attempts to keep the Peace,
Till tolls the Bell, and Strife on both Sides cease,—
Calls for our praise; his Labour Praise deserves,
But not our Pity; *Reuben* has no Nerves:
'Mid Noise and Dirt, and Stench, and Play and Prate,
He calmly cuts the Pen or views the Slate.

But *Leonard!*—Yes, for *Leonard's* Fate I grieve,
Who loaths the Station which he dares not leave;
He cannot dig, he will not beg his Bread,
All his dependence rests upon his Head;

And deeply skill'd in Sciences and Arts,
On vulgar Lads he wastes superior Parts.

Alas! what Grief that feeling Mind sustains,
In guiding Hands and stirring torpid Brains;
He whose proud Mind from Pole to Pole will move,
And view the Wonders of the Worlds above;
Who thinks and reasons strongly:—hard his Fate,
Confin'd for ever to the Pen and Slate;
True, he submits, and when the long dull Day
Has slowly past, in weary Tasks, away,
To other Worlds with cheerful view he looks,
And parts the Night between Repose and Books.

Amid his Labours, he has sometimes tried
To turn a little from his Cares aside;
Pope, Milton, Dryden, with delight has seiz'd,
His Soul engag'd and of his Trouble eas'd;
When, with an heavy Eye and ill-done Sum,
No part conceiv'd, a stupid Boy will come:
Then *Leonard* first subdues the rising frown
And bids the Blockhead lay his Blunders down;
O'er which disgusted he will turn his Eye,
To his sad Duty his sound Mind apply,
And, vex'd in Spirit, throws his Pleasures by.

Turn we to Schools which more than these afford
The sound Instruction and the wholesome Board;
And first our School for Ladies:—Pity calls
For one soft Sigh, when we behold these Walls,
Plac'd near the Town, and where, from Window high,
The Fair, confin'd, may our free Crowds espy,
With many a Stranger gazing up and down,
And all the envied tumult of the Town;
May, in the smiling Summer-eve, when they
Are sent to sleep the pleasant Hours away,

Behold the Poor (whom they conceive the blest)
Employ'd for hours, and griev'd they cannot rest.

Here the fond Girl, whose days are sad and few
Since dear Mamma pronounc'd the last Adieu,
Looks to the Road, and fondly thinks she hears
The Carriage-wheels and struggles with her Tears:
All yet is new, the Misses great and small,
Madam herself, and Teachers, odious all;
From Laughter, Pity, nay Command, she turns,
But melts in softness, or with anger burns;
Nauseates her Food, and wonders who can sleep
On such mean Beds, where she can only weep:
She scorns Condolence—but to all she hates
Slowly at length her Mind accommodates;
Then looks on Bondage with the same concern
As others felt, and finds that she must learn
As others learn'd—the common Lot to share,
To search for Comfort and submit to Care.

There are, 'tis said, who on these Seats attend,
And to these ductile Minds Destruction vend;
Wretches to Virtue, Peace, and Nature, Foes
To these soft Minds, their wicked Trash expose;
Seize on the Soul, ere Passions take the sway,
And lead the Heart, ere yet it feels, astray:
Smugglers obscene!—and can there be who take
Infernal pains, the sleeping Vice to wake?
Can there be those, by whom the Thought defil'd
Enters the spotless Bosom of a Child?
By whom the Ill is to the Heart convey'd,
Who lend the Foe, not yet in Arms, their Aid,
And sap the City-walls before the Siege be laid?

Oh! rather skulking in the By-ways steal,
And rob the poorest Traveller of his Meal;

Burst through the humblest Trader's bolted Door;
Bear from the Widow's hut her Winter-Store;
With stolen Steed, on Highways take your stand,
Your Lips with Curses arm'd, with Death your Hand;—
Take all but Life—the virtuous more would say,
Take Life itself, dear as it is, away,
Rather than guilty thus the guileless Soul betray.

Years pass away—let us suppose them past,
Th' accomplish'd Nymph for Freedom looks at last:
All Hardship over, which a School contains,
The Spirit's Bondage and the Body's Pains;
Where Teachers make the heartless, trembling set
Of Pupils suffer for their own regret;
Where Winter's Cold, attack'd by one poor Fire,
Chills the fair Child, commanded to retire;
She felt it keenly in the morning Air,
Keenly she felt it at the Evening Prayer.
More pleasant Summer; but then Walks were made,
Not a sweet Ramble, but a slow Parade;
They mov'd by Pairs beside the Hawthorn-hedge,
Only to set their Feelings on an edge;
And now at eve, when all their Spirits rise,
Are sent to rest, and all their Pleasure dies;
Where yet they all the Town alert can see,
And distant plough-boys pacing o'er the Lea.

These and the Tasks successive Masters brought—
The French they conn'd, the curious Works they wrought:
The hours they made their taper Fingers strike,
Note after Note, all dull to them alike;
Their Drawings, Dancings on appointed days,
Playing with Globes, and getting Parts of Plays;
The tender Friendships made 'twixt Heart and Heart,
When the dear Friends had nothing to impart:—

All! All! are over;—now th' accomplish'd Maid
Longs for the World, of nothing there afraid:
Dreams of Delight invade her gentle Breast,
And fancied Lovers rob the Heart of rest;
At the paternal Door a Carriage stands,
Love knits their Hearts and *Hymen* joins their Hands.

Ah!—World unknown! how charming is thy View,
Thy Pleasures many, and each Pleasure new:
Ah!—World experienc'd! what of thee is told?
How few thy Pleasures, and those few how old!

Within a silent Street, and far apart
From Noise of Business, from a Quay or Mart,
Stands an old spacious Building, and the Din
You hear without explains the Work within;
Unlike the whispering of the Nymphs, this noise
Loudly proclaims a "Boarding-School for Boys:"
The Master heeds it not, for thirty years
Have render'd all familiar to his ears;
He sits in comfort, 'mid the various sound
Of mingled tones for ever flowing round;
Day after day he to his Task attends,—
Unvaried toil, and care that never ends:
Boys in their works proceed; while his employ
Admits no change, or changes but the Boy;
Yet time has made it easy; he beside
Has Power supreme, and Power is sweet to Pride:
But grant him Pleasure;—what can Teachers feel,
Dependent Helpers always at the Wheel?
Their Power despis'd, their Compensation small,
Their Labour dull, their life Laborious all;
Set after set the lower Lads to make
Fit for the Class which their Superiors take;
The Road of Learning for a time to track

In roughest state, and then again go back:
Just the same way on other Troops to wait,—
Attendants fix'd at Learning's lower Gate.

The Day-tasks now are over,—to their Ground
Rush the gay Crowd with joy-compelling sound;
Glad to illude the Burdens of the day,
The eager Parties hurry to their Play:
Then in these hours of Liberty we find
The native bias of the opening Mind;
They yet possess not skill the Mask to place,
And hide the Passions glowing in the Face;
Yet some are found—the close, the sly, the mean,
Who know already all must not be seen.

Lo! one who walks apart, although so young,
He lays restraint upon his eye and tongue;
Nor will he into scrapes or dangers get,
And half the School are in the Stripling's debt:
Suspicious, timid, he is much afraid
Of Trick and Plot:—he dreads to be betray'd;
He shuns all Friendships, for he finds they lend,
When Lads begin to call each other Friend:
Yet Self with Self has war; the tempting sight
Of Fruit on sale provokes his Appetite;—
See! how he walks the sweet Seduction by,
That he is tempted, costs him first a sigh,—
'Tis dangerous to indulge! 'tis grievous to deny:
This he will choose, and whispering asks the Price,
The Purchase dreadful, but the Portion nice;
Within the Pocket he explores the Pence,
Without, Temptation strikes on either Sense,
The sight, the Smell;—but then he thinks again,
Of Money wasted! when no taste remain.
Meantime there comes an eager thoughtless Boy,
Who gives the Price and only feels the Joy:
Example dire! the youthful Miser stops,

And slowly back the treasur'd Coinage drops:
Heroic deed! for should he now comply,
Can he to-morrow's Appetite deny?
Beside, these Spendthrifts who so freely live,
Cloy'd with their Purchase, will a portion give:—
Here ends Debate, he buttons up his Store,
And feels the comfort that it burns no more.

Unlike to him the Tyrant-boy, whose sway
All Hearts acknowledge; him the Crowds obey:
At his Command they break through every Rule;
Whoever governs, he controls the School:
'Tis not the distant Emperor moves their Fear,
But the proud Viceroy who is ever near.

Verres could do that mischief in a day,
For which not Rome, in all its power, could pay;
And these Boy-tyrants will their Slaves distress,
And do the Wrongs no Master can redress:
The Mind they load with fear; it feels disdain
For its own baseness; yet it tries in vain
To shake th' admitted power;—The Coward comes again:
'Tis more than present pain these Tyrants give,
Long as we've Life some strong impressions live;
And these young Ruffians in the Soul will sow
Seeds of all Vices that on Weakness grow.

Hark! at his word the trembling Younglings flee,
Where he is walking none must walk but he;
See! from the Winter-fire the Weak retreat,
His the warm Corner, his the favourite Seat,
Save when he yields it to some Slave to keep
Awhile, then back, at his return, to creep;
At his command his poor Dependants fly,
And humbly bribe him as a proud Ally;

Verres: tyrannous governor of Sicily, famous because of Cicero's oration
against him

Flatter'd by all, the notice he bestows
Is gross abuse, and bantering and blows;
Yet he's a Dunce, and spite of all his fame
Without the Desk; within he feels his shame:
For there the weaker Boy who felt his scorn,
For him corrects the Blunders of the Morn;
And he is taught, unpleasant truth! to find
The trembling Body has the prouder Mind.

Hark! to that shout, that burst of empty noise,
From a rude set of bluff, obstreperous Boys;
They who, like Colts let loose, with vigour bound,
And thoughtless spirit, o'er the beaten ground;
Fearless they leap, and every Youngster feels
His *Alma* active in his hands and heels.

These are the Sons of Farmers, and they come
With partial fondness for the Joys of Home;
Their Minds are coursing in their Fathers' Fields,
And e'en the Dream a lively pleasure yields;
They, much enduring, sit th' allotted hours,
And o'er a Grammar waste their sprightly powers:
They dance; but them can measur'd steps delight,
Whom Horse and Hounds to daring deeds excite?
Nor could they bear to wait from meal to meal,
Did they not slily to the chamber steal,
And there the produce of the basket seize,
The Mother's Gift! still studious of their ease.
Poor *Alma,* thus opprest, forbears to rise,
But rests or revels in the arms and thighs.

"But is it sure that Study will repay
The more attentive and forbearing?"—Nay!

Alma: "Should any of my Readers find themselves at a loss in this place, I beg leave to refer them to a Poem of Prior, called *Alma,* or *The Progress of the Mind.*" [G. C.]

The Farm, the Ship, the humble Shop have each
Gains which severest Studies seldom reach.

At College place a Youth, who means to raise
His State by Merit and his Name by Praise;
Still much he hazards; there is serious strife
In the contentions of a Scholar's life:
Not all the Mind's attention, care, distress,
Nor Diligence itself ensure success:
His jealous heart a Rival's powers may dread,
Till its strong feelings have confus'd his head,
And, after days and months, nay, years of pain,
He finds just lost the object he would gain.

But grant him this and all such Life can give,
For other Prospects he begins to live;
Begins to feel that Man was form'd to look,
And long for other object than a Book:
In his Mind's eye his House and Glebe he sees,
And farms and talks with Farmers at his ease;
And Time is lost, till Fortune sends him forth
To a rude World unconscious of his worth;
There in some petty Parish to reside,
The College-boast, then turn'd the Village-guide;
And though awhile his Flock and Dairy please,
He soon reverts to former Joys and Ease,
Glad when a Friend shall come to break his rest,
And speak of all the Pleasures they possess'd,—
Of Masters, Fellows, Tutors, all with whom
They shar'd those Pleasures, never more to come;
Till both conceive the times by Bliss endear'd,
Which once so dismal and so dull appear'd.

But fix our Scholar, and suppose him crown'd
With all the Glory gain'd on Classic ground;
Suppose the World without a sigh resign'd,

And to his College all his care confin'd;
Give him all Honours that such states allow,
The Freshman's terror and the Tradesman's bow;
Let his Apartments with his taste agree,
And all his Views be those he loves to see;
Let him each day behold the savory treat,
For which he pays not, but is paid to eat;
These Joys and Glories soon delight no more,
Although withheld, the Mind is vex'd and sore:
The Honour too is to the place confin'd,
Abroad they know not each superior Mind:
Strangers no *Wranglers* in these Figures see,
Nor give they Worship to an high degree;
Unlike the Prophets is the Scholar's case,
His Honour all is in his Dwelling-place:
And there such Honours are familiar things,
What is a Monarch in a crowd of Kings?
Like other Sovereigns he's by Forms addressed,
By Statutes govern'd, and with Rules oppressed.

When all these Forms and Duties die away,
And the day passes like the former day,
Then of exterior things at once bereft,
He's to himself and one Attendant left;
Nay, *John* too goes; nor aught of Service more
Remains for him; he gladly quits the door,
And, as he whistles to the College-gate,
He kindly pities his poor Master's fate.

Books cannot always please, however good;
Minds are not ever craving for their Food;
But Sleep will soon the weary Soul prepare
For Cares to-morrow, that were this day's Care;
For Forms, for Feasts, that sundry times have past,
And formal Feasts that will for ever last.

"But then from Study will no Comforts rise?"—
Yes! such as studious Minds alone can prize;
Comforts, yea!—Joys ineffable they find,
Who seek the prouder Pleasures of the Mind:
The Soul, collected in those happy hours,
Then makes her efforts, then enjoys her powers;
And in those seasons feels herself repaid,
For Labours past and Honours long delay'd.

No! 'tis not worldly Gain, although by chance
The Sons of Learning may to Wealth advance;
Nor Station high, though in some favouring hour
The Sons of Learning may arrive at Power;
Nor is it Glory, though the public Voice
Of honest Praise will make the Heart rejoice:
But 'tis the Mind's own Feelings give the Joy,
Pleasures she gathers in her own employ—
Pleasures that Gain or Praise cannot bestow,
Yet can dilate and raise them when they flow.

For this the Poet looks the World around,
Where Form and Life and reasoning Man are found;
He loves the Mind, in all its modes, to trace,
And all the Manners of the changing Race;
Silent he walks the Road of Life along,
And views the aims of its tumultuous throng:
He finds what shapes the Proteus-Passions take,
And what strange waste of Life and Joy they make,
And loves to show them in their varied ways,
With honest Blame or with unflattering Praise:
'Tis good to know, 'tis pleasant to impart,
These turns and movements of the human Heart;
The stronger features of the Soul to paint,
And make distinct the latent and the faint;
Man as he is, to place in all men's view,

Yet none with rancour, none with scorn pursue:
Nor be it ever of my Portraits told—
"Here the strong lines of Malice we behold."

This let me hope, that when in public view
I bring my Pictures, Men may feel them true;
"This is a Likeness," may they all declare,
"And I have seen him, but I know not where:"
For I should mourn the mischief I had done,
If as the Likeness all would fix on One.

Man's Vice and Crime I combat as I can,
But to his God and Conscience leave the Man;
I search (a Quixote!) all the Land about,
To find its Giants and Enchanters out,
(The Giant-Folly, the Enchanter-Vice,
Whom doubtless I shall vanquish in a trice:)
But is there Man whom I would injure?—No!
I am to him a Fellow, not a Foe,—
A Fellow-Sinner, who must rather dread
The Bolt than hurl it at another's head.

No! let the Guiltless, if there such be found,
Launch forth the Spear, and deal the deadly Wound;
How can I so the cause of Virtue aid,
Who am myself attainted and afraid?
Yet as I can, I point the powers of Rhyme,
And, sparing Criminals, attack the Crime.

✷✷ "Paid to eat" is an allusion to sumptuous dinners of "dons,"
that is, professors on old endowments at Oxford and Cambridge.
  The age-old, never-ending war of the "two nations" is taken up
again by Bunting (p. 313) a century later. Suffolk or Northumberland, the conflict remains.

Robert Burns
[1759–1796]

THE BIRKS OF ABERFELDY

Bonnie lassie, will ye go,
Will ye go, will ye go,
Bonnie lassie, will ye go,
    To the Birks of Aberfeldy?

Now simmer blinks on flowery braes,
And o'er the crystal streamlets plays,
Come let us spend the lightsome days
    In the Birks of Aberfeldy.

The little birdies blythely sing,
While o'er their heads the hazels hing,
Or lightly flit on wanton wing
    In the Birks of Aberfeldy.

The braes ascend like lofty wa's,
The foaming stream deep-roaring fa's,
O'erhung wi' fragrant spreading shaws—
    The Birks of Aberfeldy.

The hoary cliffs are crown'd wi' flowers,
White o'er the linns the burnie pours,
And rising, weets wi' misty showers
    The Birks of Aberfeldy.

Let fortune's gifts at random flee,
They ne'er shall draw a wish frae me,
Supremely blest wi' love and thee,
    In the Birks of Aberfeldy.

BONNIE LESLEY

O saw ye bonnie Lesley
   As she gaed o'er the Border?
She's gane, like Alexander,
   To spread her conquests farther.

To see her is to love her,
   And love but her for ever;
For Nature made her what she is,
   And never made anither!

Thou art a queen, fair Lesley,
   Thy subjects we, before thee:
Thou art divine, fair Lesley,
   The hearts o' men adore thee.

The Deil he could na skaith thee,
   Or aught that wad belang thee;
He'd look into thy bonnie face,
   And say, 'I canna wrang thee.'

The Powers aboon will tent thee;
   Misfortune sha'na steer thee;
Thou'rt like themsel' sae lovely,
   That ill they'll ne'er let near thee.

Return again, fair Lesley,
   Return to Caledonie!
That we may brag we hae a lass
   There's nane again sae bonnie.

GREEN GROW THE RASHES

Green grow the rashes O,
　Green grow the rashes O;
The sweetest hours that e'er I spend,
　Are spent amang the lasses O!

There's nought but care on ev'ry han',
　In ev'ry hour that passes O;
What signifies the life o' man,
　An' 'twere na for the lasses O?

The warly race may riches chase,
　An' riches still may fly them O;
An' tho' at last they catch them fast,
　Their hearts can ne'er enjoy them O.

But gie me a canny hour at e'en,
　My arms about my dearie O;
An' warly cares, an' warly men,
　May a' gae tapsalteerie O!

For you sae douce, ye sneer at this,
　Ye're nought but senseless asses O:
The wisest man the warl' saw,
　He dearly lov'd the lasses O.

Auld nature swears, the lovely dears
　Her noblest work she classes O;
Her prentice han' she tried on man,
　An' then she made the lasses O.

Walter Savage Landor
[1775–1864]

PAST RUIN'D ILION HELEN LIVES

Past ruin'd Ilion Helen lives,
   Alcestis rises from the shades;
Verse calls them forth; 'tis verse that gives
   Immortal youth to mortal maids.

DIRCE

Stand close around, ye Stygian set,
   With Dirce in one bark conveyed!
Or Charon, seeing, may forget
   That he is old and she a shade.

❀ ❀ That savage old Boeotian Walter Landor,
   Who took for swan Dan Southey's gander.
               —BYRON

George Gordon, Lord Byron
[1788–1824]

from D O N   J U A N

> *Difficile est proprie communia dicere.*—HORACE

> Dost thou think, because thou art virtuous, there shall be no
> more cakes and ale? Yes, by Saint Anne, and ginger shall be
> hot i' the mouth, too!   —SHAKESPEARE, *Twelfth Night*

FRAGMENT
On the back of the MS. of Canto I

I would to heaven that I were so much clay,
    As I am blood, bone, marrow, passion feeling—
Because at least the past were passed away,
    And for the future—(but I write this reeling,
Having got drunk exceedingly to-day,
    So that I seem to stand upon the ceiling)
I say—the future is a serious matter—
And so—for God's sake—hock and soda-water!

DEDICATION

I
Bob Southey! You're a poet—Poet-laureate,
    And representative of all the race;
Although 'tis true that you turn'd out a Tory at
    Last,—yours has lately been a common case;
And now, my Epic Renegade! what are ye at?
    With all the Lakers, in and out of place?
A nest of tuneful persons, to my eye
Like "four and twenty Blackbirds in a pye;

II

"Which pye being open'd they began to sing,"
  (This old song and new simile holds good),
"A dainty dish to set before the King,"
  Or Regent, who admires such kind of food;—
And Coleridge, too, has lately taken wing,
  But like a hawk encumber'd with his hood,—
Explaining Metaphysics to the nation—
I wish he would explain his Explanation.

III

You, Bob! are rather insolent, you know,
  At being disappointed in your wish
To supersede all warblers here below,
  And be the only Blackbird in the dish;
And then you overstrain yourself, or so,
  And tumble downward like the flying fish
Gasping on deck, because you soar too high, Bob,
And fall, for lack of moisture, quite a-dry, Bob!

IV

And Wordsworth, in a rather long "Excursion,"
  (I think the quarto holds five hundred pages),
Has given a sample from the vasty version
  Of this new system to perplex the sages;
'Tis poetry—at least by his assertion,
  And may appear so when the dog-star rages—
And he who understands it would be able
To add a story to the Tower of Babel.

V

You—Gentlemen! by dint of long seclusion
  From better company, have kept your own
At Keswick, and, through still continued fusion
  Of one another's minds, at last have grown
To deem as a most logical conclusion,
  That Poesy has wreaths for you alone:

There is a narrowness in such a notion,
Which makes me wish you'd change your lakes for Ocean.

VI

I would not imitate the petty thought,
    Nor coin my self-love to so base a vice,
For all the glory your conversion brought,
    Since gold alone should not have been its price.
You have your salary; was't for that you wrought?
    And Wordsworth has his place in the Excise.
You're shabby fellows—true—but poets still,
And duly seated on the Immortal Hill.

VII

Your bays may hide the baldness of your brows—
    Perhaps some virtuous blushes;—let them go—
To you I envy neither fruit nor boughs—
    And for the fame you would engross below,
The field is universal, and allows
    Scope to all such as feel the inherent glow:
Scott, Rogers, Campbell, Moore, and Crabbe, will try
'Gainst you the question with posterity.

VIII

For me, who, wandering with pedestrian Muses,
    Contend not with you on the wingéd steed,
I wish your fate may yield ye, when she chooses,
    The fame you envy, and the skill you need;
And, recollect, a poet nothing loses
    In giving to his brethren their full meed
Of merit—and complaint of present days
Is not the certain path to future praise.

IX

He that reserves his laurels for posterity
    (Who does not often claim the bright reversion)
Has generally no great crop to spare it, he

Being only injured by his own assertion;
And although here and there some glorious rarity
    Arise like Titan from the sea's immersion,
The major part of such appellants go
To—God knows where—for no one else can know.

X

If, fallen in evil days on evil tongues,
    Milton appealed to the Avenger, Time,
If Time, the Avenger, execrates his wrongs,
    And makes the word "Miltonic" mean *"Sublime,"*
He deigned not to belie his soul in songs,
    Nor turn his very talent to a crime;
He did not loathe the Sire to laud the Son,
But closed the tyrant-hater he begun.

XI

Think'st thou, could he—the blind Old Man—arise
    Like Samuel from the grave, to freeze once more
The blood of monarchs with his prophecies,
    Or be alive again—again all hoar
With time and trials, and those helpless eyes,
    And heartless daughters—worn—and pale—and poor;
Would *he* adore a sultan? *he* obey
The intellectual eunuch Castlereagh?

XII

Cold-blooded, smooth-faced, placid miscreant!
    Dabbling its sleek young hands in Erin's gore,
And thus for wider carnage taught to pant,
    Transferred to gorge upon a sister shore,
The vulgarest tool that Tyranny could want,
    With just enough of talent, and no more,
To lengthen fetters by another fixed,
And offer poison long already mixed.

XIII

An orator of such set trash of phrase
    Ineffably—legitimately vile,
That even its grossest flatterers dare not praise,
    Nor foes—all nations—condescend to smile,—
Not even a sprightly blunder's spark can blaze
    From that Ixion grindstone's ceaseless toil,
That turns and turns to give the world a notion
Of endless torments and perpetual motion.

XIV

A bungler even in its disgusting trade,
    And botching, patching, leaving still behind
Something of which its masters are afraid—
    States to be curbed, and thoughts to be confined,
Conspiracy or Congress to be made—
    Cobbling at manacles for all mankind—
A tinkering slave-maker, who mends old chains,
With God and man's abhorrence for its gains.

XV

If we may judge of matter by the mind,
    Emasculated to the marrow *It*
Hath but two objects, how to serve, and bind,
    Deeming the chain it wears even men may fit,
Eutropius of its many masters,—blind
    To worth as freedom, wisdom as to wit,
Fearless—because *no* feeling dwells in ice,
Its very courage stagnates to a vice.

XVI

Where shall I turn me not to *view* its bonds,
    For I will never *feel* them?—Italy!
Thy late reviving Roman soul desponds
    Beneath the lie this State-thing breathed o'er thee—

Thy clanking chain, and Erin's yet green wounds,
   Have voices—tongues to cry aloud for me.
Europe has slaves—allies—kings—armies still—
And Southey lives to sing them very ill.

XVII

Meantime, Sir Laureate, I proceed to dedicate,
   In honest simple verse, this song to you,
And, if in flattering strains I do not predicate,
   'Tis that I still retain my "buff and blue;"
My politics as yet are all to educate:
   Apostasy's so fashionable, too,
To keep *one* creed's a task grown quite Herculean;
Is it not so, my Tory, ultra-Julian?

❊❊ Any instructor with an interest in the vital parts of Byron's
mind, rather than in Sunday-supplement trivialities, might find
G. S. Street's comments useful in exciting his students. *Vide*
"Byron" in Street's *A Book of Essays* and in *Ghosts of Piccadilly*,
p. 91.

Fitz-Greene Halleck

   [1790–1867]

❊❊ It has been argued that the gap between the quality of Eng-
lish versification and early American is considerably less apparent
if measured as between Byron and Fitz-Greene Halleck, than it
appears during the next half-century. At any rate a few people
think that he has been disproportionately neglected.

from F A N N Y

I

Fanny was younger once than she is now,
　　And prettier of course; I do not mean
To say that there are wrinkles on her brow;
　　Yet, to be candid, she is past eighteen—
Perhaps past twenty—but the girl is shy
About her age, and Heaven forbid that I

II

Should get myself in trouble by revealing,
　　A secret of this sort; I have too long
Loved pretty women with a poet's feeling,
　　And when a boy, in day-dream and in song,
Have knelt me down and worshipped them: alas!
They never thanked me for't—but let that pass.

　　. . . . .

V

Her father kept, some fifteen years ago,
　　A retail dry-goods shop in Chatham Street,
And nursed his little earnings, sure though slow,
　　Till, having mustered wherewithal to meet
The gaze of the great world, he breathed the air
Of Pearl Street—and "set up" in Hanover Square.

　　. . . . .

XLI

Since that wise pedant, Johnson, was in fashion,
　　Manners have changed as well as moons; and he
Would fret himself once more into a passion,
　　Should he return (which Heaven forbid!) and see,

How strangely from his standard dictionary
The meaning of some words is made to vary.

XLII

For instance, an *undress* at present means
    The wearing a pelisse, a shawl, or so;
Or anything you please, in short, that screens
    The face, and hides the form from top to toe;
Of power to brave a quizzing-glass, or storm—
'Tis worn in summer, when the weather's warm.

XLIII

But a full dress is for a winter's night.
    The most genteel is made of "woven air";
That kind of classic cobweb, soft and light,
    Which Lady Morgan's Ida used to wear.
And ladies, this aërial manner dressed in,
Look Eve-like, angel-like, and interesting.

   . . . . .

CXIV

She had been noticed at some public places
    (The Battery, and the balls of Mr. Whale),
For hers was one of those attractive faces,
    That when you gaze upon them, never fail
To bid you look again; there was a beam,
A lustre in her eye, that oft would seem

CXV

A little like effrontery; and yet
    The lady meant no harm; her only aim
Was but to be admired by all she met,
    And the free homage of the heart to claim;
And if she showed too plainly this intention,
Others have done the same—'twas not of her invention.

   . . . . .

                    —talked as loudly too

CXVII

As any beauty of the highest grade,
  To the gay circle in the box beside her;
And when the pit—half vexed and half afraid,
  With looks of smothered indignation eyed her,
She calmly met their gaze, and stood before 'em
Smiling at vulgar taste and mock decorum.

. . . . .

CXLVI

He was a trustee of a Savings Bank,
  And lectured soundly every evil-doer,
Gave dinners daily to wealth, power, and rank,
  And sixpence every Sunday to the poor;
He was a wit, in the pun-making line—
Past fifty years of age, and five feet nine.

. . . . .

CLXXII

Her father sent to Albany a prayer
  For office, told how fortune had abused him,
And modestly requested to be Mayor—
  The Council very civilly refused him;
Because, however much they might desire it,
The "public good," it seems, did not require it.

. . . . .

❊ ❊ The original edition of *Fanny* appeared in 1821; there is no harm in comparing the clarity of Halleck's writing with Byron's, and the inferiority of American verse is not in the least apparent to present anthologist. At least in the present strophes of the 175. If there is a gap between English and American standards, it is not so great as it was thirty years later.

Felicia Dorothea Hemans
[1793–1835]

from THE BRERETON OMEN

Yes! I have seen the ancient oak
On the dark deep water cast,
And it was not felled by the woodman's stroke,
Or the rush of the sweeping blast;
For the axe might never touch that tree,
And the air was still as a summer sea.

. . . . .

'Tis fallen! but think thou not I weep
For the forest's pride o'erthrown;
An old man's tears lie far too deep,
To be poured for this alone!
But by that sign too well I know
That a youthful head must soon be low!

. . . . .

He must, he must! in that deep dell,
By that dark water's side,
'Tis known that ne'er a proud tree fell
But an heir of his fathers died.
And he—there's laughter in his eye,
Joy in his voice—yet he must die.

. . . . .

Say not 'tis vain! I tell thee, some
Are warned by a meteor's light,
Or a pale bird flitting calls them home,
Or a voice on the winds by night;

And they must go! and he too, he—
Woe for the fall of the glorious tree.

✳ ✳ The once popular Hemans illustrates the "romantic" style
of that era as well as some of the still famous writers.

John Keats

[1795–1821]

from ENDYMION

✳ ✳ Read it aloud, noting the punctuation; do not stop at the
end of each line.

A thing of beauty is a joy for ever:
Its loveliness increases; it will never
Pass into nothingness; but still will keep
A bower quiet for us, and a sleep
Full of sweet dreams, and health, and quiet breathing.
Therefore, on every morrow, are we wreathing
A flowery band to bind us to the earth,
Spite of despondence, of the inhuman dearth
Of noble natures, of the gloomy days,
Of all the unhealthy and o'er-darkened ways
Made for our searching: yes, in spite of all,
Some shape of beauty moves away the pall
From our dark spirits. Such the sun, the moon,
Trees old and young sprouting a shady boon
For simple sheep; and such are daffodils
With the green world they live in; and clear rills
That for themselves a cooling covert make

'Gainst the hot season; the mid forest brake,
Rich with a sprinkling of fair musk-rose blooms:
And such too is the grandeur of the dooms
We have imagined for the mighty dead;
All lovely tales that we have heard or read:
An endless fountain of immortal drink,
Pouring unto us from the heaven's brink.

Nor do we merely feel these essences
For one short hour; no, even as the trees
That whisper round a temple become soon
Dear as the temple's self, so does the moon,
The passion poesy, glories infinite,
Haunt us till they become a cheering light
Unto our souls, and bound to us so fast,
That, whether there be shine, or gloom o'ercast,
They alway must be with us, or we die.

Therefore, 'tis with full happiness that I
Will trace the story of Endymion.
The very music of the name has gone
Into my being, and each pleasant scene
Is growing fresh before me as the green
Of our own vallies: so I will begin
Now while I cannot hear the city's din;
Now while the early budders are just new,
And run in mazes of the youngest hue
About old forests; while the willow trails
Its delicate amber; and the dairy pails
Bring home increase of milk. And, as the year
Grows lush in juicy stalks, I'll smoothly steer
My little boat, for many quiet hours,
With streams that deepen freshly into bowers.
Many and many a verse I hope to write,

Before the daisies, vermeil rimm'd and white,
Hide in deep herbage. . . .

❋❋ One of *The Quarterly Review's* "young," or old, men
gained a certain permanence in English literary tradition by
such phrases as: "Mr. Keats (if that be his real name, for we
almost doubt that any man in his senses put his real name to
such a rhapsody)," etc. . . . Byron was presumably correct in
stating that the review did not kill Keats, as some later sob
sisters maintained. But it did not, on the other hand, kill the
Quarterly.

Thomas Lovell Beddoes
[1803–1849]

from DEATH'S JEST BOOK

MANDRAKE: Have reverence, I pray thee. To-morrow I know thee
not. In truth, I mark our noble faculty is in decay. The world
will see its ears in a glass no longer; so we are laid aside and shall
soon be forgotten; for why should the feast of asses come but
once a year, when all the days are foaled of one mother? O world,
world! The gods and fairies left thee, for thou wert too wise;
and now, thou Socratic star, thy demon, the great Pan, Folly, is
parting from thee. The oracles still talked in their sleep, shall our
grandchildren say, till Master Merriman's kingdom was broken
up: now is every man his own fool, and the world's cheerless.

ATHULF: A fair and bright assembly: never strode
Old arched Grüssau over such a tide
Of helmed chivalry, as when to-day
Our tourney guests swept, leaping billow-like,

Its palace-banked streets. Knights shut in steel,
Whose shields, like water, glassed the soul-eyed maidens,
That softly did attend their armed tread,
Flower-cinctured on the temples, whence gushed down
A full libation of star-numbered tresses,
Hallowing the neck unto love's silent kiss,
Veiling its innocent white: and then came squires,
And those who bore war's silken tapestries,
And chequered heralds: 'twas a human river,
Brimful and beating as if the great god,
Who lay beneath it, would arise. So swings
Time's sea, which Age snows into and encreases,
When from the rocky side of the dim future,
Leaps into it a mighty destiny,
Whose being to endow great souls have been
Centuries hoarded, and the world meanwhile
Sate like a beggar upon Heaven's threshold,
Muttering its wrongs.

    Act II, Scene 3

❋❋ "At anchor, rot while Beddoes breasts the tide!" *Vide*
R. Browning's "The Two Poets of Croisic." Beddoes is full of
magnificent phrasing at the Elizabethan level which is not at
all mere rhetoric or bumbast, as witness:

                     . . . he, whose world
Grows in his thoughts, methinks, alone is happy.
                (*Torrismond,* I, 1)

And *Death's Jest Book,* I, 2:

                   . . . whose love-spurned hearts
Hunger for goblin immortality.

Elizabeth Barrett Browning
[1806–1861]

from SONNETS FROM THE PORTUGUESE

VII

The face of all the world is changed, I think,
Since first I heard the footsteps of thy soul
Move still, oh, still, beside me, as they stole
Betwixt me and the dreadful outer brink
Of obvious death, where I, who thought to sink,
Was caught up into love, and taught the whole
Of life in a new rhythm. The cup of dole
God gave for baptism, I am fain to drink,
And praise its sweetness, Sweet, with thee anear.
The names of country, heaven, are changed away
For where thou art or shalt be, there or here;
And this . . . this lute song . . . loved yesterday,
(The singing angels know) are only dear
Because thy name moves right in what they say.

IX

Can it be right to give what I can give?
To let thee sit beneath the fall of tears
As salt as mine, and hear the sighing years
Re-sighing on my lips renunciative
Through those infrequent smiles which fail to live
For all thy adjurations? O my fears,
That this can scarce be right! We are not peers,
So to be lovers; and I own, and grieve,
That givers of such gifts as mine are, must

Be counted with the ungenerous. Out, alas!
I will not soil thy purple with my dust,
Nor breathe my poison on thy Venice-glass,
Nor give thee any love—which were unjust.
Beloved, I only love thee! let it pass.

X

Yet, love, mere love, is beautiful indeed
And worthy of acceptation. Fire is bright,
Let temple burn, or flax; an equal light
Leaps in the flame from cedar-plank or weed:
And love is fire. And when I say at need
I love thee . . . mark! *. . . I love thee!*—in thy sight
I stand transfigured, glorified aright,
With conscience of the new rays that proceed
Out of my face toward thine. There's nothing low
In love, when love the lowest: meanest creatures
Who love God, God accepts while loving so.
And what I *feel,* across the inferior features
Of what I *am,* doth flash itself, and show
How that great work of Love enhances Nature's.

XIV

If thou must love me, let it be for nought
Except for love's sake only. Do not say
"I love her for her smile—her look—her way
Of speaking gently,—for a trick of thought
That falls in well with mine, and certes brought
A sense of pleasant ease on such a day"—
For these things in themselves, Belovèd, may
Be changed, or change for thee,—and love so wrought,
May be unwrought so. Neither love me for
Thine own dear pity's wiping my cheeks dry,—

A creature might forget to weep, who bore
Thy comfort long, and lose thy love thereby!
But love me for love's sake, that evermore
Thou mayst love on, through love's eternity.

XXXVIII

First time he kissed me, he but only kissed
The fingers of this hand wherewith I write;
And ever since, it grew more clean and white,
Slow to world-greetings, quick with its "Oh, list,"
When the angels speak. A ring of amethyst
I could not wear here, plainer to my sight,
Than that first kiss. The second passed in height
The first, and sought the forehead, and half missed,
Half falling on the hair. O beyond meed!
That was the chrism of love, which love's own crown,
With sanctifying sweetness, did precede.
The third upon my lips was folded down
In perfect, purple state; since when, indeed,
I have been proud and said, "My love, my own."

XLIII

How do I love thee? Let me count the ways.
I love thee to the depth and breadth and height
My soul can reach, when feeling out of sight
For the ends of Being and ideal Grace.
I love thee to the level of everyday's
Most quiet need, by sun and candle-light.
I love thee freely, as men strive for Right;
I love thee purely, as they turn from Praise.
I love thee with the passion put to use
In my old griefs, and with my childhood's faith.
I love thee with a love I seemed to lose

With my lost saints!—I love thee with the breath,
Smiles, tears, of all my life!—and, if God choose,
I shall but love thee better after death.

❀ ❀ The second: that is, a sonnet sequence surpassed in English
by one other alone. I would argue for that.

John Greenleaf Whittier

[1807–1892]

BARBARA FRIETCHIE

Up from the meadows rich with corn,
Clear in the cool September morn,

The clustered spires of Frederick stand
Green-walled by the hills of Maryland.

Round about them orchards sweep,
Apple and peach tree fruited deep,

Fair as the garden of the Lord
To the eyes of the famished rebel horde,

On that pleasant morn of the early fall
When Lee marched over the mountain-wall,—

Over the mountains winding down,
Horse and foot, into Frederick town.

Forty flags with their silver stars,
Forty flags with their crimson bars,

Flapped in the morning wind: the sun
Of noon looked down, and saw not one.

Up rose old Barbara Frietchie then,
Bowed with her fourscore years and ten;

Bravest of all in Frederick town,
She took up the flag the men hauled down;

In her attic window the staff she set,
To show that one heart was loyal yet.

Up the street came the rebel tread,
Stonewall Jackson riding ahead.

Under his slouched hat left and right
He glanced; the old flag met his sight.

"Halt!"—the dust-brown ranks stood fast.
"Fire!"—out blazed the rifle-blast.

It shivered the window, pane and sash;
It rent the banner with seam and gash.

Quick, as it fell, from the broken staff
Dame Barbara snatched the silken scarf.

She leaned far out on the window-sill,
And shook it forth with a royal will.

"Shoot, if you must, this old gray head,
But spare your country's flag," she said.

A shade of sadness, a blush of shame,
Over the face of the leader came;

The nobler nature within him stirred
To life at that woman's deed and word:

"Who touches a hair of yon gray head
Dies like a dog! March on!" he said.

All day long through Frederick street
Sounded the tread of marching feet:

All day long that free flag tost
Over the heads of the rebel host.

Ever its torn folds rose and fell
On the loyal winds that loved it well;

And through the hill-gaps sunset light
Shone over it with a warm good-night.

Barbara Frietchie's work is o'er,
And the Rebel rides on his raids no more.

Honor to her! and let a tear
Fall, for her sake, on Stonewall's bier.

Over Barbara Frietchie's grave,
Flag of Freedom and Union, wave!

Peace and order and beauty draw
Round thy symbol of light and law;

And ever the stars above look down
On the stars below in Frederick town!

Théophile Gautier
[1811–1872]

from ARS VICTRIX

All passes. Art alone
    Enduring stays to us;
The bust outlasts the throne;
    The coin, Tiberius.

Even the gods must go;
    Only the lofty rime,
Not countless years o'erthrow,
    Nor long array of time.

Translated by H. Austin Dobson

❊ ❊ A fragment quoted from the introduction to von Noppen's translation of Vondel's *Lucifer* (New York, 1898). Dobson catches Gautier's quality, in the lines given here, though he misses it in the other eight strophes he translated.

Robert Browning
[1812–1889]

HOW IT STRIKES A CONTEMPORARY

I only knew one poet in my life:
And this, or something like it, was his way.

You saw go up and down Valladolid,
A man of mark, to know next time you saw.
His very serviceable suit of black
Was courtly once and conscientious still,
And many might have worn it, though none did:
The cloak, that somewhat shone and showed the threads,
Had purpose, and the ruff, significance.
He walked and tapped the pavement with his cane,
Scenting the world, looking it full in face,
An old dog, bald and blindish, at his heels.
They turned up, now, the alley by the church,
That leads no whither; now, they breathed themselves
On the main promenade just at the wrong time:
You'd come upon his scrutinizing hat,
Making a peaked shade blacker than itself
Against the single window spared some house
Intact yet with its mouldered Moorish work,—
Or else surprise the ferule of his stick
Trying the mortar's temper 'tween the chinks
Of some new shop a-building, French and fine.
He stood and watched the cobbler at his trade,
The man who slices lemons into drink,
The coffee-roaster's brasier, and the boys
That volunteer to help him turn its winch.
He glanced o'er books on stalls with half an eye,
And fly-leaf ballads on the vendor's string,
And broad-edge bold-print posters by the wall.
He took such cognisance of men and things,
If any beat a horse, you felt he saw;
If any cursed a woman, he took note;
Yet stared at nobody,—they stared at him,
And found, less to their pleasure than surprise,
He seemed to know them and expect as much.
So, next time that a neighbour's tongue was loosed,
It marked the shameful and notorious fact,
We had among us, not so much a spy,
As a recording chief-inquisitor,

The town's true master if the town but knew!
We merely kept a Governor for form,
While this man walked about and took account
Of all thought, said and acted, then went home,
And wrote it fully to our Lord the King
Who has an itch to know things, He knows why,
And reads them in His bed-room of a night.
Oh, you might smile! there wanted not a touch,
A tang of . . . well, it was not wholly ease
As back into your mind the man's look came—
Stricken in years a little,—such a brow
His eyes had to live under!—clear as flint
On either side the formidable nose
Curved, cut and coloured like an eagle's claw.
Had he to do with A.'s surprising fate?
When altogether old B. disappeared
And young C. got his mistress,—was't our friend,
His letter to the King, that did it all?
What paid the bloodless man for so much pains?
Our Lord the King has favourites manifold,
And shifts His ministry some once a month;
Our city gets new Governors at whiles,—
But never word or sign, that I could hear,
Notified to this man about the streets
The King's approval of those letters conned
The last thing duly at the dead of night.
Did the man love his office? frowned our Lord,
Exhorting when none heard—"Beseech Me not!
Too far above My people,—beneath Me!
I set the watch,—how should the people know?
Forget them, keep Me all the more in mind!"
Was some such understanding 'twixt the Two?

      I found no truth in one report at least—
That if you tracked him to his home, down lanes
Beyond the Jewry, and as clean to pace,
You found he ate his supper in a room

Blazing with lights, four Titians on the wall,
And twenty naked girls to change his plate!
Poor man, he lived another kind of life
In that new, stuccoed, third house by the bridge,
Fresh-painted, rather smart than otherwise!
The whole street might o'erlook him as he sat,
Leg crossing leg, one foot on the dog's back,
Playing a decent cribbage with his maid
(Jacynth, you're sure her name was) o'er the cheese
And fruit, three red halves of starved winter-pears,
Or treat of radishes in April! nine,
Ten, struck the church clock, straight to bed went he.

My father, like the man of sense he was,
Would point him out to me a dozen times;
"St—St," he'd whisper, "the Corregidor!"
I had been used to think that personage
Was one with lacquered breeches, lustrous belt,
And feathers like a forest in his hat,
Who blew a trumpet and proclaimed the news,
Announced the bull-fights, gave each church its turn,
And memorized the miracle in vogue!
He had a great observance from us boys;
We were in error; that was not the man.

I'd like now, yet had haply been afraid,
To have just looked, when this man came to die,
And seen who lined the clean gay garret's sides
And stood about the neat low truckle-bed,
With the heavenly manner of relieving guard.
Here had been, mark, the general-in-chief,
Thro' a whole campaign of the world's life and death,
Doing the King's work all the dim day long,
In his old coat and up to his knees in mud,
Smoked like a herring, dining on a crust,—
And, now the day was won, relieved at once!
No further show or need for that old coat,

You are sure, for one thing! Bless us, all the while
How sprucely we are dressed out, you and I!
A second, and the angels alter that.
Well, I could never write a verse,—could you?
Let's to the Prado and make the most of time.

PICTOR IGNOTUS
Florence, 15———

I could have painted pictures like that youth's
    Ye praise so. How my soul springs up! No bar
Stayed me—ah, thought which saddens while it soothes!
    —Never did fate forbid me, star by star,
To outburst on your night with all my gift
    Of fires from God: nor would my flesh have shrunk
From seconding my soul, with eyes uplift
    And wide to heaven, or, straight like thunder, sunk
To the centre, of an instant; or around
    Turned calmly and inquisitive, to scan
The licence and the limit, space and bound,
    Allowed to Truth made visible in Man.
And, like that youth ye praise so, all I saw,
    Over the canvas could my hand have flung,
Each face obedient to its passion's law,
    Each passion clear proclaimed without a tongue;
Whether Hope rose at once in all the blood,
    A-tiptoe for the blessing of embrace,
Or Rapture drooped the eyes, as when her brood
    Pull down the nesting dove's heart to its place;
Or Confidence lit swift the forehead up,
    And locked the mouth fast, like a castle braved,—
O human faces, hath it spilt, my cup?
    What did ye give me that I have not saved?
Nor will I say I have not dreamed (how well!)
    Of going—I, in each new picture,—forth,
As, making new hearts beat and bosoms swell,

To Pope or Kaiser, East, West, South or North,
Bound for the calmly satisfied great State,
    Or glad aspiring little burgh, it went,
Flowers cast upon the car which bore the freight,
    Through old streets named afresh from its event,
Till it reached home, where learned Age should greet
    My face, and Youth, the star not yet distinct
Above his hair, lie learning at my feet!—
    Oh, thus to live, I and my picture, linked
With love about, and praise, till life should end,
    And then not go to heaven, but linger here,
Here on my earth, earth's every man my friend,—
    The thought grew frightful, 'twas so wildly dear!
But a voice changed it! Glimpses of such sights
    Have scared me, like the revels through a door
Of some strange House of Idols at its rites;
    This world seemed not the world it was before:
Mixed with my loving trusting ones there trooped
    . . . Who summoned those cold faces that begun
To press on me and judge me? Though I stooped
    Shrinking, as from the soldiery a nun,
They drew me forth, and spite of me . . . enough!
    These buy and sell our pictures, take and give,
Count them for garniture and household-stuff,
    And where they live our pictures needs must live
And see their faces, listen to their prate,
    Partakers of their daily pettiness,
Discussed of,—"This I love, or this I hate,
    This likes me more, and this affects me less!"
Wherefore I chose my portion. If at whiles
    My heart sinks, as monotonous I paint
These endless cloisters and eternal aisles
    With the same series, Virgin, Babe and Saint,
With the same cold, calm, beautiful regard,
    At least no merchant traffics in my heart;
The sanctuary's gloom at least shall ward
    Vain tongues from where my pictures stand apart:

Only prayer breaks the silence of the shrine
  While, blackening in the daily candle-smoke,
They moulder on the damp wall's travertine,
  'Mid echoes the light footstep never woke.
So die, my pictures; surely, gently die!
  Oh, youth, men praise so,—holds their praise its worth?
Blown harshly, keeps the trump its golden cry?
  Tastes sweet the water with such specks of earth?

GARDEN FANCIES

I   The.Flower's.Name

I

Here's the garden she walked across,
  Arm in my arm, such a short while since:
Hark, now I push its wicket, the moss
  Hinders the hinges and makes them wince!
She must have reached this shrub ere she turned,
  As back with that murmur the wicket swung;
For she laid the poor snail, my chance foot spurned,
  To feed and forget it the leaves among.

II

Down this side of the gravel-walk
  She went while her robe's edge brushed the box:
And here she paused in her gracious talk
  To point me a moth on the milk-white phlox.
Roses, ranged in valiant row,
  I will never think that she passed you by!
She loves you, noble roses, I know;
  But yonder, see, where the rock-plants lie:

III

This flower she stopped at, finger on lip,
  Stooped over, in doubt, as settling its claim;

Till she gave me, with pride to make no slip,
    Its soft meandering Spanish name:
What a name! was it love, or praise?
    Speech half-asleep, or song half-awake?
I must learn Spanish, one of these days,
    Only for that slow sweet name's sake.

IV

Roses, if I live and do well,
    I may bring her, one of these days,
To fix you fast with as fine a spell,
    Fit you each with his Spanish phrase;
But do not detain me now; for she lingers
    There, like sunshine over the ground,
And ever I see her soft white fingers
    Searching after the bud she found.

V

Flower, you Spaniard, look that you grow not,
    Stay as you are and be loved for ever!
Bud, if I kiss you 'tis that you blow not,
    Mind, the shut pink mouth opens never!
For while thus it pouts, her fingers wrestle,
    Twinkling the audacious leaves between,
Till round they turn and down they nestle—
    Is not the dear mark still to be seen?

VI

Where I find her not, beauties vanish;
    Whither I follow her, beauties flee;
Is there no method to tell her in Spanish
    June's twice June since she breathed it with me?
Come, bud, show me the least of her traces,
    Treasure my lady's lightest footfall
—Ah, you may flout and turn up your faces—
    Roses, you are not so fair after all!

II   *Sibrandus . Schafnaburgensis*

I

Plague take all your pedants, say I!
    He who wrote what I hold in my hand,
Centuries back was so good as to die,
    Leaving this rubbish to cumber the land;
This, that was a book in its time,
    Printed on paper and bound in leather,
Last month in the white of a matin-prime
    Just when the birds sang all together.

II

Into the garden I brought it to read,
    And under the arbute and laurustine
Read it, so help me grace in my need,
    From title-page to closing line.
Chapter on chapter did I count,
    As a curious traveller counts Stonehenge;
Added up the mortal amount;
    And then proceeded to my revenge.

III

Yonder's a plum-tree with a crevice
    An owl would build in, were he but sage;
For a lap of moss, like a fine pont-levis
    In a castle of the middle age,
Joins to a lip of gum, pure amber;
    When he'd be private, there might he spend
Hours alone in his lady's chamber:
    Into this crevice I dropped our friend.

IV

Splash, went he, as under he ducked,
    —I knew at the bottom rain-drippings stagnate;
Next a handful of blossoms I plucked
    To bury him with, my bookshelf's magnate;

Then I went indoors, brought out a loaf,
　　Half a cheese, and a bottle of Chablis;
Lay on the grass and forgot the oaf
　　Over a jolly chapter of Rabelais.

V

Now, this morning, betwixt the moss
　　And gum that locked our friend in limbo,
A spider had spun his web across,
　　And sat in the midst with arms akimbo:
So, I took pity, for learning's sake,
　　And, *de profundis, accentibus laetis,*
Cantate! quoth I, as I got a rake,
　　And up I fished his delectable treatise.

VI

Here you have it, dry in the sun,
　　With all the binding all of a blister,
And great blue spots where the ink has run,
　　And reddish streaks that wink and glister
O'er the page so beautifully yellow:
　　Oh, well have the droppings played their tricks!
Did he guess how toadstools grow, this fellow?
　　Here's one stuck in his chapter six!

VII

How did he like it when the live creatures
　　Tickled and toused and browsed him all over,
And worm, slug, eft, with serious features,
　　Came in, each one, for his right of trover?
—When the water-beetle with great blind deaf face
　　Made of her eggs the stately deposit,
And the newt borrowed just so much of the preface
　　As tiled in the top of his black wife's closet?

VIII

All that life and fun and romping,
  All that frisking and twisting and coupling,
While slowly our poor friend's leaves were swamping
  And clasps were cracking and covers suppling!
As if you had carried sour John Knox
  To the play-house at Paris, Vienna or Munich,
Fastened him into a front-row box,
  And danced off the ballet with trousers and tunic.

IX

Come, old martyr! What, torment enough is it?
  Back to my room shall you take your sweet self!
Good-bye, mother-beetle; husband-eft, *sufficit!*
  See the snug niche I have made on my shelf.
A.'s book shall prop you up, B.'s shall cover you,
  Here's C. to be grave with, or D. to be gay,
And with E. on each side, and F. right over you,
  Dry-rot at ease till the Judgment-day!

FRA LIPPO LIPPI

I am poor brother Lippo, by your leave!
You need not clap your torches to my face.
Zooks, what's to blame? you think you see a monk!
What, it's past midnight, and you go the rounds,
And here you catch me at an alley's end
Where sportive ladies leave their doors ajar?
The Carmine's my cloister: hunt it up,
Do,—harry out, if you must show your zeal,
Whatever rat, there, haps on his wrong hole,
And nip each softling of a wee white mouse,
Weke, weke, that's crept to keep him company!

Aha, you know your betters? Then, you'll take
Your hand away that's fiddling on my throat,
And please to know me likewise. Who am I?
Why, one, sir, who is lodging with a friend
Three streets off—he's a certain . . . how d'ye call?
Master—a . . . Cosimo of the Medici,
In the house that caps the corner. Boh! you were best!
Remember and tell me, the day you're hanged,
How you affected such a gullet's-gripe!
But you, sir, it concerns you that your knaves
Pick up a manner nor discredit you.
Zooks, are we pilchards, that they sweep the streets
And count fair prize what comes into their net?
He's Judas to a tittle, that man is!
Just such a face! why, sir, you make amends.
Lord, I'm not angry! Bid your hangdogs go
Drink out this quarter-florin to the health
Of the munificent House that harbours me
(And many more beside, lads! more beside!)
And all's come square again. I'd like his face—
His, elbowing on his comrade in the door
With the pike and lantern,—for the slave that holds
John Baptist's head a-dangle by the hair
With one hand ('look you, now,' as who should say)
And his weapon in the other, yet unwiped!
It's not your chance to have a bit of chalk,
A wood-coal or the like? or you should see!
Yes, I'm the painter, since you style me so.
What, brother Lippo's doings, up and down,
You know them and they take you? like enough!
I saw the proper twinkle in your eye—
'Tell you, I liked your looks at very first.
Let's sit and set things straight now, hip to haunch.
Here's spring come, and the nights one makes up bands
To roam the town and sing out carnival,
And I've been three weeks shut within my mew,
A-painting for the great man, saints and saints

And saints again. I could not paint all night—
Ouf! I leaned out of window for fresh air.
There came a hurry of feet and little feet,
A sweep of lute-strings, laughs, and whifts of song,—
Flower o' the broom,
Take away love, and our earth is a tomb!
Flower o' the quince,
I let Lisa go, and what good's in life since?
Flower o' the thyme—and so on. Round they went.
Scarce had they turned the corner when a titter
Like the skipping of rabbits by moonlight,—three slim shapes—
And a face that looked up . . . zooks, sir, flesh and blood,
That's all I'm made of! Into shreds it went,
Curtain and counterpane and coverlet,
All the bed-furniture—a dozen knots,
There was a ladder! down I let myself,
Hands and feet, scrambling somehow, and so dropped,
And after them. I came up with the fun
Hard by Saint Laurence, hail fellow, well met,—
Flower o' the rose,
If I've been merry, what matter who knows?
And so as I was stealing back again
To get to bed and have a bit of sleep
Ere I rise up to-morrow and go work
On Jerome knocking at his poor old breast
With his great round stone to subdue the flesh,
You snap me of the sudden. Ah, I see!
Though your eye twinkles still, you shake your head—
Mine's shaved,—a monk, you say—the sting's in that!
If Master Cosimo announced himself,
Mum's the word naturally; but a monk!
Come, what am I a beast for? tell us, now!
I was a baby when my mother died
And father died and left me in the street.
I starved there, God knows how, a year or two
On fig skins, melon-parings, rinds and shucks,
Refuse and rubbish. One fine frosty day

My stomach being empty as your hat,
The wind doubled me up and down I went.
Old Aunt Lapaccia trussed me with one hand,
(Its fellow was a stinger as I knew)
And so along the wall, over the bridge,
By the straight cut to the convent. Six words, there,
While I stood munching my first bread that month:
'So, boy, you're minded,' quoth the good fat father
Wiping his own mouth, 'twas refection-time,—
'To quit this very miserable world?
Will you renounce' . . . The mouthful of bread? thought I;
By no means! Brief, they made a monk of me;
I did renounce the world, its pride and greed,
Palace, farm, villa, shop and banking-house,
Trash, such as these poor devils of Medici
Have given their hearts to—all at eight years old.
Well, sir, I found in time, you may be sure,
'Twas not for nothing—the good bellyful,
The warm serge and the rope that goes all round,
And day-long blessed idleness beside!
'Let's see what the urchin's fit for'—that came next.
Not overmuch their way, I must confess.
Such a to-do! they tried me with their books.
Lord, they'd have taught me Latin in pure waste!
Flower o' the clove,
All the Latin I construe is, 'amo' I love!
But, mind you, when a boy starves in the streets
Eight years together, as my fortune was,
Watching folk's faces to know who will fling
The bit of half-stripped grape-bunch he desires,
And who will curse or kick him for his pains—
Which gentleman processional and fine,
Holding a candle to the Sacrament
Will wink and let him lift a plate and catch
The droppings of the wax to sell again,
Or holla for the Eight and have him whipped,—
How say I?—nay, which dog bites, which lets drop

His bone from the heap of offal in the street,—
Why, soul and sense of him grow sharp alike,
He learns the look of things, and none the less
For admonitions from the hunger-pinch.
I had a store of such remarks, be sure,
Which, after I found leisure, turned to use:
I drew men's faces on my copy-books,
Scrawled them within the antiphonary's marge,
Joined legs and arms to the long music-notes,
Found nose and eyes and chin for A's and B's,
And made a string of pictures of the world
Betwixt the ins and outs of verb and noun,
On the wall, the bench, the door. The monks looked black.
'Nay,' quoth the Prior, 'turn him out, d'ye say?
In no wise. Lose a crow and catch a lark.
What if at last we get our man of parts,
We Carmelites, like those Camaldolese
And Preaching Friars, to do our church up fine
And put the front on it that ought to be!'
And hereupon they bade me daub away.
Thank you! my head being crammed, their walls a blank,
Never was such prompt disemburdening.
First, every sort of monk, the black and white,
I drew them, fat and lean: then, folks at church,
From good old gossips waiting to confess
Their cribs of barrel-droppings, candle-ends,—
To the breathless fellow at the altar-foot,
Fresh from his murder, safe and sitting there
With the little children round him in a row
Of admiration, half for his beard and half
For that white anger of his victim's son
Shaking a fist at him with one fierce arm,
Signing himself with the other because of Christ
(Whose sad face on the cross sees only this
After the passion of a thousand years)
Till some poor girl, her apron o'er her head,
Which the intense eyes looked through, came at eve

On tip-toe, said a word, dropped in a loaf,
Her pair of earrings and a bunch of flowers
The brute took growling, prayed, and then was gone.
I painted all, then cried ' 'tis ask and have—
Choose, for more's ready!'—laid the ladder flat,
And showed my covered bit of cloister-wall.
The monks closed in a circle and praised loud
Till checked,—taught what to see and not to see,
Being simple bodies,—'that's the very man!
Look at the boy who stoops to pat the dog!
That woman's like the Prior's niece who comes
To care about his asthma: it's the life!'
But there my triumph's straw-fire flared and funked—
Their betters took their turn to see and say:
The Prior and the learned pulled a face
And stopped all that in no time. 'How? what's here?
Quite from the mark of painting, bless us all!
Faces, arms, legs and bodies like the true
As much as pea and pea! it's devil's-game!
Your business is not to catch men with show,
With homage to the perishable clay,
But lift them over it, ignore it all,
Make them forget there's such a thing as flesh.
Your business is to paint the souls of men—
Man's soul, and it's a fire, smoke . . . no it's not . . .
It's vapour done up like a new-born babe—
(In that shape when you die it leaves your mouth)
It's . . . well, what matters talking, it's the soul!
Give us no more of body than shows soul!
Here's Giotto, with his Saint a-praising God,
That sets you praising,—why not stop with him?
Why put all thoughts of praise out of our heads
With wonder at lines, colours, and what not?
Paint the soul, never mind the legs and arms!
Rub all out, try at it a second time.
Oh, that white smallish female with the breasts,
She's just my niece . . . Herodias, I would say,—

Who went and danced and got men's heads cut off—
Have it all out!' Now, is this sense, I ask?
A fine way to paint soul, by painting body
So ill, the eye can't stop there, must go further
And can't fare worse! Thus, yellow does for white
When what you put for yellow's simply black,
And any sort of meaning looks intense
When all beside itself means and looks nought.
Why can't a painter lift each foot in turn,
Left foot and right foot, go a double step,
Make his flesh liker and his soul more like,
Both in their order? Take the prettiest face,
The Prior's niece . . . patron-saint—is it so pretty
You can't discover if it means hope, fear,
Sorrow or joy? won't beauty go with these?
Suppose I've made her eyes all right and blue,
Can't I take breath and try to add life's flash,
And then add soul and heighten them threefold?
Or say there's beauty with no soul at all—
(I never saw it—put the case the same—)
If you get simple beauty and nought else,
You get about the best thing God invents,—
That's somewhat. And you'll find the soul you have missed,
Within yourself, when you return Him thanks.
'Rub all out!' Well, well, there's my life, in short.
And so the thing has gone on ever since.
I'm grown a man no doubt, I've broken bounds—
You should not take a fellow eight years old
And make him swear to never kiss the girls.
I'm my own master, paint now as I please—
Having a friend, you see, in the Corner-house!
Lord, it's fast holding by the rings in front—
Those great rings serve more purposes than just
To plant a flag in, or tie up a horse!
And yet the old schooling sticks, the old grave eyes
Are peeping o'er my shoulder as I work,
The heads shake still—'It's Art's decline, my son!

You're not of the true painters, great and old;
Brother Angelico's the man, you'll find;
Brother Lorenzo stands his single peer:
Fag on at flesh, you'll never make the third!'
Flower o' the pine,
You keep your mistr . . . *manners, and I'll stick to mine!*
I'm not the third, then: bless us, they must know!
Don't you think they're the likeliest to know,
They with their Latin? so, I swallow my rage,
Clench my teeth, suck my lips in tight, and paint
To please them—sometimes do, and sometimes don't,
For, doing most, there's pretty sure to come
A turn, some warm eve finds me at my saints—
A laugh, a cry, the business of the world—
(*Flower o' the peach,*
Death for us all, and his own life for each!)
And my whole soul revolves, the cup runs over,
The world and life's too big to pass for a dream,
And I do these wild things in sheer despite,
And play the fooleries you catch me at,
In pure rage! the old mill-horse, out at grass
After hard years, throws up his stiff heels so,
Although the miller does not preach to him
The only good of grass is to make chaff.
What would men have? Do they like grass or no—
May they or mayn't they? all I want's the thing
Settled for ever one way: as it is,
You tell too many lies and hurt yourself.
You don't like what you only like too much,
You do like what, if given you at your word,
You find abundantly detestable.
For me, I think I speak as I was taught—
I always see the Garden and God there
A-making man's wife—and, my lesson learned,
The value and significance of flesh,
I can't unlearn ten minutes afterwards.

Lorenzo: Lorenzo Monaco, an eminent painter, a monk

You understand me: I'm a beast, I know.
But see, now—why, I see as certainly
As that the morning-star's about to shine,
What will hap some day. We've a youngster here
Comes to our convent, studies what I do,
Slouches and stares and lets no atom drop—
His name is Guidi—he'll not mind the monks—
They call him Hulking Tom, he lets them talk—
He picks my practice up—he'll paint apace,
I hope so—though I never live so long,
I know what's sure to follow. You be judge!
You speak no Latin more than I, belike—
However, you're my man, you've seen the world
—The beauty and the wonder and the power,
The shapes of things, their colours, lights and shades,
Changes, surprises,—and God made it all!
—For what? do you feel thankful, ay or no,
For this fair town's face, yonder river's line,
The mountain round it and the sky above,
Much more the figures of man, woman, child,
These are the frame to? What's it all about?
To be passed over, despised? or dwelt upon,
Wondered at? oh, this last of course!—you say.
But why not do as well as say,—paint these
Just as they are, careless what comes of it?
God's works—paint anyone, and count it crime
To let a truth slip. Don't object, 'His works
Are here already—nature is complete:
Suppose you reproduce her—(which you can't)
There's no advantage! you must beat her, then.'
For, don't you mark, we're made so that we love
First when we see them painted, things we have passed
Perhaps a hundred times nor cared to see;
And so they are better, painted—better to us,
Which is the same thing. Art was given for that—
God uses us to help each other so,

Guidi: Tommaso Guidi, a painter

Lending our minds out. Have you noticed, now,
Your cullion's hanging face? A bit of chalk,
And trust me but you should, though! How much more,
If I drew higher things with the same truth!
That were to take the Prior's pulpit-place,
Interpret God to all of you! oh, oh,
It makes me mad to see what men shall do
And we in our graves! This world's no blot for us,
Nor blank—it means intensely, and means good:
To find its meaning is my meat and drink.
'Ay, but you don't so instigate to prayer!'
Strikes in the Prior: 'when your meaning's plain
It does not say to folks—remember matins,
Or, mind you fast next Friday!' Why, for this
What need of art at all? A skull and bones,
Two bits of stick nailed cross-wise, or, what's best,
A bell to chime the hour with, does as well.
I painted a Saint Laurence six months since
At Prato, splashed the fresco in fine style:
'How looks my painting, now the scaffold's down?'
I ask a brother: 'Hugely,' he returns—
'Already not one phiz of your three slaves
That turn the Deacon off his toasted side,
But's scratched and prodded to our heart's content,
The pious people have so eased their own
When coming to say prayers there in a rage:
We get on fast to see the bricks beneath.
Expect another job this time next year,
For pity and religion grow i' the crowd—
Your painting serves its purpose!' Hang the fools!

    —That is—you'll not mistake an idle word
Spoke in a huff by a poor monk, God wot,
Tasting the air this spicy night which turns
The unaccustomed head like Chianti wine!
Oh, the church knows! don't misreport me, now!
It's natural a poor monk out of bounds

Should have his apt word to excuse himself:
And hearken how I plot to make amends.
I have bethought me: I shall paint a piece
. . . There's for you! Give me six months, then go, see
Something in Sant' Ambrogio's! Bless the nuns!
They want a cast of my office. I shall paint
God in the midst, Madonna and her babe,
Ringed by a bowery, flowery angel-brood,
Lilies and vestments and white faces, sweet
As puff on puff of grated orris-root
When ladies crowd to church at mid-summer.
And then in the front, of course a saint or two—
Saint John, because he saves the Florentines,
Saint Ambrose, who puts down in black and white
The convent's friends and gives them a long day,
And Job, I must have him there past mistake,
The man of Uz, (and Us without the z,
Painters who need his patience). Well, all these
Secured at their devotions, up shall come
Out of a corner when you least expect,
As one by a dark stair into a great light,
Music and talking, who but Lippo! I!—
Mazed, motionless and moon-struck—I'm the man!
Back I shrink—what is this I see and hear?
I, caught up with my monk's things by mistake,
My old serge gown and rope that goes all round,
I, in this presence, this pure company!
Where's a hole, where's a corner for escape?
Then steps a sweet angelic slip of a thing
Forward, puts out a soft palm—'Not so fast!'
—Addresses the celestial presence, 'nay—
He made you and devised you, after all,
Though he's none of you! Could Saint John there, draw—
His camel-hair make up a painting-brush?
We come to brother Lippo for all that,
Iste perfecit opus!' So, all smile—
I shuffle sideways with my blushing face

Under the cover of a hundred wings
Thrown like a spread of kirtles when you're gay
And play hot cockles, all the doors being shut,
Till, wholly unexpected, in there pops
The hothead husband! Thus I scuttle off
To some safe bench behind, not letting go
The palm of her, the little lily thing
That spoke the good word for me in the nick,
Like the Prior's niece . . . Saint Lucy, I would say.
And so all's saved for me, and for the church
A pretty picture gained. Go, six months hence!
Your hand, sir, and good-bye: no lights, no lights!
The street's hushed, and I know my own way back,
Don't fear me! There's the grey beginning. Zooks!

ANDREA DEL SARTO
Called 'The Faultless Painter'

But do not let us quarrel any more,
No, my Lucrezia; bear with me for once:
Sit down and all shall happen as you wish.
You turn your face, but does it bring your heart?
I'll work then for your friend's friend, never fear,
Treat his own subject after his own way,
Fix his own time, accept too his own price,
And shut the money into this small hand
When next it takes mine. Will it? tenderly?
Oh, I'll content him,—but to-morrow, Love!
I often am much wearier than you think,
This evening more than usual, and it seems
As if—forgive now—should you let me sit
Here by the window with your hand in mine
And look a half hour forth on Fiesole,
Both of one mind, as married people use,
Quietly, quietly, the evening through,
I might get up to-morrow to my work

Cheerful and fresh as ever. Let us try.
To-morrow how you shall be glad for this!
Your soft hand is a woman of itself,
And mine the man's bared breast she curls inside.
Don't count the time lost, either; you must serve
For each of the five pictures we require—
It saves a model. So! keep looking so—
My serpentining beauty, rounds on rounds!
—How could you ever prick those perfect ears,
Even to put the pearl there! oh, so sweet—
My face, my moon, my everybody's moon,
Which everybody looks on and calls his,
And, I suppose, is looked on by in turn,
While she looks—no one's: very dear, no less!
You smile? why, there's my picture ready made.
There's what we painters call our harmony!
A common greyness silvers everything,—
All in a twilight, you and I alike
—You, at the point of your first pride in me
(That's gone you know),—but I, at every point;
My youth, my hope, my art, being all toned down
To yonder sober pleasant Fiesole.
There's the bell clinking from the chapel-top;
That length of convent-wall across the way
Holds the trees safer, huddled more inside;
The last monk leaves the garden; days decrease
And autumn grows, autumn in everything.
Eh? The whole seems to fall into a shape
As if I saw alike my work and self
And all that I was born to be and do,
A twilight-piece. Love, we are in God's hand.
How strange now, looks the life He makes us lead!
So free we seem, so fettered fast we are!
I feel He laid the fetter: let it lie!
This chamber for example—turn your head—
All that's behind us! you don't understand
Nor care to understand about my art,

But you can hear at least when people speak;
And that cartoon, the second from the door
—It is the thing, Love! so such things should be—
Behold Madonna, I am bold to say.
I can do with my pencil what I know,
What I see, what at bottom of my heart
I wish for, if I ever wish so deep—
Do easily, too—when I say perfectly
I do not boast, perhaps: yourself are judge
Who listened to the Legate's talk last week,
And just as much they used to say in France.
At any rate 'tis easy, all of it,
No sketches first, no studies, that's long past—
I do what many dream of all their lives
—Dream? strive to do, and agonise to do,
And fail in doing. I could count twenty such
On twice your fingers, and not leave this town,
Who strive—you don't know how the others strive
To paint a little thing like that you smeared
Carelessly passing with your robes afloat,—
Yet do much less, so much less, Someone says,
(I know his name, no matter) so much less!
Well, less is more, Lucrezia! I am judged.
There burns a truer light of God in them,
In their vexed, beating, stuffed and stopped-up brain,
Heart, or whate'er else, than goes on to prompt
This low-pulsed forthright craftsman's hand of mine.
Their works drop groundward, but themselves, I know,
Reach many a time a heaven that's shut to me,
Enter and take their place there sure enough,
Though they come back and cannot tell the world.
My works are nearer heaven, but I sit here.
The sudden blood of these men! at a word—
Praise them, it boils, or blame them, it boils too.
I, painting from myself and to myself,
Know what I do, am unmoved by men's blame
Or their praise either. Somebody remarks

Morello's outline there is wrongly traced,
His hue mistaken—what of that? or else,
Rightly traced and well ordered—what of that?
Speak as they please, what does the mountain care?
Ah, but a man's reach should exceed his grasp,
Or what's a Heaven for? all is silver-grey
Placid and perfect with my art—the worse!
I know both what I want and what might gain—
And yet how profitless to know, to sigh
'Had I been two, another and myself,
Our head would have o'erlooked the world!' No doubt.
Yonder's a work, now, of that famous youth
The Urbinate who died five years ago.
('Tis copied, George Vasari sent it me.)
Well, I can fancy how he did it all,
Pouring his soul, with kings and popes to see,
Reaching, that Heaven might so replenish him,
Above and through his art—for it gives way;
That arm is wrongly put—and there again—
A fault to pardon in the drawing's lines,
Its body, so to speak: its soul is right,
He means right—that, a child may understand.
Still, what an arm! and I could alter it.
But all the play, the insight and the stretch—
Out of me! out of me! And wherefore out?
Had you enjoined them on me, given me soul,
We might have risen to Rafael, I and you.
Nay, Love, you did give all I asked, I think—
More than I merit, yes, by many times.
But had you—oh, with the same perfect brow,
And perfect eyes, and more than perfect mouth,
And the low voice my soul hears, as a bird
The fowler's pipe, and follows to the snare—
Had you, with these the same, but brought a mind!
Some women do so. Had the mouth there urged
'God and the glory! never care for gain.

Morello: one of the Apennines

The Present by the Future, what is that?
Live for fame, side by side with Angelo—
Rafael is waiting: Up to God all three!'
I might have done it for you. So it seems—
Perhaps not. All is as God over-rules.
Beside, incentives come from the soul's self;
The rest avail not. Why do I need you?
What wife had Rafael, or has Angelo?
In this world, who can do a thing, will not—
And who would do it, cannot, I perceive:
Yet the will's somewhat—somewhat, too, the power—
And thus we half-men struggle. At the end,
God, I conclude, compensates, punishes.
'Tis safer for me, if the award be strict,
That I am something underrated here,
Poor this long while, despised, to speak the truth.
I dared not, do you know, leave home all day,
For fear of chancing on the Paris lords.
The best is when they pass and look aside;
But they speak sometimes; I must bear it all.
Well may they speak! That Francis, that first time,
And that long festal year at Fontainebleau!
I surely then could sometimes leave the ground,
Put on the glory, Rafael's daily wear,
In that humane great monarch's golden look,—
One finger in his beard or twisted curl
Over his mouth's good mark that made the smile,
One arm about my shoulder, round my neck,
The jingle of his gold chain in my ear,
I painting proudly with his breath on me,
All his court round him, seeing with his eyes,
Such frank French eyes, and such a fire of souls
Profuse, my hand kept plying by those hearts,—
And, best of all, this, this, this face beyond,
This in the background, waiting on my work,
To crown the issue with a last reward!

A good time, was it not, my kingly days?
And had you not grown restless—but I know—
'Tis done and past; 'twas right, my instinct said;
Too live the life grew, golden and not grey,
And I'm the weak-eyed bat no sun should tempt
Out of the grange whose four walls make his world.
How could it end in any other way?
You called me, and I came home to your heart.
The triumph was, to have ended there; then if
I reached it ere the triumph, what is lost?
Let my hands frame your face in your hair's gold,
You beautiful Lucrezia that are mine!
'Rafael did this, Andrea painted that—
The Roman's is the better when you pray,
But still the other's Virgin was his wife—'
Men will excuse me. I am glad to judge
Both pictures in your presence; clearer grows
My better fortune, I resolve to think.
For, do you know, Lucrezia, as God lives,
Said one day Angelo, his very self,
To Rafael . . . I have known it all these years . . .
(When the young man was flaming out his thoughts
Upon a palace-wall for Rome to see,
Too lifted up in heart because of it)
'Friend, there's a certain sorry little scrub
Goes up and down our Florence, none cares how,
Who, were he set to plan and execute
As you are, pricked on by your popes and kings,
Would bring the sweat into that brow of yours!'
To Rafael's!—And indeed the arm is wrong.
I hardly dare—yet, only you to see,
Give the chalk here—quick, thus the line should go!
Ay, but the soul! he's Rafael! rub it out!
Still, all I care for, if he spoke the truth,
(What he? why, who but Michael Angelo?
Do you forget already words like those?)

If really there was such a chance, so lost,—
Is, whether you're—not grateful—but more pleased.
Well, let me think so. And you smile indeed!
This hour has been an hour! Another smile?
If you would sit thus by me every night
I should work better, do you comprehend?
I mean that I should earn more, give you more.
See, it is settled dusk now; there's a star;
Morello's gone, the watch-lights show the wall,
The cue-owls speak the name we call them by.
Come from the window, Love,—come in, at last,
Inside the melancholy little house
We built to be so gay with. God is just.
King Francis may forgive me: Oft at nights
When I look up from painting, eyes tired out,
The walls become illumined, brick from brick
Distinct, instead of mortar, fierce bright gold,
That gold of his I did cement them with!
Let us but love each other. Must you go?
That Cousin here again? he waits outside?
Must see you—you, and not with me? Those loans?
More gaming debts to pay? you smiled for that?
Well, let smiles buy me! have you more to spend?
While hand and eye and something of a heart
Are left me, work's my ware, and what's it worth?
I'll pay my fancy. Only let me sit
The grey remainder of the evening out,
Idle, you call it, and muse perfectly
How I could paint, were I but back in France,
One picture, just one more—the Virgin's face,
Not your's this time! I want you at my side
To hear them—that is, Michael Angelo—
Judge all I do and tell you of its worth.
Will you? To-morrow, satisfy your friend.
I take the subjects for his corridor,
Finish the portrait out of hand—there, there,

And throw him in another thing or two
If he demurs; the whole should prove enough
To pay for this same Cousin's freak. Beside,
What's better and what's all I care about,
Get you the thirteen scudi for the ruff.
Love, does that please you? Ah, but what does he,
The Cousin! what does he to please you more?

   I am grown peaceful as old age to-night.
I regret little, I would change still less.
Since there my past life lies, why alter it?
The very wrong to Francis!—it is true
I took his coin, was tempted and complied,
And built this house and sinned, and all is said.
My father and my mother died of want.
Well, had I riches of my own? you see
How one gets rich! Let each one bear his lot.
They were born poor, lived poor, and poor they died:
And I have laboured somewhat in my time
And not been paid profusely. Some good son
Paint my two hundred pictures—let him try!
No doubt, there's something strikes a balance. Yes,
You loved me quite enough, it seems to-night.
This must suffice me here. What would one have?
In Heaven, perhaps, new chances, one more chance—
Four great walls in the New Jerusalem
Meted on each side by the angel's reed,
For Leonard, Rafael, Angelo and me
To cover—the three first without a wife,
While I have mine! So—still they overcome
Because there's still Lucrezia,—as I choose.

Again the Cousin's whistle! Go, my Love.

YOUTH AND ART

1

It once might have been, once only:
    We lodged in a street together,
You, a sparrow on the housetop lonely,
    I, a lone she-bird of his feather.

2

Your trade was with sticks and clay,
    You thumbed, thrust, patted and polished,
Then laughed, 'They will see some day
    Smith made, and Gibson demolished.'

3

My business was song, song, song;
    I chirped, cheeped, trilled and twittered,
'Kate Brown's on the boards ere long,
    And Grisi's existence embittered!'

4

I earned no more by a warble
    Than you by a sketch in plaster;
You wanted a piece of marble,
    I needed a music-master.

5

We studied hard in our styles,
    Chipped each at a crust like Hindoos,
For air, looked out on the tiles,
    For fun, watched each other's windows.

6

You lounged, like a boy of the South,
    Cap and blouse—nay, a bit of beard too;
Or you got it, rubbing your mouth
    With fingers the clay adhered to.

7

And I—soon managed to find
   Weak points in the flower-fence facing,
Was forced to put up a blind
   And be safe in my corset-lacing.

8

No harm! It was not my fault
   If you never turned your eyes' tail up,
As I shook upon E *in alt,*
   Or ran the chromatic scale up:

9

For spring bade the sparrows pair,
   And the boys and girls gave guesses,
And stalls in our street looked rare
   With bulrush and watercresses.

10

Why did not you pinch a flower
   In a pellet of clay and fling it?
Why did not I put a power
   Of thanks in a look, or sing it?

11

I did look, sharp as a lynx,
   (And yet the memory rankles)
When models arrived, some minx
   Tripped up-stairs, she and her ankles.

12

But I think I gave you as good!
   'That foreign fellow,—who can know
How she pays, in a playful mood,
   For his tuning her that piano?'

13

Could you say so, and never say
  'Suppose we join hands and fortunes,
And I fetch her from over the way,
  Her, piano, and long tunes and short tunes?'

14

No, no: you would not be rash,
  Nor I rasher and something over:
You've to settle yet Gibson's hash,
  And Grisi yet lives in clover.

15

But you meet the Prince at the Board,
  I'm queen myself at *bals-paré,*
I've married a rich old lord,
  And you're dubbed knight and an R.A.

16

Each life's unfulfilled, you see;
  It hangs still, patchy and scrappy:
We have not sighed deep, laughed free,
  Starved, feasted, despaired,—been happy.

17

And nobody calls you a dunce,
  And people suppose me clever:
This could but have happened once,
  And we missed it, lost it for ever.

A FACE

If one could have that little head of hers
Painted upon a background of pale gold,
Such as the Tuscan's early art prefers!
No shade encroaching on the matchless mould

Of those two lips, which should be opening soft
In the pure profile; not as when she laughs,
For that spoils all: but rather as if aloft
Yon hyacinth, she loves so, leaned its staff's
Burthen of honey-coloured buds to kiss
And capture 'twixt the lips apart for this.
Then her lithe neck, three fingers might surround,
How it should waver on the pale gold ground
Up to the fruit-shaped, perfect chin it lifts!
I know, Correggio loves to mass, in rifts
Of heaven, his angel faces, orb on orb
Breaking its outline, burning shades absorb:
But these are only massed there, I should think,
Waiting to see some wonder momently
Grow out, stand full, fade slow against the sky
(That's the pale ground you'd see this sweet face by),
All heaven, meanwhile, condensed into one eye
Which fears to lose the wonder, should it wink.

A LIKENESS

Some people hang portraits up
In a room where they dine or sup:
And the wife clinks tea-things under,
And her cousin, he stirs his cup,
Asks, 'Who was the lady, I wonder?'
' 'Tis a daub John bought at a sale,'
Quoth the wife,—looks black as thunder:
'What a shade beneath her nose!
Snuff-taking, I suppose,—'
Adds the cousin, while John's corns ail.

Or else, there's no wife in the case,
But the portrait's queen of the place,
Alone mid the other spoils
Of youth,—masks, gloves and foils,

And pipe-sticks, rose, cherry-tree, jasmine,
And the long whip, the tandem-lasher,
And the cast from a fist ('not, alas! mine,
But my master's, the Tipton Slasher')
And the cards where pistol-balls mark ace,
And a satin shoe used for cigar-case,
And the chamois-horns ('shot in the Chablais')
And prints—Rarey drumming on Cruiser,
And Sayers, our champion, the bruiser,
And the little edition of Rabelais:
Where a friend, with both hands in his pockets,
May saunter up close to examine it,
And remark a good deal of Jane Lamb in it,
'But the eyes are half out of their sockets;
That hair's not so bad, where the gloss is,
But they've made the girl's nose a proboscis:
Jane Lamb, that we danced with at Vichy!
What, is not she Jane? Then, who is she?'

All that I own is a print,
An etching, a mezzotint;
'Tis a study, a fancy, a fiction,
Yet a fact (take my conviction)
Because it has more than a hint
Of a certain face, I never
Saw elsewhere touch or trace of
In women I've seen the face of:
Just an etching, and, so far, clever.

I keep my prints, an imbroglio,
Fifty in one portfolio.
When somebody tries my claret,
We turn round chairs to the fire,
Chirp over days in a garret,
Chuckle o'er increase of salary,
Taste the good fruits of our leisure,
Talk about pencil and lyre,

And the National Portrait Gallery:
Then I exhibit my treasure.
After we've turned over twenty,
And the debt of wonder my crony owes
Is paid to my Marc Antonios,
He stops me—'*Festina lentè!*
What's that sweet thing there, the etching?'
How my waistcoat-strings want stretching,
How my cheeks grow red as tomatoes,
How my heart leaps! But hearts, after leaps, ache.

'By the by, you must take, for a keepsake,
That other, you praised, of Volpato's.'

The fool! would he try a flight further and say
He never saw, never before to-day,
What was able to take his breath away,
A face to lose youth for, to occupy age
With the dream of, meet death with,—why, I'll not engage
But that, half in a rapture and half in a rage,
I should toss him the thing's self—' 'Tis only a duplicate,
A thing of no value! Take it, I supplicate!'

ORPHEUS AND EURYDICE
A Picture by Leighton

But give them me, the mouth, the eyes, the brow!
Let them once more absorb me! One look now
   Will lap me round for ever, not to pass
Out of its light, though darkness lie beyond:
Hold me but safe again within the bond
   Of one immortal look! All woe that was,
Forgotten, and all terror that may be,
Defied,—no past is mine, no future: look at me!

Herman Melville
[1819–1891]

THE RAVAGED VILLA

In shards the sylvan vases lie,
  Their links of dance undone,
And brambles wither by thy brim,
  Choked fountain of the sun!
The spider in the laurel spins,
  The weed exiles the flower:
And, flung to kiln, Apollo's bust
  Makes lime for Mammon's tower.

Walt Whitman
[1819–1892]

I SING THE BODY ELECTRIC

1
I sing the body electric,
The armies of those I love engirth me and I engirth them,
They will not let me off till I go with them, respond to them,
And discorrupt them, and charge them full with the charge of
  the soul.

Was it doubted that those who corrupt their own bodies conceal
  themselves?
And if those who defile the living are as bad as they who defile the
  dead?

And if the body does not do fully as much as the soul?
And if the body were not the soul, what is the soul?

2

The love of the body of man or woman balks account, the body
    itself balks account,
That of the male is perfect, and that of the female is perfect.

The expression of the face balks account,
But the expression of a well-made man appears not only in his
    face,
It is in his limbs and joints also, it is curiously in the joints of
    his hips and wrists,
It is in his walk, the carriage of his neck, the flex of his waist and
    knees, dress does not hide him,
The strong sweet quality he has strikes through the cotton and
    broadcloth,
To see him pass conveys as much as the best poem, perhaps more,
You linger to see his back, and the back of his neck and shoulder-
    side.

The sprawl and fulness of babes, the bosoms and heads of women,
    the folds of their dress, their style as we pass in the street, the
    contour of their shape downwards,
The swimmer naked in the swimming-bath, seen as he swims
    through the transparent green-shine, or lies with his face up
    and rolls silently to and fro in the heave of the water,
The bending forward and backward of rowers in row-boats, the
    horseman in his saddle,
Girls, mothers, house-keepers, in all their performances,
The group of laborers seated at noon-time with their open din-
    ner kettles, and their wives waiting,
The female soothing a child, the farmer's daughter in the garden
    or cow-yard,
The young fellow hoeing corn, the sleigh-driver driving his six
    horses through the crowd,

The wrestle of wrestlers, two apprentice-boys, quite grown, lusty, good-natured, native-born, out on the vacant lot at sundown after work,

The coats and caps thrown down, the embrace of love and re-sistance,

The upper-hold and under-hold, the hair rumpled over and blinding the eyes;

The march of firemen in their own costumes, the play of mascu-line muscle through clean-setting trowsers and waist-straps,

The slow return from the fire, the pause when the bell strikes suddenly again, and the listening on the alert,

The natural, perfect, varied attitudes, the bent head, the curv'd neck and the counting;

Such-like I love—I loosen myself, pass freely, am at the mother's breast with the little child,

Swim with the swimmers, wrestle with wrestlers, march in line with the firemen, and pause, listen, count.

3

I knew a man, a common farmer, the father of five sons,

And in them the fathers of sons, and in them the fathers of sons.

This man was of wonderful vigor, calmness, beauty of person,

The shape of his head, the pale yellow and white of his hair and beard, the immeasurable meaning of his black eyes, the rich-ness and breadth of his manners,

These I used to go and visit him to see, he was wise also,

He was six feet tall, he was over eighty years old, his sons were massive, clean, bearded, tan-faced, handsome,

They and his daughters loved him, all who saw him loved him,

They did not love him by allowance, they loved him with per-sonal love,

He drank water only, the blood show'd like scarlet through the clear-brown skin of his face,

He was a frequent gunner and fisher, he sail'd his boat himself, he had a fine one presented to him by a ship-joiner, he had fowling-pieces presented to him by men that loved him,

When he went with his five sons and many grand-sons to hunt or
fish, you would pick him out as the most beautiful and vigor-
ous of the gang,
You would wish long and long to be with him, you would wish
to sit by him in the boat that you and he might touch each
other.

4
I have perceiv'd that to be with those I like is enough,
To stop in company with the rest at evening is enough,
To be surrounded by beautiful, curious, breathing, laughing flesh
is enough,
To pass among them or touch any one, or rest my arm ever so
lightly round his or her neck for a moment, what is this then?
I do not ask any more delight, I swim in it as in a sea.

There is something in staying close to men and women and look-
ing on them, and in the contact and odor of them, that pleases
the soul well,
All things please the soul, but these please the soul well.

5
This is the female form,
A divine nimbus exhales from it from head to foot,
It attracts with fierce undeniable attraction,
I am drawn by its breath as if I were no more than a helpless
vapor, all falls aside but myself and it,
Books, art, religion, time, the visible and solid earth, and what
was expected of heaven or fear'd of hell, are now consumed,
Mad filaments, ungovernable shoots play out of it, the response
likewise ungovernable,
Hair, bosom, hips, bend of legs, negligent falling hands all dif-
fused, mine too diffused,
Ebb stung by the flow and flow stung by the ebb, love-flesh swell-
ing and deliciously aching,

Limitless limpid jets of love hot and enormous, quivering jelly
  of love, white-blow and delirious juice,
Bridegroom night of love working surely and softly into the
  prostrate dawn,
Undulating into the willing and yielding day,
Lost in the cleave of the clasping and sweet-flesh'd day.

This the nucleus—after the child is born of woman, man is born
  of woman,
This the bath of birth, this the merge of small and large, and the
  outlet again.

Be not ashamed women, your privilege encloses the rest, and is
  the exit of the rest,
You are the gates of the body, and you are the gates of the soul.

The female contains all qualities and tempers them,
She is in her place and moves with perfect balance,
She is all things duly veil'd, she is both passive and active,
She is to conceive daughters as well as sons, and sons as well as
  daughters.

As I see my soul reflected in Nature,
As I see through a mist, One with inexpressible completeness,
  sanity, beauty,
See the bent head and arms folded over the breast, the Female
  I see.

6
The male is not less the soul nor more, he too is in his place,
He too is all qualities, he is action and power,
The flush of the known universe is in him,
Scorn becomes him well, and appetite and defiance become him
  well,
The wildest largest passions, bliss that is utmost, sorrow that is
  utmost become him well, pride is for him,

The full-spread pride of man is calming and excellent to the
    soul,
Knowledge becomes him, he likes it always, he brings every thing
    to the test of himself,
Whatever the survey, whatever the sea and the sail he strikes
    soundings at last only here,
(Where else does he strike soundings except here?)

The man's body is sacred and the woman's body is sacred,
No matter who it is, it is sacred—is it the meanest one in the
    laborers' gang?
Is it one of the dull-faced immigrants just landed on the wharf?
Each belongs here or anywhere just as much as the well-off, just
    as much as you,
Each has his or her place in the procession.

(All is a procession,
The universe is a procession with measured and perfect motion.)

Do you know so much yourself that you call the meanest igno-
    rant?
Do you suppose you have a right to a good sight, and he or she
    has no right to a sight?
Do you think matter has cohered together from its diffuse float,
    and the soil is on the surface, and water runs and vegetation
    sprouts,
For you only, and not for him and her?

7
A man's body at auction,
(For before the war I often go to the slave-mart and watch the
    sale,)
I help the auctioneer, the sloven does not half know his business.

Gentlemen look on this wonder,
Whatever the bids of the bidders they cannot be high enough
  for it,
For it the globe lay preparing quintillions of years without one
  animal or plant,
For it the revolving cycles truly and steadily roll'd.

In this head the all-baffling brain,
In it and below it the makings of heroes.

Examine these limbs, red, black, or white, they are cunning in
  tendon and nerve,
They shall be stript that you may see them.

Exquisite senses, life-lit eyes, pluck, volition,
Flakes of breast-muscle, pliant backbone and neck, flesh not
  flabby, good-sized arms and legs,
And wonders within there yet.

Within there runs blood,
The same old blood! the same red-running blood!
There swells and jets a heart, there all passions, desires, reach-
  ings, aspirations,
(Do you think they are not there because they are not express'd
  in parlors and lecture-rooms?)

This is not only one man, this the father of those who shall be
  fathers in their turns,
In him the start of populous states and rich republics,
Of him countless immortal lives with countless embodiments
  and enjoyments.

How do you know who shall come from the offspring of his off-
  spring through the centuries?
(Who might you find you have come from yourself, if you could
  trace back through the centuries?)

8

A woman's body at auction,
She too is not only herself, she is the teeming mother of mothers,
She is the bearer of them that shall grow and be mates to the
    mothers.

Have you ever loved the body of a woman?
Have you ever loved the body of a man?
Do you not see that these are exactly the same to all in all na-
    tions and times all over the earth?

If any thing is sacred the human body is sacred,
And the glory and sweet of a man is the token of manhood un-
    tainted,
And in man or woman a clean, strong, firm-fibred body, is more
    beautiful than the most beautiful face.

Have you seen the fool that corrupted his own live body? or the
    fool that corrupted her own live body?
For they do not conceal themselves, and cannot conceal them-
    selves.

9

O my body! I dare not desert the likes of you in other men and
    women, nor the likes of the parts of you,
I believe the likes of you are to stand or fall with the likes of the
    soul, (and that they are the soul,)
I believe the likes of you shall stand or fall with my poems, and
    that they are my poems,
Man's, woman's, child's, youth's, wife's, husband's, mother's,
    father's, young man's, young woman's poems,
Head, neck, hair, ears, drop and tympan of the ears,
Eyes, eye-fringes, iris of the eye, eyebrows, and the waking or
    sleeping of the lids,
Mouth, tongue, lips, teeth, roof of the mouth, jaws, and the jaw-
    hinges,

Nose, nostrils of the nose, and the partition,

Cheeks, temples, forehead, chin, throat, back of the neck, neck-slue,

Strong shoulders, manly beard, scapula, hind-shoulders, and the ample side-round of the chest,

Upper-arm, armpit, elbow-socket, lower-arm, arm-sinews, arm-bones,

Wrist and wrist-joints, hand, palm, knuckles, thumb, forefinger, finger-joints, finger-nails,

Broad breast-front, curling hair of the breast, breast-bone, breast-side,

Ribs, belly, backbone, joints of the backbone,

Hips, hip-sockets, hip-strength, inward and outward round, man-balls, man-root,

Strong set of thighs, well carrying the trunk above,

Leg-fibres, knee, knee-pan, upper-leg, under-leg,

Ankles, instep, foot-ball, toes, toe-joints, the heel;

All attitudes, all the shapeliness, all the belongings of my or your body or of any one's body, male or female,

The lung-sponges, the stomach-sac, the bowels sweet and clean,

The brain in its folds inside the skull-frame,

Sympathies, heart-valves, palate-valves, sexuality, maternity,

Womanhood, and all that is a woman, and the man that comes from woman,

The womb, the teats, nipples, breast-milk, tears, laughter, weeping, love-looks, love-perturbations and risings,

The voice, articulation, language, whispering, shouting aloud,

Food, drink, pulse, digestion, sweat, sleep, walking, swimming,

Poise on the hips, leaping, reclining, embracing, arm-curving and tightening,

The continual changes of the flex of the mouth, and around the eyes,

The skin, the sunburnt shade, freckles, hair,

The curious sympathy one feels when feeling with the hand the naked meat of the body,

The circling rivers the breath, and breathing it in and out,

The beauty of the waist, and thence of the hips, and thence
    downward toward the knees,
The thin red jellies within you or within me, the bones and the
    marrow in the bones,
The exquisite realization of health;
O I say these are not the parts and poems of the body only, but of
    the soul,
O I say now these are the soul!

THE CENTENARIAN'S STORY

*Volunteer of 1861–2 (at Washington Park, Brooklyn, assisting
the Centenarian)*

Give me your hand old Revolutionary,
The hill-top is nigh, but a few steps, (make room gentlemen,)
Up the path you have follow'd me well, spite of your hundred
    and extra years.
You can walk old man, though your eyes are almost done,
Your faculties serve you, and presently I must have them serve
    me.

Rest, while I tell what the crowd around us means,
On the plain below recruits are drilling and exercising,
There is the camp, one regiment departs to-morrow,
Do you hear the officers giving their orders?
Do you hear the clank of the muskets?

Why what comes over you now old man?
Why do you tremble and clutch my hand so convulsively?
The troops are but drilling, they are yet surrounded with smiles,
Around them at hand the well-drest friends and the women,
While splendid and warm the afternoon sun shines down,
Green the midsummer verdure and fresh blows the dallying
    breeze,
O'er proud and peaceful cities and arm of the sea between.

But drill and parade are over, they march back to quarters,
Only hear that approval of hands! hear what a clapping!

As wending the crowds now part and disperse—but we old man,
Not for nothing have I brought you hither—we must remain,
You to speak in your turn, and I to listen and tell.

The Centenarian

When I clutch'd your hand it was not with terror,
But suddenly pouring about me here on every side,
And below there where the boys were drilling, and up the slopes
    they ran,
And where tents are pitch'd, and wherever you see south and
    south-east and south-west,
Over hills, across lowlands and in the skirts of woods,
And along the shores in mire (now fill'd over) came again and
    suddenly raged,
As eighty-five years a-gone no mere parade receiv'd with applause
    of friends,
But a battle which I took part in myself—aye, long ago as it is,
    I took part in it,
Walking then this hilltop, this same ground.

Aye, this is the ground,
My blind eyes even as I speak behold it re-peopled from graves,
The years recede, pavements and stately houses disappear,
Rude forts appear again, the old hoop'd guns are mounted,
I see the lines of rais'd earth stretching from river to bay,
I mark the vista of waters, I mark the uplands and slopes;
Here we lay encamp'd, it was this time in summer also.

As I talk I remember all, I remember the Declaration,
It was read here, the whole army paraded, it was read to us here,

By his staff surrounded the General stood in the middle, he held
   up his unsheath'd sword,
It glitter'd in the sun in full sight of the army.

'Twas a bold act then—the English war-ships had just arrived,
We could watch down the lower bay where they lay at anchor,
And the transports swarming with soldiers.

A few days more and they landed, and then the battle.

Twenty thousand were brought against us,
A veteran force furnish'd with good artillery.

I tell not now the whole of the battle,
But one brigade early in the forenoon order'd forward to engage
   the red-coats,
Of that brigade I tell, and how steadily it march'd,
And how long and well it stood confronting death.

Who do you think that was marching steadily sternly confronting
   death?
It was the brigade of the youngest men, two thousand strong,
Rais'd in Virginia and Maryland, and most of them known per-
   sonally to the General.

Jauntily forward they went with quick step toward Gowanus'
   waters,
Till of a sudden unlook'd for by defiles through the woods, gain'd
   at night,
The British advancing, rounding in from the east, fiercely playing
   their guns,
That brigade of the youngest was cut off and at the enemy's
   mercy.

The General watch'd them from this hill,

They made repeated desperate attempts to burst their environ-
ment,
Then drew close together, very compact, their flag flying in the
middle,
But O from the hills how the cannon were thinning and thinning
them!

It sickens me yet, that slaughter!
I saw the moisture gather in drops on the face of the General.
I saw how he wrung his hands in anguish.

Meanwhile the British manœuvr'd to draw us out for a pitch'd
battle,
But we dared not trust the chances of a pitch'd battle.

We fought the fight in detachments,
Sallying forth we fought at several points, but in each the luck
was against us,
Our foe advancing, steadily getting the best of it, push'd us back
to the works on this hill,
Till we turn'd menacing here, and then he left us.

That was the going out of the brigade of the youngest men, two
thousand strong,
Few return'd, nearly all remain in Brooklyn.

That and here my General's first battle,
No women looking on nor sunshine to bask in, it did not con-
clude with applause,
Nobody clapp'd hands here then.

But in darkness in mist on the ground under a chill rain,
Wearied that night we lay foil'd and sullen,
While scornfully laugh'd many an arrogant lord off against us
encamp'd,
Quite within hearing, feasting, clinking wineglasses together over
their victory.

So dull and damp and another day,
But the night of that, mist lifting, rain ceasing,
Silent as a ghost while they thought they were sure of him, my
  General retreated.

I saw him at the river-side,
Down by the ferry lit by torches, hastening the embarcation;
My General waited till the soldiers and wounded were all pass'd
  over,
And then, (it was just ere sunrise,) these eyes rested on him for
  the last time.

Every one else seem'd fill'd with gloom,
Many no doubt thought of capitulation.

But when my General pass'd me,
As he stood in his boat and look'd toward the coming sun,
I saw something different from capitulation.

Terminus

Enough, the Centenarian's story ends,
The two, the past and present, have interchanged,
I myself as connecter, as chansonnier of a great future, am now
  speaking.

And is this the ground Washington trod?
And these waters I listlessly daily cross, are these the waters he
  cross'd,
As resolute in defeat as other generals in their proudest triumphs?

I must copy the story, and sent it eastward and westward,
I must preserve that look as it beam'd on you rivers of Brooklyn.

See—as the annual round returns the phantoms return,
It is the 27th of August and the British have landed,

The battle begins, and goes against us, behold through the smoke
   Washington's face,
The brigade of Virginia and Maryland have march'd forth to
   intercept the enemy,
They are cut off, murderous artillery from the hills plays upon
   them,
Rank after rank falls, while over them silently droops the flag,
Baptized that day in many a young man's bloody wounds,
In death, defeat, and sisters', mothers' tears.

Ah, hills and slopes of Brooklyn! I perceive you are more valu-
   able than your owners supposed;
In the midst of you stands an encampment very old,
Stands forever the camp of that dead brigade.

TO THE STATES

To the States or any one of them, or any city of the States, *Resist
   much, obey little,*
Once unquestioning obedience, once fully enslaved,
Once fully enslaved, no nation, state, city of this earth, ever after-
   ward resumes its liberty.

❊ ❊ The U.S. during the first century of its existence as an inde-
pendent nation was full of exhilarating ferment; Halleck's rollick-
ing satire (see p. 206) was not far enough below the English level
to bother anyone. Longfellow, Ticknor, Bayard Taylor were deter-
mined to bring in at least a knowledge of foreign literatures.
Agassiz enlivened the mind, and Whitman took a place in world
literature, proclaiming himself American and not mentioning
Asiatic components of his outlook.

Dante Gabriel Rossetti
[1828–1882]

from THE HOUSE OF LIFE

SONG IV: SUDDEN LIGHT

I have been here before,
    But when or how I cannot tell:
I know the grass beyond the door,
    The sweet keen smell,
The sighing sound, the lights around the shore.

You have been mine before,—
    How long ago I may not know:
But just when at that swallow's soar
    Your neck turned so,
Some veil did fall,—I knew it all of yore.

Has this been thus before?
    And shall not thus time's eddying flight
Still with our lives our love restore
    In death's despite,
And day and night yield one delight once more?

Algernon Charles Swinburne
[1837–1909]

from ATALANTA IN CALYDON

CHORUS

When the hounds of spring are on winter's traces,
  The mother of months in meadow or plain
Fills the shadows and windy places
  With lisp of leaves and ripple of rain;
And the brown bright nightingale amorous
Is half assuaged for Itylus,
For the Thracian ships and the foreign faces,
  The tongueless vigil, and all the pain.

Come with bows bent and with emptying of quivers,
  Maiden most perfect, lady of light,
With a noise of winds and many rivers,
  With a clamour of waters, and with might;
Bind on thy sandals, O thou most fleet,
Over the splendour and speed of thy feet;
For the faint east quickens, the wan west shivers,
  Round the feet of the day and the feet of the night.

Where shall we find her, how shall we sing to her,
  Fold our hands round her knees, and cling?
O that man's heart were as fire and could spring to her,
  Fire, or the strength of the streams that spring!
For the stars and the winds are unto her
As raiment, as songs of the harp-player;
For the risen stars and the fallen cling to her,
  And the south-west wind and the west wind sing.

For winter's rains and ruins are over,
   And all the season of snows and sins;
The days dividing lover and lover,
   The light that loses, the night that wins;
And time remembered is grief forgotten,
And frosts are slain and flowers begotten,
And in green underwood and cover
   Blossom by blossom the spring begins.

The full streams feed on flower of rushes,
   Ripe grasses trammel a travelling foot,
The faint fresh flame of the young year flushes
   From leaf to flower and flower to fruit;
And fruit and leaf are as gold and fire,
And the oat is heard above the lyre,
And the hoofèd heel of a satyr crushes
   The chestnut-husk at the chestnut-root.

And Pan by noon and Bacchus by night,
   Fleeter of foot than the fleet-foot kid,
Follows with dancing and fills with delight
   The Maenad and the Bassarid;
And soft as lips that laugh and hide
The laughing leaves of the trees divide,
And screen from seeing and leave in sight
   The god pursuing, the maiden hid.

The ivy falls with the Bacchanal's hair
   Over her eyebrows hiding her eyes;
The wild vine slipping down leaves bare,
   Her bright breast shortening into sighs;
The wild vine slips with the weight of its leaves,
But the berried ivy catches and cleaves
To the limbs that glitter, the feet that scare
   The wolf that follows, the fawn that flies.

Francis Bret Harte

[1836–1902]

PLAIN LANGUAGE FROM TRUTHFUL JAMES
Table Mountain, 1870

Which I wish to remark,
  And my language is plain,
That for ways that are dark
  And for tricks that are vain,
The heathen Chinee is peculiar,
  Which the same I would rise to explain.

Ah Sin was his name;
  And I shall not deny,
In regard to the same,
  What that name might imply;
But his smile it was pensive and childlike,
  As I frequent remarked to Bill Nye.

It was August the third,
  And quite soft was the skies;
Which it might be inferred
  That Ah Sin was likewise;
Yet he played it that day upon William
  And me in a way I despise.

Which we had a small game,
  And Ah Sin took a hand:
It was Euchre. The same
  He did not understand;
But he smiled as he sat by the table,
  With the smile that was childlike and bland.

Yet the cards they were stocked
    In a way that I grieve,
And my feelings were shocked
    At the state of Nye's sleeve,
Which was stuffed full of aces and bowers,
    And the same with intent to deceive.

But the hands that were played
    By that heathen Chinee,
And the points that he made,
    Were quite frightful to see,—
Till at last he put down a right bower,
    Which the same Nye had dealt unto me.

Then I looked up at Nye,
    And he gazed upon me;
And he rose with a sigh,
    And said, "Can this be?
We are ruined by Chinese cheap labor,"—
    And he went for that heathen Chinee.

In the scene that ensued
    I did not take a hand,
But the floor it was strewed
    Like the leaves on the strand
With the cards that Ah Sin had been hiding,
    In the game "he did not understand."

In his sleeves, which were long,
    He had twenty-four jacks,—
Which was coming it strong,
    Yet I state but the facts;
And we found on his nails, which were taper,
    What is frequent in tapers,—that's wax.

Which is why I remark,
    And my language is plain,

That for ways that are dark
   And for tricks that are vain,
The heathen Chinee is peculiar,—
   Which the same I am free to maintain.

James Whitcomb Riley

   [1849–1916]

GOOD-BY ER HOWDY-DO

Say good-by er howdy-do—
What's the odds betwixt the two?
Comin'—goin', ev'ry day—
Best friends first to go away—
Grasp of hands you'd ruther hold
Than their weight in solid gold
Slips their grip while greetin' you.—
Say good-by er howdy-do!

Howdy-do, and then, good-by—
Mixes jes' like laugh and cry;
Deaths and births, and worst and best,
Tangled their contrariest;
Ev'ry jinglin' weddin'-bell
Skeerin' up some funer'l knell.—
Here's my song, and there's your sigh.—
Howdy-do, and then, good-by!

Say good-by er howdy-do—
Jes' the same to me and you;
'Taint worth while to make no fuss,
'Cause the job's put up on us!

Some One's runnin' this concern
That's got nothin' else to learn:
Ef *He's* willin', we'll pull through—
Say good-by er howdy-do!

Benjamin Franklin King, Jr.
[1857–1894]

from THE SUM OF LIFE

Nothing to do but work,
   Nothing to eat but food,
Nothing to wear but clothes,
   To keep one from going nude.

Nothing to breathe but air,
   Quick as a flash 'tis gone;
Nowhere to fall but off,
   Nowhere to stand but on.
    . . . . .

Nothing to sing but songs,
   Ah, well, alas! alack!
Nowhere to go but out,
   Nowhere to come but back.
    . . . . .

Nothing to strike but a gait;
   Everything moves that goes.
Nothing at all but common sense
   Can ever withstand these woes.

Anonymous

[Egyptian, c. 1200–1169 B.C.]

from CONVERSATIONS IN COURTSHIP

✳✳ The original of this Egyptian poem, perhaps by several hands, is from a papyrus of the XXth Dynasty, 1200–1169 B.C. or thereabouts. It is placed here, out of chronological order, on the excuse that Egyptian poetry has not formed a known part of English tradition, though it did filter into the general course of occidental writing via Theocritus and Alexandria. The other reason for the displacement is to jolt the reader into seeing how much Hardy (see pp. 283–86) brought into our verse that had not been there before him.

He says:
Darling, you only, there is no duplicate,
More lovely than all other womanhood,
   Luminous, perfect,
A star coming over the sky-line at new year,
   a good year,
Splendid in colours
   with allure in the eye's turn.
Her lips are enchantment,
   her neck the right length
      and her breasts a marvel;
Her hair lapis lazuli in its glitter,
   her arms more splendid than gold.
Her fingers make me see petals,
   the lotus' are like that.
Her flanks are modeled as should be,
   her legs beyond all other beauty.

Noble her walking
   (vera incessu)
My heart would be a slave should she enfold me.

Every neck turns—that is her fault—
   to look at her.
Fortune's who can utterly embrace her;
   he would stand first among all young lovers.
Deo mi par esse
   Every eye keeps following her
      even after she has stepped out of range,
A single goddess,
   uniquely.

She says:
His voice unquiets my heart,
   It's the voice's fault if I suffer.
My mother's neighbor!
     But I can't go see him,
   Ought she to enrage me?

Mother:
Oh, stop talking about that fellow,
   the mere thought of him is revolting.

She:
I am made prisoner 'cause I love him.

Mother:
But he's a mere kid with no brains.

She:
So am I, I am just like him
   and he don't know I want to put my arms round him.
     That would make mama talk . . .

May the golden goddess make fate,
   and make him my destiny.

Come to where I can see you.
   My father and mother will then be happy
      Because everyone likes to throw parties for you
        And they would get to doing it too.
    . . . . .

She says:
I wanted to come out here where it's lovely
   and get some rest,
Now I meet Mehy in his carriage
   with a gang of other young fellows,
      How can I turn back?

Can I walk in front of him
   as if it did not matter?
Oh, the river is the only way to get by
   and I can't walk on the water.

   My soul, you are all in a muddle.
If I walk in front of him my secret will show,
   I'll blurt out my secrets; say:
               Yours!

And he will mention my name and
   hand me over to just any one of them
     who merely wants a good time.
    . . . . .

She says:
My heart runs out if I think how I love him,
   I can't just act like anyone else.
It, my heart, is all out of place,
   It won't let me choose a dress
     or hide back of my fan.

I can't put on my eye make-up
                        or pick a perfume.

"Don't stop, come into the house."
    That's what my heart said, one time,
And does, every time I think of my beloved.
    Don't play the fool with me, oh heart,
        Why *are* you such an idiot?
Sit quiet! keep calm
            and he'll come to you.
And my alertness won't let people say:
    This girl is unhinged with love.
When you remember him
    stand firm and be solid,
        don't escape me.

He says:
I adore the gold-gleaming Goddess,
    Hathor the dominant,
        and I praise her.

I exalt the Lady of Heaven,
    I give thanks to the Patron.
She hears my invocation
    and has fated me to my lady,
Who has come here, herself, to find me.
    What felicity came in with her!
I rise exultant
    in hilarity
        and triumph when I have said:
                                Now,
And behold her.
    Look at it!
        The young fellows fall at her feet.
Love is breathed into them.

I make vows to my Goddess,
 because she has given me this girl for my own.
I have been praying three days,
 calling her name.
For five days she has abandoned me.

She says:
I went to his house, and the door was open.
 My beloved was at his ma's side
  with brothers and sisters about him.
Everybody who passes has sympathy for him,
 an excellent boy, none like him,
  a friend of rare quality.
He looked at me when I passed
 and my heart was in jubilee.
If my mother knew what I am thinking
 she would go to him at once.

O Goddess of Golden Light,
 put that thought into her,
  Then I could visit him
And put my arms round him while people were looking
And not weep because of the crowd,
 But would be glad that they knew it
  and that you know me.
What a feast I would make to my Goddess,
 My heart revolts at the thought of exit,
If I could see my darling tonight,
 Dreaming is loveliness.

He says:
Yesterday. Seven days and I have not seen her.
 My malady increases;
  limbs heavy!
   I know not myself any more.

High priest is no medicine, exorcism is useless:
   a disease beyond recognition.

I said: She will make me live,
   her name will rouse me,
Her messages are the life of my heart
   coming and going.
My beloved is the best of medicine,
   more than all pharmacopoeia.
My health is in her coming,
   I shall be cured at the sight of her.

Let her open my eyes
   and my limbs are alive again;
Let her speak and my strength returns.
Embracing her will drive out my malady.
   Seven days and
               she has abandoned me.

*Translated from the Italian version of
Boris de Rachewiltz by Ezra Pound*

Thomas Hardy
[1840–1928]

HEREDITY

I am the family face;
Flesh perishes, I live on,
Projecting trait and trace
Through time to times anon,
And leaping from place to place
Over oblivion.

The years-heired feature that can
In curve and voice and eye
Despise the human span
Of durance—that is I;
The eternal thing in man,
That heeds no call to die.

UNDER THE WATERFALL

"Whenever I plunge my arm, like this,
In a basin of water, I never miss
The sweet sharp sense of a fugitive day
Fetched back from its thickening shroud of gray.
    Hence the only prime
    And real love-rhyme
    That I know by heart,
    And that leaves no smart,
Is the purl of a little valley fall
About three spans wide and two spans tall
Over a table of solid rock,
And into a scoop of the self-same block;
The purl of a runlet that never ceases
In stir of kingdoms, in wars, in peaces;
With a hollow boiling voice it speaks
And has spoken since hills were turfless peaks."

"And why gives this the only prime
Idea to you of a real love-rhyme?
And why does plunging your arm in a bowl
Full of spring water, bring throbs to your soul?"

"Well, under the fall, in a crease of the stone,
Though where precisely none ever has known,

Jammed darkly, nothing to show how prized,
And by now with its smoothness opalized,
    Is a drinking-glass:
    For, down that pass
    My lover and I
    Walked under a sky
Of blue with a leaf-wove awning of green,
In the burn of August, to paint the scene,
And we placed our basket of fruit and wine
By the runlet's rim, where we sat to dine;
And when we had drunk from the glass together,
Arched by the oak-copse from the weather,
I held the vessel to rinse in the fall,
Where it slipped, and sank, and was past recall,
Though we stooped and plumbed the little abyss
With long bared arms. There the glass still is.
And, as said, if I thrust my arm below
Cold water in basin or bowl, a throe
From the past awakens a sense of that time,
And the glass we used, and the cascade's rhyme.
The basin seems the pool, and its edge
The hard smooth face of the brook-side ledge,
And the leafy pattern of china-ware
The hanging plants that were bathing there.

"By night, by day, when it shines or lours,
There lies intact that chalice of ours,
And its presence adds to the rhyme of love
Persistently sung by the fall above.
No lip has touched it since his and mine
In turns therefrom sipped lovers' wine."

FAINTHEART IN A RAILWAY TRAIN

At nine in the morning there passed a church,
At ten there passed me by the sea,
At twelve a town of smoke and smirch,
At two a forest of oak and birch,
    And then, on a platform, she:

A radiant stranger, who saw not me.
I said, "Get out to her do I dare?"
But I kept my seat in search for a plea,
And the wheels moved on. O could it but be
    That I had alighted there!

THE YOUNG GLASS-STAINER

"These Gothic windows, how they wear me out
With cusp and foil, and nothing straight or square,
Crude colours, leaden borders roundabout,
And fitting in Peter here, and Matthew there!

"What a vocation! Here do I draw now
The abnormal, loving the Hellenic norm;
Martha I paint, and dream of Hera's brow,
Mary, and think of Aphrodite's form."

❀❀ Pre-Imagist concision and firmness; the Swinburnian revolt
in contents; cf. his longer "The Abbey Mason: Inventor of the
Perpendicular Style of Gothic Architecture," Macmillan collected
edition, p. 379, for Hardy's personal aesthetic.
    For a longer note on Hardy, see Appendix I.

William Butler Yeats

[1865–1939]

DOWN BY THE SALLEY GARDENS

Down by the salley gardens my love and I did meet;
She passed the salley gardens with little snow-white feet.
She bid me take love easy, as the leaves grow on the tree;
But I, being young and foolish, with her would not agree.

In a field by the river my love and I did stand,
And on my leaning shoulder she laid her snow-white hand.
She bid me take life easy, as the grass grows on the weirs;
But I was young and foolish, and now am full of tears.

WHEN YOU ARE OLD

When you are old and grey and full of sleep,
And nodding by the fire, take down this book,
And slowly read, and dream of the soft look
Your eyes had once, and of their shadows deep;

How many loved your moments of glad grace,
And loved your beauty with love false or true,
But one man loved the pilgrim soul in you,
And loved the sorrows of your changing face;

And bending down beside the glowing bars,
Murmur, a little sadly, how Love fled
And paced upon the mountains overhead
And hid his face amid a crowd of stars.

THE MOODS

Time drops in decay,
Like a candle burnt out,
And the mountains and woods
Have their day, have their day;
What one in the rout
Of the fire-born moods
Has fallen away?

HE REMEMBERS FORGOTTEN BEAUTY

When my arms wrap you round I press
My heart upon the loveliness
That has long faded from the world;
The jewelled crowns that kings have hurled
In shadowy pools, when armies fled;
The love-tales wrought with silken thread
By dreaming ladies upon cloth
That has made fat the murderous moth;
The roses that of old time were
Woven by ladies in their hair,
The dew-cold lilies ladies bore
Through many a sacred corridor
Where such grey clouds of incense rose
That only God's eyes did not close:
For that pale breast and lingering hand
Come from a more dream-heavy land,
A more dream-heavy hour than this;
And when you sigh from kiss to kiss
I hear white Beauty sighing, too,
For hours when all must fade like dew,
But flame on flame, and deep on deep,
Throne over throne where in half sleep,
Their swords upon their iron knees,
Brood her high lonely mysteries.

HE THINKS OF THOSE WHO HAVE SPOKEN EVIL OF HIS BELOVED

Half close your eyelids, loosen your hair,
And dream about the great and their pride;
They have spoken against you everywhere,
But weigh this song with the great and their pride;
I made it out of a mouthful of air,
Their children's children shall say they have lied.

THE COLD HEAVEN

Suddenly I saw the cold and rook-delighting heaven
That seemed as though ice burned and was but the more ice,
And thereupon imagination and heart were driven
So wild that every casual thought of that and this
Vanished, and left but memories, that should be out of season
With the hot blood of youth, of love crossed long ago;
And I took all the blame out of all sense and reason,
Until I cried and trembled and rocked to and fro,
Riddled with light. Ah! when the ghost begins to quicken,
Confusion of the death-bed over, is it sent
Out naked on the roads, as the books say, and stricken
By the injustice of the skies for punishment?

TO A POET, WHO WOULD HAVE ME PRAISE CERTAIN BAD POETS, IMITATORS OF HIS AND MINE

You say, as I have often given tongue
In praise of what another's said or sung,
'Twere politic to do the like by these;
But was there ever dog that praised his fleas?

Ford Madox Ford

[1873–1939]

ON HEAVEN
To V. H., who asked for a working Heaven

I
That day the sunlight lay on the farms;
On the morrow the bitter frost that there was!
That night my young love lay in my arms,
    The morrow how bitter it was!

And because she is very tall and quaint
And golden, like a *quattrocento* saint,
I desire to write about Heaven;
To tell you the shape and the ways of it,
And the joys and the toil in the maze of it,
For these there must be in Heaven,
Even in Heaven!

For God is a good man, God is a kind man,
And God's a good brother, and God is no blind man,
And God is our father.

            I will tell you how this thing began:
How I waited in a little town near Lyons many years,
And yet knew nothing of passing time, or of her tears,
But, for nine slow years, lounged away at my table in the shadowy
        sunlit square
Where the small cafés are.

The *Place* is small and shaded by great planes,
Over a rather human monument
Set up to *Louis Dixhuit* in the year
Eighteen fourteen; a funny thing with dolphins

About a pyramid of green-dripped, sordid stone.
But the enormous, monumental planes
Shade it all in, and in the flecks of sun
Sit market women. There's a paper shop
Painted all blue, a shipping agency,
Three or four cafés; dank, dark colonnades
Of an eighteen-forty *Maîrie*. I'd no wish
To wait for her where it was picturesque,
Or ancient or historic, or to love
Over well any place in the land before she came
And loved it too. I didn't even go
To Lyons for the opera; Arles for the bulls,
Or Avignon for glimpses of the Rhone.
Not even to Beaucaire! I sat about
And played long games of dominoes with the *maire*,
Or passing *commis-voyageurs*. And so
I sat and watched the trams come in, and read
The *Libre Parole* and sipped the thin, fresh wine
They call Piquette, and got to know the people,
The kindly, southern people . . .

Until, when the years were over, she came in her swift red car,
Shooting out past a tram; and she slowed and stopped and lighted
    absently down,
A little dazed, in the heart of the town;
And nodded imperceptibly.
With a sideways look at me.

So our days here began.

And the wrinkled old woman who keeps the café,
And the man
Who sells the *Libre Parole*,
And the sleepy gendarme,
And the fat *facteur* who delivers letters only in the shady,
Pleasanter kind of streets;
And the boy I often gave a penny,

And the *maire* himself, and the little girl who loves toffee
And me because I have given her many sweets;
And the one-eyed, droll
Bookseller of the *rue Grand de Provence,*—
Chancing to be going home to bed,
Smiled with their kindly, fresh benevolence,
Because they knew I had waited for a lady
Who should come in a swift, red, English car,
To the square where the little cafés are.
And the old, old woman touched me on the wrist
With a wrinkled finger,
And said: "Why do you linger?—
Too many kisses can never be kissed!
And comfort her—nobody here will think harm—
Take her instantly to your arm!
It is a little strange, you know, to your dear,
To be dead!"

But one is English,
Though one be never so much of a ghost;
And if most of your life have been spent in the craze to relinquish
What you want most,
You will go on relinquishing,
You will go on vanquishing
Human longings, even
In Heaven.

God! You will have forgotten what the rest of the world is on fire
        for—
The madness of desire for the long and quiet embrace,
The coming nearer of a tear-wet face;
Forgotten the desire to slake
The thirst, and the long, slow ache,
And to interlace
Lash with lash, lip with lip, limb with limb, and the fingers of the
        hand with the hand
And . . .

You will have forgotten . . .

But they will all awake;
Aye, all of them shall awaken
In this dear place.
And all that then we took
Of all that we might have taken,
Was that one embracing look,
Coursing over features, over limbs, between eyes, a making sure,
    and a long sigh,
Having the tranquillity
Of trees unshaken,
And the softness of sweet tears,
And the clearness of a clear brook
To wash away past years.
(For that too is the quality of Heaven,
That you are conscious always of great pain
Only when it is over
And shall not come again.
Thank God, thank God, it shall not come again,
Though your eyes be never so wet with the tears
Of many years!)

II
And so she stood a moment by the door
Of the long, red car. Royally she stepped down,
Settling on one long foot and leaning back
Amongst her russet furs. And she looked round . . .
Of course it must be strange to come from England
Straight into Heaven. You must take it in,
Slowly, for a long instant, with some fear . . .
Now that *affiche,* in orange, on the kiosque:
*"Six Spanish bulls will fight on Sunday next
At Arles, in the arena"* . . . Well, it's strange
Till you get used to our ways. And, on the *Maîrie,*
The untidy poster telling of the *concours
De vers de soie,* of silkworms. The cocoons
Pile, yellow, all across the little Places

Of ninety townships in the environs
Of Lyons, the city famous for her silks.
What if she's pale? It must be more than strange,
After these years, to come out here from England
To a strange place, to the stretched-out arms of me,
A man never fully known, only divined,
Loved, guessed at, pledged to, in your Sussex mud,
Amongst the frost-bound farms by the yeasty sea.
Oh, the long look; the long, long searching look!
And how my heart beat!

                  Well, you see, in England
She had a husband. And four families—
His, hers, mine, and another woman's too—
Would have gone crazy. And, with all the rest,
Eight parents, and the children, seven aunts
And sixteen uncles and a grandmother.
There were, besides, our names, a few real friends,
And the decencies of life. A monstrous heap!
They made a monstrous heap. I've lain awake
Whole aching nights to tot the figures up!
Heap after heaps, of complications, griefs,
Worries, tongue-clackings, nonsenses and shame
For not making good. You see the coil there was!
And the poor strained fibres of our tortured brains,
And the voice that called from depth in her to depth
In me . . . my God, in the dreadful nights,
Through the roar of the great black winds, through the sound of
    the sea!
Oh agony! Agony! From out my breast
It called whilst the dark house slept, and stairheads creaked;
From within my breast it screamed and made no sound;
And wailed. . . . And made no sound.
And howled like the damned. . . . No sound! No sound!
Only the roar of the wind, the sound of the sea,
The tick of the clock . . .
And our two voices, noiseless through the dark.
O God! O God!

(That night my young love lay in my arms . . .

There was a bitter frost lay on the farms
In England, by the shiver
And the crawling of the tide;
By the broken silver of the English Channel,
Beneath the aged moon that watched alone—
Poor, dreary, lonely old moon to have to watch alone,
Over the dreary beaches mantled with ancient foam
Like shrunken flannel;
The moon, an intent, pale face, looking down
Over the English Channel.

But soft and warm she lay in the crook of my arm,
And came to no harm since we had come quietly home
Even to Heaven;
Which is situate in a little old town
Not very far from the side of the Rhone,
That mighty river
That is, just there by the Crau, in the lower reaches,
Far wider than the Channel.)

But, in the market place of the other little town,
Where the Rhone is a narrower, greener affair,
When she had looked at me, she beckoned with her long white
    hand,
A little languidly, since it is a strain, if a blessed strain, to have
    just died.
And, going back again,
Into the long, red, English racing car,
Made room for me amongst the furs at her side.
And we moved away from the kind looks of the kindly people
Into the wine of the hurrying air.
And very soon even the tall grey steeple
Of Lyons cathedral behind us grew little and far
And then was no more there . . .
And, thank God, we had nothing any more to think of,

And thank God, we had nothing any more to talk of;
Unless, as it chanced, the flashing silver stalk of the pampas
Growing down to the brink of the Rhone,
On the lawn of a little château, giving onto the river.
And we were alone, alone, alone . . .
At last alone . . .

The poplars on the hill-crests go marching rank on rank,
And far away to the left, like a pyramid, marches the ghost of
        Mont Blanc.
There are vines and vines and vines, all down to the river bank.
There will be a castle here,
And an abbey there;
And huge quarries and a long, white farm,
With long thatched barns and a long wine shed,
As we ran alone, all down the Rhone.

And that day there was no puncturing of the tyres to fear;
And no trouble at all with the engine and gear;
Smoothly and softly we ran between the great poplar alley
All down the valley of the Rhone.
For the dear, good God knew how we needed rest and to be alone.
But, on other days, just as you must have perfect shadows to
        make perfect Rembrandts,
He shall afflict us with little lets and hindrances of His own
Devising—just to let us be glad that we are dead . . .
Just for remembrance.

III

Hard by the castle of God in the Alpilles,
In the eternal stone of the Alpilles,
There's this little old town, walled round by the old, grey gar-
        dens . . .
There were never such olives as grow in the gardens of God,
The green-grey trees, the wardens of agony
And failure of gods.
Of hatred and faith, of truth, of treachery

They whisper; they whisper that none of the living prevail;
They whirl in the great mistral over the white, dry sods,
Like hair blown back from white foreheads in the enormous gale
Up to the castle walls of God . . .

But, in the town that's our home,
Once you are past the wall,
Amongst the trunks of the planes,
Though they roar never so mightily overhead in the day,
All this tumult is quieted down, and all
The windows stand open because of the heat of the night
That shall come.
And, from each little window, shines in the twilight a light,
And, beneath the eternal planes
With the huge, gnarled trunks that were aged and grey
At the creation of Time,
The Chinese lanthorns, hung out of the doors of hotels,
Shimmering in the dusk, here on an orange tree, there on a sweet-
    scented lime,
There on a golden inscription: "Hotel of the Three Holy Bells."
Or "Hotel Sublime," or "Inn of the Real Good Will."
And, yes, it is very warm and still,
And all the world is afoot after the heat of the day,
In the cool of the even in Heaven . . .
And it is here that I have brought my dear to pay her all that I
    owed her,
Amidst this crowd, with the soft voices, the soft footfalls, the re-
    joicing laughter.
And after the twilight there falls such a warm, soft darkness,
And there will come stealing under the planes a drowsy odour,
Compounded all of cyclamen, of oranges, or rosemary and bay,
To take the remembrance of the toil of the day away.

So we sat at a little table, under an immense plane,
And we remembered again
The blisters and foments
And terrible harassments of the tired brain,

The cold and the frost and the pain,
As if we were looking at a picture and saying: "This is true!
Why this is a truly painted
Rendering of that street where—you remember?—I fainted."
And we remembered again
Tranquilly, our poor few tranquil moments,
The falling of the sunlight through the panes,
The flutter for ever in the chimney of the quiet flame,
The mutter of our two poor tortured voices, always a-whisper
And the endless nights when I would cry out, running through all
      the gamut of misery even to a lisp, her name;
And we remembered our kisses, nine, maybe, or eleven—
If you count two that I gave and she did not give again.

And always the crowd drifted by in the cool of the even,
And we saw the faces of friends,
And the faces of those to whom one day we must make amends,
Smiling in welcome.
And I said: "On another day—
And such a day may well come soon—
We will play dominoes with Dick and Evelyn and Frances
For a whole afternoon.
And, in the time to come, Genée
Shall dance for us, fluttering over the ground as the sunlight
      dances."
And *Arlésiennes* with the beautiful faces went by us,
And gipsies and Spanish shepherds, noiseless in sandals of straw,
      sauntered nigh us,
Wearing slouch hats and old sheep-skins, and casting admiring
      glances
From dark, foreign eyes at my dear . . .
(And ah, it is Heaven alone, to have her alone and so near!)
So all this world rejoices
In the cool of the even
In Heaven . . .
And, when the cool of the even was fully there,
Came a great ha-ha of voices.

Many children run together, and all laugh and rejoice and call,
Hurrying with little arms flying, and little feet flying, and little
    hurrying haunches,
From the door of a stable,
Where, in an *olla podrida,* they had been playing at the *corrida*
With the black Spanish bull, whose nature
Is patience with children. And so, through the gaps of the
    branches
Of jasmine on our screen beneath the planes,
We saw, coming down from the road that leads to the olives and
    Alpilles,
A man of great stature,
In a great cloak,
With a great stride,
And a little joke
For all and sundry, coming down with a hound at his side.
And he stood at the cross-roads, passing the time of day
In a great, kind voice, the voice of a man-and-a-half!—
With a great laugh, and a great clap on the back,
For a fellow in black—a priest I should say,
Or may be a lover,
Wearing black for his mistress's mood.
"A little toothache," we could hear him say; "but that's so good
When it gives over." So he passed from sight
In the soft twilight, into the soft night,
In the soft riot and tumult of the crowd.

And a magpie flew down, laughing, holding up his beak to us.
And I said: "That was God! Presently, when he has walked
    through the town
And the night has settled down,
So that you may not be afraid,
In the darkness, he will come to our table and speak to us."
And past us many saints went walking in a company—
The kindly, thoughtful saints, devising and laughing and talking,
And smiling at us with their pleasant solicitude.
And because the thick of the crowd followed to the one side God,

Or to the other the saints, we sat in solitude.
In the distance the saints went singing all in chorus,
And our Lord went by on the other side of the street,
Holding a little boy.
Taking him to pick the musk-roses that open at dusk,
For wreathing the statue of Jove,
Left on the Alpilles above
By the Romans; since Jove,
Even Jove,
Must not want for his quota of honour and love;
But round about him there must be,
With all its tender jollity,
The laughter of children in Heaven,
Making merry with roses in Heaven.

Yet never he looked at us, knowing that that would be such joy
As must be over-great for hearts that needed quiet;
Such a riot and tumult of joy as quiet hearts are not able
To taste to the full . . .

. . . And my dear one sat in the shadows; very softly she wept:—
Such joy is in Heaven,
In the cool of the even,
After the burden and toil of the days,
After the heat and haze
In the vine-hills; or in the shady
Whispering groves in high passes up in the Alpilles,
Guarding the castle of God.

And I went on talking towards her unseen face:
"So it is, so it goes, in this beloved place,
There shall be never a grief but passes; no, not any;
There shall be such bright light and no blindness;
There shall be so little awe and so much loving-kindness;
There shall be a little longing and enough care,
There shall be a little labour and enough of toil
To bring back the lost flavour of our human coil;

Not enough to taint it;
And all that we desire shall prove as fair as we can paint it."
For, though that may be the very hardest trick of all
God set Himself, who fashioned this goodly hall.
Thus He has made Heaven;
Even Heaven.

For God is a very clever mechanician;
And if He made this proud and goodly ship of the world,
From the maintop to the hull,
Do you think He could not finish it to the full,
With a flag and all,
And make it sail, tall and brave,
On the waters, beyond the grave?
It should cost but very little rhetoric
To explain for you that last, fine, conjuring trick;
Nor does God need to be a very great magician
To give to each man after his heart,
Who knows very well what each man has in his heart:
To let you pass your life in a night-club where they dance,
If that is your idea of heaven; if you will, in the South of France;
If you will, on the turbulent sea; if you will, in the peace of the
        night;
Where you will; how you will;
Or in the long death of a kiss, that may never pall:
He would be a very little God if He could not do all this,
And He is still
The great God of all.

For God is a good man; God is a kind man;
In the darkness He came walking to our table beneath the planes,
And spoke
So kindly to my dear,
With a little joke,
Giving Himself some pains
To take away her fear
Of His stature,

So as not to abash her,
In no way at all to dash her new pleasure beneath the planes,
In the cool of the even
In Heaven.

That, that is God's nature.
For God's a good brother, and God is no blind man,
And God's a good mother and loves sons who're rovers,
And God is our father and loves all good lovers.
He has a kindly smile for many a poor sinner;
He takes note to make it up to poor wayfarers on sodden roads;
Such as bear heavy loads
He takes note of, and of all that toil on bitter seas and frosty
      lands,
He takes care that they shall have good at His hands;
Well He takes note of a poor old cook,
Cooking your dinner;
And much He loves sweet joys in such as ever took
Sweet joy on earth. He has a kindly smile for a kiss
Given in a shady nook.
And in the golden book
Where the accounts of His estate are kept,
All the round, golden sovereigns of bliss,
Known by poor lovers, married or never yet married,
Whilst the green world waked, or the black world quietly slept;
All joy, all sweetness, each sweet sigh that's sighed—
Their accounts are kept,
And carried
By the love of God to His own credit's side.
So that is why He came to our table to welcome my dear, dear
      bride,
In the cool of the even
In front of a café in Heaven.

WHAT THE ORDERLY DOG SAW
A Winter Landscape

I

The seven white peacocks against the castle wall
In the high trees and the dusk are like tapestry,
The sky being orange, the high wall a purple barrier
The canal, dead silver in the dusk
    And you are far away.
Yet I can see infinite miles of mountains.
Little lights shining in rows in the dark of them;
Infinite miles of marshes.
Thin wisps of mist, shimmering like blue webs
Over the dusk of them, great curves and horns of sea
And dusk and dusk and the little village
    And you, sitting in the firelight.

II

Around me are the two hundred and forty men of B Company
Mud-coloured.
Going about their avocations,
Resting between their practice of the art
Of killing men,
As I too rest between my practice
Of the art of killing men.
Their pipes glow above the mud and their mud colour, moving
    like fireflies beneath the trees,
I too being mud-coloured
Beneath the trees and the peacocks.
When they come up to me in the dusk
They start, stiffen and salute, almost invisibly.
And the forty-two prisoners from the Battalion guardroom
Crouch over the tea cans in the shadow of the wall.
And the bread hunks glimmer, beneath the peacocks,
    And you are far away.

III
Presently I shall go in,
I shall write down the names of the forty-two
Prisoners in the Battalion guardroom
On fair white foolscap.
Their names, rank, and regimental numbers,
Corps, Companies, Punishments and Offences,
Remarks, and By whom Confined.
Yet in spite of all I shall see only
The infinite miles of dark mountain,
The infinite miles of dark marshland,
Great curves and horns of sea
The little village.
And you,
Sitting in the firelight.

"WHEN THE WORLD WAS IN BUILDING..."

Thank Goodness, the moving is over,
They've swept up the straw in the passage
And life will begin . . .
This tiny, white, tiled cottage by the bridge! . . .
When we've had tea I will punt you
To Paradise for the sugar and onions . . .
We will drift home in the twilight,
The trout will be rising . . .

THE OLD HOUSES OF FLANDERS

The old houses of Flanders,
They watch by the high cathedrals;
They overtop the high town-halls;

They have eyes, mournful, tolerant and sardonic, for the ways of
    men
In the high, white, tiled gables.

The rain and the night have settled down on Flanders;
It is all wet darkness; you can see nothing.

Then those old eyes, mournful, tolerant and sardonic,
Look at great, sudden, red lights,
Look upon the shades of the cathedrals;
And the golden rods of the illuminated rain,
For a second . . .

And those old eyes,
Very old eyes that have watched the ways of men for generations,
Close for ever.
The high, white shoulders of the gables
Slouch together for a consultation,
Slant drunkenly over in the lea of the flaming cathedrals.

They are no more, the old houses of Flanders.

Padraic Colum

[1881–   ]

"I SHALL NOT DIE FOR THEE"

O woman, shapely as the swan,
On your account I shall not die:
The men you've slain—a trivial clan—
Were less than I.

I ask me shall I die for these—
For blossom teeth and scarlet lips?
And shall that delicate swan-shape
Bring me eclipse?

Well-shaped the breasts and smooth the skin,
The cheeks are fair, the tresses free—
And yet I shall not suffer death,
God over me!

Those even brows, that hair like gold,
Those languorous tones, that virgin way,
The flowing limbs, the rounded heel
Slight men betray!

Thy spirit keen through radient mien,
Thy shining throat and smiling eye,
Thy little palm, thy side like foam—
I cannot die!

O woman, shapely as the swan,
In a cunning house hard-reared was I:
O bosom white, O well-shaped palm,
I shall not die!

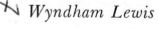 *Wyndham Lewis*

[1883–1957]

from ONE-WAY SONG

I would set all things whatsoever front to back,
All that go upright—by these tactics show

How the bold Fronts depend upon this knack
Of nature's—how our one-way bodies grow—
Always *Eyes-front!* Creatures of Progress! suited
Only for one-way travel, in Time bodily rooted.

Try and walk backwards: you will quickly see
How you were meant only *one-way* to be!
Attempt to gaze out of your bricked-up back:
You will soon discover what we *One-ways* lack!

William Carlos Williams

[1883–1963]

THE HIGH BRIDGE ABOVE THE TAGUS RIVER AT TOLEDO

A young man, alone, on the high bridge over the Tagus which
   was too narrow to allow the sheep driven by the lean, enor-
   mous dogs whose hind legs worked slowly on cogs
to pass easily . . .
   (he didn't speak the language)

Pressed against the parapet either side by the crowding sheep,
   the relentless pressure of the dogs communicated itself to
   him also
above the waters in the gorge below.

They were hounds to him rather than sheep dogs because of their
   size and savage appearance, dog tired from the day's work.
The stiff jerking movement of the hind legs, the hanging heads
   at the shepherd's heels, slowly followed the excited and crowd-
   ing sheep.

The whole flock, the shepherd and the dogs, were covered with
dust as if they had been all day long on the road. The pace of
the sheep, slow in the mass,
governed the man and the dogs. They were approaching the city
at nightfall, the long journey completed.

In old age they walk in the old man's dreams and will still walk
in his dreams, peacefully continuing in his verse forever.

** Dr. Williams' criticism of himself may be examined in a list
of ten poems ("Pastoral" ["When I was younger"], "Virtue,"
"Nantucket," "Between Walls," "It is a living coral," "Spring
and All," "Primrose," "To a Poor Old Woman," "The Sea Ele-
phant," "The Red-wing Blackbird") on which he comments:
"This brief selection is as much as the casual reader will find
illustrative of what I have been doing with myself for the past
30 years." [M. S.]

Ezra Pound

[1885–   ]

VILLANELLE:
THE PSYCHOLOGICAL HOUR

I
I had over-prepared the event,
          that much was ominous.
With middle-ageing care
          I had laid out just the right books.
I had almost turned down the pages.

          Beauty is so rare a thing.
          So few drink of my fountain.

So much barren regret,
So many hours wasted!
And now I watch, from the window,
              the rain, the wandering busses.

"Their little cosmos is shaken"—
              the air is alive with that fact.
In their parts of the city
              they are played on by diverse forces.
How do I know?
              Oh, I know well enough.
For them there is something afoot.
              As for me;
I had over-prepared the event—

              Beauty is so rare a thing,
              So few drink of my fountain.

Two friends: a breath of the forest . . .
Friends? Are people less friends
       because one has just, at last, found them?
Twice they promised to come.

              "Between the night and morning?"

Beauty would drink of my mind.
Youth would awhile forget
              my youth is gone from me.

II
("Speak up! You have danced so stiffly?
       Someone admired your works,
       And said so frankly.

       "Did you talk like a fool,
       The first night?
       The second evening?"

"*But* they promised again:
              'To-morrow at tea-time.' ")

III

Now the third day is here—
          no word from either;
No word from her nor him,
Only another man's note:
        "Dear Pound, I am leaving England."

ENVOI (1919)

Go, dumb-born book,
Tell her that sang me once that song of Lawes:
Hadst thou but song
As thou hast subjects known,
Then were there cause in thee that should condone
Even my faults that heavy upon me lie,
And build her glories their longevity.

Tell her that sheds
Such treasure in the air,
Recking naught else but that her graces give
Life to the moment,
I would bid them live
As roses might, in magic amber laid,
Red overwrought with orange and all made
One substance and one colour
Braving time.

Tell her that goes
With song upon her lips
But sings not out the song, nor knows
The maker of it, some other mouth,
May be as fair as hers,
Might, in new ages, gain her worshippers,
When our two dusts with Waller's shall be laid,
Siftings on siftings in oblivion,
Till change hath broken down
All things save Beauty alone.

H. D. [*Hilda Doolittle*]

[1886–1961]

"NEVER MORE WILL THE WIND"

Never more will the wind
cherish you again,
never more will the rain.

Never more
shall we find you bright
in the snow and wind.

The snow is melted,
the snow is gone,
and you are flown:

Like a bird out of our hand,
like a light out of our heart,
you are gone.

Marianne Moore

[1886–   ]

O TO BE A DRAGON

If I, like Solomon, . . .
could have my wish—

my wish . . . O to be a dragon,
a symbol of the power of Heaven—of silkworm
size or immense; at times invisible.
    Felicitous phenomenon!

❈ ❈ Selection by Marianne Moore follows a suggestion from her; we had intended using instead the poem which contains the reference to causes of war in oneself. [M. S.]

T. S. Eliot
   [1888–   ]

from WHISPERS OF IMMORTALITY

Webster was much possessed by death
And saw the skull beneath the skin;
And breastless creatures under ground
Leaned backward with a lipless grin.

Daffodil bulbs instead of balls
Stared from the sockets of the eyes!
He knew that thought clings round dead limbs
Tightening its lusts and luxuries.

Donne, I suppose, was such another
Who found no substitute for sense,
To seize and clutch and penetrate;
Expert beyond experience,

He knew the anguish of the marrow
The ague of the skeleton;

No contact possible to flesh
Allayed the fever of the bone.

. . . . .

Grishkin is nice: her Russian eye
Is underlined for emphasis;
Uncorseted, her friendly bust
Gives promise of pneumatic bliss.

The couched Brazilian jaguar
Compels the scampering marmoset
With subtle effluence of cat;
Grishkin has a maisonette;

The sleek Brazilian jaguar
Does not in its arboreal gloom
Distil so rank a feline smell
As Grishkin in a drawing-room.

And even the Abstract Entities
Circumambulate her charm;
But our lot crawls between dry ribs
To keep our metaphysics warm.

Basil Bunting

[1900–   ]

GIN THE GOODWIFE STINT

The ploughland has gone to bent
And the pasture to heather;

bent: tough, tussocky grass

Gin the goodwife stint
She'll keep the house together.

Gin the goodwife stint
And the bairns hunger
The Duke can get his rent
One year longer.

The Duke can get his rent
And we can get our ticket
Twa pund emigrant
On a C.P.R. packet.

gin: if   *C.P.R.:* In 1920 it was still possible for an emigrant pledged
to agricultural labor to cross from England to Canada on a Canadian Pacific
Railway boat for two pounds.

THE COMPLAINT OF THE MORPETHSHIRE FARMER

On the up-platform at Morpeth station
In the market-day throng
I overheard a Morpethshire farmer
Muttering this song:

Must ye bide, my good stone house,
To keep a townsman dry?
To hear the flurry of the grouse
But not the lowing of the kye?

To see the bracken choke the clod
The coulter will na turn?
The bit level neebody
Will drain soak up the burn?

Where are ye, my seven score sheep?
Feeding on other braes!

kye: cattle   *coulter:* plowshare

My brand has faded from your fleece,
Another has its place.

The fold beneath the rowan
Where ye were dipt before,
Its cowpit walls are overgrown,
Ye would na heed them more.

And thou! Thou's idled all the spring,
I doubt thou's spoiled, my Meg!
But a sheepdog's faith is aye something.
We'll hire together in Winnipeg.

Canada's a cold land.
Thou and I must share
A straw bed and a hind's wages
And the bitter air.

Canada's a bare land
For the north wind and the snow.
Northumberland's a bare land
For men have made it so

Sheep and cattle are poor men's food,
Grouse is sport for the rich;
Heather grows where the sweet grass might grow
For the cost of cleaning the ditch

A liner lying in the Clyde
Will take me to Quebec.
My sons'll see the land I am leaving
As barren as her deck.

cowpit: overturned   *hind:* farm laborer

✳ ✳ The stylistic reform, or the change in language, was a means
not an end. After the war of 1914–19 there was definitely an ex-
tension of subject matter. This anthology cannot analyze the

results, it is a lead up, but the poetry of the last forty years definitely breeds a discontent with a great deal that had been accepted in 1900. Of the poets who appeared in the 1920's it has been asserted that Cummings and Bunting show a deeper concern with basic human problems in relation to the state of the times, Cummings with irony, Bunting in more glum sobriety. We have chosen two of Bunting's poems that are easiest to grasp, but they lead up to such passages as:

> "The sea is his and he
> made it."—Who
> made Holland and whose is it?
> MAN IS NOT AN END-PRODUCT,
>   MAGGOT ASSERTS.

There are unforgettable lines in his "Villon."

e e cummings

[1894–1963]

from ONE TIMES ONE

XIII

plato told

him:he couldn't
believe it(jesus

told him;he
wouldn't believe
it)lao

tsze
certainly told
him,and general
(yes

mam)
sherman;
and even
(believe it
or

not)you
told him:i told
him;we told him
(he didn't believe it,**no**

sir)it took
a nipponized bit of
the old sixth

avenue
el;in the top of his head:to tell

him

❊ ❊ Eva Hesse has translated Cummings' poem into German:

platon sagt

es ihm: er konnt'
es nicht glauben (jesus

sagt es ihm ; er
wollt' es nicht
glauben) lao

tse
sagt es ihm und ob

und general
(ja

wohl)
sherman;
und sogar
(ob du's glaubst
oder

nicht) du
sagest es ihm: ich sagte
es ihm; wir sagten es ihm
(er glaubte es einfach nicht im befehl

nein) erst als ein
japanisiertes stuck von
der alten sixth

avenue
s-bahn in seinem Hirnkasten stak
sa musst' er daran glauben.

Postscript

Postscript

Urbanity in externals, virtu in internals
        some in high style for the rites
some in humble;
for Emperors; for the people . . . ,

wrote Chun Tchi in his preface to the Confucian Odes. This
breadth of scope will perhaps explain the inclusion of Whitcomb
Riley and Bret Harte, once esteemed reading matter in the U.S.
but whose presence in a draft selection has already puzzled
several professors.

The Confucian Anthology was the basis of an education, as
were the Homeric poems, as was Dante to a limited aristocracy
of the mind, as Shakespeare would presumably have wished to
be, had not the necessity of appealing to a theatre audience pre-
vented his concentration on several subjects in which he took
personal interest.

If I started with the hope of selecting passages of Cicero suffi-
ciently lively to interest my contemporaries in 1907, my aesthetic
period may in the long run look like an interlude. At any rate
"education" has for the past twenty or more years seemed to me
to mean civic education. That is to say education that fits the
pupil to function in literate human society at whatever level his
talents and destiny land him.

A few years ago I ploughed through the memoirs of Hull,
LeMay, Stillwell, and Madame de Chambrun, all of 'em ham ig-
norant of things they should have learned in high school. If I
had spent my 'teen years in the same town with my granddad I
would have known vital facts at seventeen that I only discovered
or began discovering at fifty.

Faced with the all but total blackout of history in our schools
and colleges, almost the sole chance of a pupil's learning any-
thing useful by the age of twenty that he will be glad to know at
forty or sixty, apart from mechanics and "scientific developments,"

some of dubious value, is via the courses in "literature," of which poetry is the most condensed form.

Felix Schelling used to say or quote that the critic is good when he praises and bad when he blames. That statement is sweeping but in the rare cases when criticism helps a reader to understand a text, it is probably due to the critic's perception of positive values and to his not having looked for something which the author never intended to put into his work—thus the scandal of Gifford's attack on Keats, which contains several acute observations, but apart from Gifford's dirty temper was due in part to an incomprehension of why Keats could expect a thing of beauty to be a joy.

Nineteenth-century rhetoric books used to recommend: clearness, force, and beauty. Medieval Latin gave it: *ut doceat, ut moveat, ut dilectet,* that it teach, move, and delight. From at least Walter Pater's time there was a distinct reaction against the didactic, which would have surprised the Elizabethans in the time of the first English queen of that name.

Some distinction among the various kinds of poetry may eliminate gross miscomprehension. Lyric and epic have their own rights. If you define an epic as a "poem including history" you admit elements improper to brief emotional utterance. Drama differs from poetry made to be sung or spoken by one person in that it is a text to be used in combination with human beings or puppets in action, gesticulating or quiet. The verbal manifest is not the whole show but can be or usually needs to be completed by movement and interplay. Apart from the sequence of lyrics from *A Midsummer Night's Dream,* and the Egyptian sequence where drama is merely hinted at, this volume is mainly lyric or narrative as in the Ovid and Crabbe, etc.

I cannot too greatly emphasize a statement in one of the prefaces that this book is intended as a start, that is mainly to arouse curiosity, but also to alert the pupil to the extent and variety of the fields where she or he can browse later with enjoyment.

E. P.

Section for Instructors

Appendix I

✸✸ Ezra Pound's note on Hardy and Ford contains so many suggestions for an approach to reading that I print it as it stands, despite the author's avoidance of the smooth syntactic flow to which one is accustomed. [M. S.]

Clear page or palimpsest, Hardy registered an age. Of conventional mind, apparently, but of a very particular sensibility; whether he saw ghosts or thought them useful to his record, he liked the feel of the past and dissented with remarkable ubiquity and vigor from the era he lived in: nothing like a crusade, simply a quiet registration of disapproval by 1860 of numerous things more people have since disapproved.

That he missed a chance once, as in not getting out of a railway train (*see* p. 286) at sight of a skirt, is registered, and the registration may seem to continue along with a determination that neither he nor anyone else should ever, ever do it again. *Carpe diem* never so coupled to an almost surprise that it, the day, should have to be seized, and usually wasn't.

Every conventional fashion, all the undergraduate efforts to use ancient metres—no man ever had so much Latin and so eschewed the least appearance of being a classicist on the surface. He did translate; he wrote verse on current events, the Boer War for example. Born three years after Swinburne, writing with the same metric heritage as Kipling but with sobriety, so that whether Kipling did it first or not, Kipling reads like a derivative, cheaper; as Housman a mere derivative, with lesser men in their wake.

Contemporary for a long time with Browning on whom he improves at his, Hardy's, best, taking over the marrow of the tradition, he comes through the underbrush with his own, largely and for long, novelist's contents: Wessex, determined to leave a record of what he knew at first hand or gathered in local story.

It should be known that Ford Madox Ford started the *English Review* in a rage that there was no place in England to print a poem by Thomas Hardy. In literary history one never knows whether things happen because of or merely after something else. Chronology is often determinable. The lift in Hardy certainly occurs after Ford's review, and Ford's criticism, and Ford's demands for a timely language. The succession from Ford might be traced in Hardy's letters to me after *Propertius* and after *Mauberley*.

In the midst of a mass (800 pages good and bad together) of quite ordinary verse and verse experiment, one wants to make a valid selection, implying the history of Hardy's technical biography, a technique consisting largely in sloughing off all that wasn't the essential Hardy and only Hardy. This one can measure whimsically—or possibly not whimsically—against the *Discorsi degli Amanti* (pp. 278–83), a microcosmos of the poetic contents since Pharaoh's time, which is inserted out of chronological order for emphasis, and as the mine from which everyone from Solomon and Theocritus, through the Afghans and Mathers' anthology of the Near East, has taken ore or slag.

Hardy was not a chameleon, yet he took on the shades of every decade, Swinburne's metric experiment, oodles of German romanticism, ghosts, etc., and having got rid of a coloring he did not return to it because it was the fashion.

No one trying to learn writing in regular, formed verse can learn better than in observing what Thomas Hardy accepted from Browning and what he pruned away from his more busteous or rambunctious predecessor.

The chronology in most of his collections is, he admits, jumbled. What I learned from an impractical suggestion was the degree in which he would have had his mind on the SUBJECT MATTER, and how little he cared about manner, which does not in the least mean that he did not care about it or had not a definite aim. Also, having printed only four poems up to the age of fifty-eight, the lifetime spent in novel-writing gave him a magnificent tool kit, and if you have the sense to read without jingling, there is emphasis as it falls in the natural phrasing. You *can* jingle just as you can ruin Golding's *Metamorphoses* if you don't think of the natural phrasing, and let the metric *scheme* swallow it.

Nobody, on occasion, ever used rhyme with less insult to statement, but the road to this accomplishment left a number of botches, and a lot of words he would not have used in writing prose.

The next phase of good poetry in English was Ford's, who refused the imagist rock-drill, intent on his own *donné*, his own. They say no angel can carry more than one message, and the most important critical act of the half-century was in the limpidity of natural speech, driven toward the just word, not slopping down, as he aimed specifically not to slop into the more ordinary Wordsworthian word.

The preface to his imperfect poems is still there as in *Poetry* about 1911, along with Whitman's occasional comments on American poetry which are worth all the essayists of New England, for example his half-page on the enjoyment of Emerson's company. This chimes with the personal recollection of Charles Grinnell in spoken tradition: "He [Emerson] didn't know a damn thing about it, but he used the literary word." A memory of the Jameses' (Henry Senior's) parlor. The word being "valor" in connection with the practice of law.

It is no secret that I learned more from Ford than from anyone else. I went to London because, as seen from Philadelphia, 1906, Yeats knew more about writing poetry than any contemporary. He had made lyrics of a single sentence, with no word out of natural order. I had got that far by 1910. Robert Bridges advised against homophones, which look different on the page, but are ambiguous if spoken. Add Hardy, Edgar Wallace, and a Roman Archbishop and you have my apprentissage as far as I had it on the hoof from other writers of my own era.

Hardy at his best stems out of Browning, as Ford does, and does so by shedding the encrustation. In 1912 nobody paid any attention to Ford's verse, or to Hardy's. Macmillan's edition of the latter asserts, by internal evidence, that he started with metrical experiment; got to solid land in "The Ball at the Phoenix," and the poem about the hangman at the inn (parallel *Caster-bridge*). He traveled, apparently after the Boer War, as best evidenced in "Gibbon's Garden." "The Family Face" is undated. He translated a Sapphic fragment labeling it "imitation" to avoid quibbling. But the poems of 1912–13 lift him to his apex, sixteen poems from "The Going to Castle Boterel," all good, and enough for a lifetime.

"The Waterfall" is the lead-up, at the end of the volume just precedent. The approach through Browning was there in

> "Time's Laughingstocks"
> "Vaulted Way"
> "Phantom"
> "Episode"
> "Sigh"
> "The Conformers"
> "Night of the Dance"
> "Church Romance"
> "One We Knew"
> "After the Visit"
> "Wessex Heights."

There had been passages in "Revisitation." There are moments of frivolity, re which he ironizes in a later preface, with the edge of the irony toward those who expected him to do the same thing all the time.

"The Two Rosalinds" show conventional nostalgia, as the opening and oft-quoted line of "The Dancing Man." There is a spate of conventional moralizing, but there is also a grappling with and registration of the real struggle of mid-Victorian doubt. One need not quibble about his idiom in the horrible title "God's Funeral" or in such a line as "that moderate man Voltaire."

He started in an era when, as Henry James remarked, "they besought the deep blue sea to roll." He did not get to a positive statement of the KOINE ENNOIA, those basic common perceptions and deep agreement that can be traced from early China through Herbert of Cherbury and Remusat, and which Dante had "with trimmings." He hadn't Swinburne's specific antidote "Hellas" but he certainly did not reject it. He merely gave it in crinoline. He did not accept the Victorian conventions re marriage, monogomy, and the divorce laws of England, but he did not, like Blake, sit naked in a London back garden.

To make up for neglect in 1912 he now stands in the restricted area of reading matter, as distinct from printed matter, into which the reputed metrists of that era are now sunk "in their Georgian Marsh," to such a degree that Ronald Duncan, in giving advice for this collection and plugging for Pope, is ready to skip 3/4ths of the nineteenth century and after, i.e. from Byron to *Mauberley*.

E. P.

Appendix II

❅ ❅ The function of an introductory anthology should, as I see it, be to show the pupil as many different kinds of poetry as possible.

On the other hand, the teacher should have some idea of the extent of the world's verbal manifestation, and the extent of that part of it which is easily available to pupils whose curiosity has been aroused.

The simplest way of knowing the extent of Greek and Latin literature is to get a Loeb Library catalog. It can be supplemented by one of the Société Guillaume Budé in Paris. The Budé is the last rock and center of civilized resistance in France against the rising tide of imprecision, vulgarity and outright brainwash and perversion that has engulfed Europe in our time. No praise can be too high for their labor. They print bilingual editions not only of Greek and Latin but other languages, and lively works of general criticism and research, such as Massai's *Plethon et le Platonisme de mistra,* not regarding the past as something to be seen in mere retrospect but as key to parts of the future.

Professor Miller has permitted the use of his syllabus for students, and we give it as hint to those who wish to extend their reading or, let us say more advisedly, to deepen their knowledge. Also as indication of where the younger generation of teachers has, as Mr. James said, "got to."

SYLLABUS

REFERENCE: General works helpful if you aim to lessen your ignorance. Put them close at hand or you will be too lazy to get up and look in them. *Realize the dangers of your position:* two things can be done with a beginner—he can be taught and he can be taken advantage of. The second approach is easier, more profitable, and the beginner likes it better.

An encyclopedia. Use only for simple facts and suspect those until you have made your own examination. You will not be able to tell whether or not what you read is an *idée réçue,* dead, dying, or maintained by an effective pressure group. When you get to know some subject well, look it up and you'll see how incomplete and dangerous the account is. Right now you must start somewhere and run yours risks. The older the edition the better.

A dictionary. Merriam Webster, American College, Webster's New World. An unabridged when you get richer than I. All are tainted with heresy. Look up Sam Johnson's preface to his dictionary. He realized that words get their precision from the expert and not the sloppy who are—in God's wisdom—more numerous. Finally "the experts" are the poets. They know a lot about words. You should learn what you can. A dictionary is a place to begin. It gives some account of "general usage." The larger the dictionary, the more of a word's history, origins, and actual use by writers will be given.

Oxford Companion to Classical Literature. A brief account of the reference, with information as to what classical author wrote about it, in what work, and where in that work. Use it to look up names, places, etc., *in order to find out where to look them up.*

A Classical Dictionary, by J. Lemprière (Everyman Library). Cheaper than the above. Where some nineteenth-century authors learned about the classical and derived the images with which to decorate their works. *Not its use.*

A MINIMUM LIST OF CLASSICS: Don't fall for the dodge that there are 5,000 things you need to know; such ideas are spread abroad by those who don't know anything well but may have invested a lot of time in getting an "education." One or two books will put you way ahead of almost everyone, if they are important books and you *know* them. The possibility of a Renaissance may depend upon the number who grasp this fact.

Homer: *Odyssey* and *Iliad* translated by W. H. D. Rouse (Pocket Books). These, along with Robert Fitzgerald's fine verse translation of the *Odyssey* (Anchor Books), are the best translations—although Fitzgerald does not have all the qualities that are in Rouse. Some are horrible. These two books are at the base of Greek wisdom. Formulated abstractly 400 years later by Aristotle and Plato, they have been a major determinant in western civilization. Aristotle and Plato are O.K., just not at the beginning but the end (i.e., they were trying to restore the civilization Homer helped build—and they failed).

Ovid: *Metamorphoses.* Another view of the pagan wisdom: how to sort out the animals. This is one of two or three books Shakespeare learned from. The stories are precise renderings of psychological truths not defined anywhere else or even perceived by most. A prose translation by Mary Innes is in Penguin Books. A lively verse translation by Rolfe Humphries is also in paperback. Humphries thinks Ovid a good dirty story teller (a mode of excellence he confuses with sophistication) and so at serious points leaves out what seem to him pedestrian details. As a result, the reader can find in the Innes translation an Ovid of whom she herself is perhaps unaware. The best translation is the one Shakespeare used, Arthur Golding's. It is available only in part, in Everyman.

Dante: *Divine Comedy.* An excellent translation by Laurence

Binyon is available in a Viking Press paperback. Don't get a poor translation or all is lost. Many bad translations are recommended by people who teach Dante and read *The New Yorker*. This is a difficult work to get at, but when you do, it will give you a large part of the little wisdom man has acquired. It contains much of what later centuries were able to add to the Greek wisdom and should be examined with this in mind. Voltaire could not understand it, which gives a measure of subsequent decline. Not that we come up to Voltaire, who did set out to clean a very nasty stable.

Shakespeare: *Plays.* Get a book you can read without a microscope and one you can carry. Separate texts are the best. You shouldn't be in a hurry to *own* them all (in our country almost everyone can do that) but to *know* a few of them. Don't read the notes. Don't read any critics. (The only ones not dangerous are D. Traversi, G. Wilson Knight—who is difficult but not trying to underrate [different thing from underpraise] the work—and Sam Johnson, who is fine within a narrow limit. These three may help to keep your teachers at bay, if that is necessary.) Remember you are much better schooled than Shakespeare's audience and they understood him without any college professors. Of course, they had learned to observe—they had to to stay alive. Notice that Shakespeare is concerned with man as a political creature in ways more directly applicable to present situations than Homer.

Confucius: *The Analects, The Chung Yung (Unwobbling Pivot), The Ta S'eu (Great Digest)*, with perhaps *The Odes* as edited by Confucius. Best translations are by Ezra Pound, the first three in paperback from The Square Dollar Series, 1419 Clifton Street, N.W., Washington 9, D.C., in two volumes, *The Odes* in a New Directions paperback. Confucius' significance is similar to Homer's. In addition, our political and social organization differs from Homer's in ways it does not differ from Confucius'. Despite our debt to Greece, therefore, these works are at least as important in helping one know where the battle is going on.

James Joyce, Ezra Pound, T. S. Eliot. All modern, all difficult. The advantage is that you aren't likely to think you understand them when you don't. They are also of use to test others' ability *and desire* to read. Open one and ask a question.

Correspondence of Jefferson and Adams. Or their works. To find out what *kind* of men they were. This is where we started and it remains to be proved that we haven't been going backward.

BOOKS OF COMMENTARY: It is generally best to avoid these. The following will do a minimum of harm. They will introduce you to many authors. Read them. These books, listed below, are not written by professors who have to make the originals sound so dull or so complex that you don't read them and therefore do not find out how dull the professors are. Remember that people like the present writer make a living by getting between a student and a work of literature and pretending the student isn't bright enough to read—or at least seeing to it he doesn't get anything except through the union. Consider the fact that professors must appeal to sophomoric minds and that first-rate authors do not: this is one "advantage" the professor can exploit.

The English Novel and *The March of Literature,* by Ford Madox Ford. For the novel in both cases. Not for poetry.

Selected Essays by T. S. Eliot. For poetry and drama. Caused the modern "revolution" in criticism in academic circles. Remember that Eliot is trying to camouflage himself as a college professor and don't be misled—a careful eye is needed but he does say many things. A history of the misstatements he has encouraged in order to get some sense into a set of professorial blockheads would constitute an account of what has and has not been accomplished in this century in academic and "literary" circles. It is the opinion of this writer that he has, in the long run, outmaneuvered himself.

A.B.C. of Reading and *Guide to Kulchur,* by Ezra Pound. Just what the titles say, how and what to read, and how to acquire culture. Remember that Pound is set against talking like a professor ("Gravity, a mysterious carriage of the body to conceal the defects of the mind"). Each sentence is an idea, and its importance you will discover slowly. Pound makes no attempt to spin a single idea into a book. But you have been taught to read that way. The adjustment will be harder than it sounds.

The Chinese Written Character as a Medium for Poetry by Ernest Fenollosa. Fenollosa was an oriental scholar and this is an essay on the Chinese language, but it defines what poetry is and how it operates, if you want to know. Square Dollar Series; also City Lights Books, 261 Columbus Avenue, San Francisco, California.

Make your own list of what first-rate authors thought of other authors. Pay no attention to whom they stole a plot from. Whom did Swift admire? Whom Dante? Shakespeare? Chaucer? Whitman? If you insist upon having the opinions of others, such a list will do you some good. Now don't go and get some book on the subject.

DON'T JOIN ANY BOOK CLUBS!!

ODDS AND ENDS: Books not essential but of importance or interest. Not complete and in no order.

Anthony Trollope's novels. He preserves what lasted of healthy vision (in both himself and his audience) into the late nineteenth century in England and is of value for this. Compare with Pope, a preserver for the eighteenth, to measure loss and/or. Jane Austen's novels. Wyndham Lewis' novels and essays: a violent mind, wrong but of great use. Ford Madox Ford's novels. The novels of Henry James: in the most serious sense, America's only significant novelist. *The Portrait of a Lady* is an attempt to assess America's chances of leading a new worldwide Renaissance. It is a mirror held up to America to disclose signs of potential health and disease; later developments confirm the diagnosis. *An Introduction to Haiku: An Anthology of Poems from Bashō to Shiki,* translated with commentary by Harold Henderson (Anchor Books). Henderson gives an excellent account, offers an anthology of translations, and gives with each poem the Japanese (phonetically) and, as best he can, literal word by word equivalents. Flaubert's *Madame Bovary*. Ben Jonson's plays. Swift's *Gulliver's Travels*, especially the last book, *and his poetry*. Pope's poetry (concentrate on the late work of his maturity). Chaucer's *Canterbury Tales* and *Troilus and Criseyde*: the most important artist on the list; the closest approach in English to what has been called the Mediterranean sanity. Remember that Chaucer was a man active in an England that was a responsible part of western civilization and was seriously concerned with the concept of equity upon which all civilization rests. Are Shakespeare's plays an analysis of the loss thereof and resultant retchings of the patient???

Don't pay any attention to book prizes! Never. To none. Not even the Nobel. They are a snare.

VINCENT MILLER

Appendix III

The most active, not to say aggressive, of younger but experienced professors insists that this book cannot be accepted as a "textbook" for class use unless it is accompanied by questions for use in class.

To constitute a method, these questions must be the same for every assignment. I therefore suggest that the teacher start by asking himself, and then asking the pupils, the following:

Why is the poem included in the anthology?
What moved the author to write it?
What does it tell the reader?

These three lines of inquiry will, or at any rate should, keep both teacher and pupil from divagating into consideration of their own personal bellyaches.

They will also fill the class period without need of variants.

E. P.

Appendix IV

The instructor can use this volume in several different ways. The faint indication of the history of the occident in the sequence of Greek, Mediterranean, and English verses could act as outline for those who prefer lecturing as a means of instruction. The development of the actual English idiom is also exposed in the sequence. All of which gives the teacher a chance to be as traditional as he likes or offers opportunity for individual taste and fantasy. Such an approach should at least keep the student from supposing that the teacher knows only what is found in one textbook.

The analysis, more or less minute, of individual poems is practiced in some universities. Nothing herein prevents it. In fact, Mr. Pound's three questions listed above in Appendix III would lend themselves to this type of instruction, as would any question designed to get the student to observe what is being said—questions about the nature of the individuals present in the poems or, on the simplest level, if one wished to start there, the objects depicted, the story told. The important thing as I see it is to get the student to look. All else will follow, that is, assuming the student has any intelligence at all. Agassiz, one of the greatest teachers of all time, was certainly aware of this. When asked what he considered his most important achievement, he said: "I have taught men to observe."

Any teacher with the same goal should read carefully Vincent Miller's syllabus (Appendix II), which has the additional aim of this anthology, i.e., of getting the best available specimens for study. His syllabus ought to be required reading for all students, preferably near the end of a literature course in which they have been taught to *look* and to *think*.

Although designed for an introductory course in poetry, this anthology can also be used in comparative literature courses, and as stimulus in composition or, if one must use the current term, "creative writing" courses.

Since compiling the collection it has been tested by reading aloud. Most of the poems fit Ezra Pound's acid test of sonority, but there are others here for practical classroom use under present teaching conditions and accepted modes of classroom operation.

The teacher who wants more extended footnotes for the anthology in a convenient form might use both Pound's *A.B.C. of Reading* and his *Literary Essays* (New Directions).

M. S.

Appendix V

❋ ❋ At the publisher's request, I have made the following selections from Ezra Pound's criticism that could function as cardinal points in the study of this anthology. Unless otherwise stated they are to be found in the *A.B.C. of Reading*. [M. S.]

You would think that anyone wanting to know about poetry would do one of two things or both. I.e., *look at* it or listen to it. He might even think about it.

And it is my firm conviction that a man can learn more about poetry by really knowing and examining a few of the best poems than by meandering about among a great many.

The reader's first and simplest test of an author will be to look for words that do not function; that contribute nothing to the meaning *or* that distract from the *most* important factor of the meaning to factors of minor importance.

One definition of beauty is: aptness to purpose.

Whether it is a good definition or not, you can readily see that a good deal of *bad* criticism has been written by men who assume that an author is trying to do what he is *not* trying to do.

Good writers are those who keep the language efficient. That is to say, keep it accurate, keep it clear.

Language is the main means of human communication.

Your legislator can't legislate for the public good, your commander can't command, your populace . . . can't instruct its "representatives," save by language.

Greece and Rome civilized *by language*. Your language is in the care of your writers.

The man of understanding can no more sit quiet and resigned while his country lets its literature decay, and lets good writing meet with contempt, than a good doctor could sit quiet and contented while some ignorant child was infecting itself with tuberculosis under the impression that it was merely eating jam tarts.

Divide writers into two main categories
A. Those who write with a sense of responsibility to the life of the mind.
B. Those who do without it. [Unpublished note from the Pound notebooks. Dated 5 February 1956.]

A writer dies when he ceases to have, and exercise, omnivorous curiosity. Compare Landor on Browning—and Henry James's estimates of impressions of Tennyson and Browning in *The Middle Years* volume of his memoirs. [Unpublished, 5 February 1956.]

When you start searching for "pure elements" in literature

you will find that literature has been created by the following classes of persons:

1. Inventors. Men who found a new process, or whose extant work gives us the first known example of a process.

2. The masters. Men who combined a number of such processes, and who used them as well as or better than the inventors.

3. The diluters. Men who came after the first two kinds of writer, and couldn't do the job quite as well.

4. Good writers without salient qualities. Men who are fortunate enough to be born when the literature of a given country is in good working order, or when some particular branch of writing is "healthy." For example, men who wrote sonnets in Dante's time, men who wrote short lyrics in Shakespeare's time or for several decades thereafter, or who wrote French novels and stories after Flaubert had shown them how.

5. Writers of belles-lettres. That is, men who didn't really invent anything, but who specialized in some particular part of writing, who couldn't be considered as "great men" or as authors who were trying to give a complete presentation of life, or of their epoch.

6. The starters of crazes.

Until the reader knows the first two categories he will never be able to "see the wood for the trees." He may know what he "likes." He may be a "compleat book-lover," with a large library of beautifully printed books, bound in the most luxurious bindings, but he will never be able to sort out what he knows or to estimate the value of one book in relation to others, and he will be more confused and even less able to make up his mind about a book where a new author is "breaking with convention" than to form an opinion about a book eighty or a hundred years old.

He will never understand why a specialist is annoyed with him for trotting out a second- or third-hand opinion about the merits of his favorite bad writer.

Until you have made your own survey and your own closer inspection you might at least beware and avoid accepting opinions:

1. From men who haven't themselves produced notable work.

2. From men who have not themselves taken the risk of printing the results of their own personal inspection and survey, even if they are seriously making one.

You can spot the bad critic when he starts by discussing the poet and not the poem.

E. P.

Indices

Index of Poets and Translators

A. W., 136-38
Aeschylus, 19-21
Aldington, Richard, *translation*, 119
Anonymous, 69-72, 77-78, 100-101, 107, 108-10, 126, 142, 278-83
Arnaut, Daniel, 84-86

Beauveau, Marie-Françoise-Catherine de, *see* Boufflers, la Marquise de
Beddoes, Thomas Lovell, 213-14
Bernart de Ventadorn, 81-82
Bertrans de Born, 80-81
Boethius, 68-69
Boufflers, Marie-Françoise-Catherine de Beauveau, la Marquise de, 178-79
Browning, Elizabeth Barrett, 215-18
Browning, Robert, 221-55
Bunting, Basil, 313-16
Burns, Robert, 197-99
Byron, George Gordon, Lord, 201-206

Catullus, 33
Cavalcanti, Guido, 91-96
Chapman, George, *translations*, 16-18
Charles d'Orléans, 108
Chaucer, Geoffrey, 102-107
Colum, Padraic, 305-306
Confucius, 3-14
Cornish, William, 124-25
Crabbe, George, 182-96
Creech, Thomas, *translation*, 25
cummings, e e, 316-18

Daniel, Samuel, 143-45
Dante Alighieri, 96-99
Davies, John, 172-73

Dobson, H. Austin, *translation*, 221
Doolittle, Hilda, *see* H.D.
Douglas, Gavin, *translation*, 34
Dryden, John, *translation*, 32
du Bellay, Joachim, 128

Eliot, T. S., 312-13
Elizabeth I, *poems*, 129-30; *translation*, 68

Folgore da San Gemignano, 90-91
Ford, Ford Madox, *poems*, 290-305; *translation*, 82
Francis of Assisi, Saint, 86-88

Gautier, Théophile, 221
Godeschalk, 75-76
Golding, Arthur, *translations*, 38-66
Greene, Robert, 139-42
Guinicelli, Guido, 88-90

H. D. (Hilda Doolittle), 311
Halleck, Fitz-Greene, 206-209
Hardy, Thomas, *poems*, 283-86; *translation*, 18
Harte, Francis Bret, 274-76
Heath, 125-26
Hemans, Felicia Dorothea, 210-11
Henry VIII, 122-24
Herrick, Robert, 174-75
Hesse, Eva, *translation*, 317
Homer, 15-18
Horace, 35-37

Jonson, Ben, 173-74

Keats, John, 211-13
King, Benjamin Franklin, Jr., 277

Landor, Walter Savage, 200

Lang, Andrew, *translations*, 79, 108, 128-29
Langland, William, 101-102
Lewis, Wyndham, 306-307
Li Po, *see* Rihaku
Longfellow, Henry Wadsworth, *translation*, 127
Lorenzo de' Medici, the Magnificent, 118-19
Lucretius, 32-33
Luther, Martin, 120-21

Marlowe, Christopher, 146-47
Medici, Lorenzo de', *see* Lorenzo de' Medici
Melville, Herman, 256
Metastasio, Pietro, 177
Michelangelo Buonarotti, 119-20
Moore, Marianne, 311-12
Munday, Anthony, 139

"Old Captive," The, 79
Orléans, Charles d', *see* Charles d'Orléans
Ovid, 37-66

Pound, Ezra, *poems*, 308-10; *translations*, 3-14, 22, 33, 35, 36, 67, 69, 72, 75, 80, 81, 84, 86, 91, 92, 93, 177, 178, 278

Rachewiltz, Boris de, *translation*, 278
Ralegh, Walter, 132-36
Rikahu (Li Po), 72-75

Riley, James Whitcomb, 276-77
Ronsard, Pierre de, 128-29
Rossetti, Dante Gabriel, *poem*, 271; *translations*, 88, 90, 96-99, 115, 117
Rutilius, 66-67

Sappho, 18
Shakespeare, William, 148-71
Simpson, Dallam, *translation*, 19
Smart, Christopher, 179-82
Sophokles, 22-25
Stryker, M. Woolsey, *translation*, 120
Swinburne, Algernon Charles, *poem*, 272-73; *translations*, 111, 114, 115

Teresa d'Avila, Santa, 127
Theocritus, 25-32
Turberville, George, 131

Villon, François, 111-17
Virgil, 34
von der Vogelweide, Walther, 82-83

Waller, Edmund, 175-77
Whitman, Walt, 256-70
Whittier, John Greenleaf, 218-20
Williams, William Carlos, 307-308
Wilson, Robert, 143
Wordsworth, William, *translation*, 119
Wyatt, Thomas, 127

Yeats, William Butler, 287-89

Index of Titles and First Lines of Poems

A Baby is born, us bliss to bring, 109
A face that should content me wonders well, 127
A fair and bright assembly: never strode, 213
A lady asks me, 93
"*A Perigord pres del muralh,*" 80
A rat too has a skin (to tan), 6
A thing of beauty is a joy for ever, 211
A Tower of Refuge is our God!, 120
A very pitiful lady, very young, 96
A young man, alone, on the high bridge over the Tagus . . . , 307
Achtung, 18
Acteon, 38
Adam lay yboundin, boundin in a bond, 107
Aeneid, the, from, 34
Again and again I kiss thy gates at departing, 67
Agamemnon, the, from, 19
Age of Gold, I bid thee come, 177
Air: Sentir avec ardeur, 178
Airs of Pei, from, 5
Alba, 11
Alisoun, 100
Aliter, 13
All passes. Art alone, 221
All that glisters is not gold—, 162
And I bowed my body and beheld all about, 102
And Paris be it or Helen dying, 115
Andrea del Sarto, 242
Ars Victrix, from, 221
As the holly groweth green, 123
As You Like It, from, 158-62
Ask not ungainly askings of the end, 36
Asleep, my love?, 154
At nine in the morning there passed a church, 286
At Perigord near to the wall, 80
Atalanta in Calydon, from, 272
Aucassin and Nicolette, from, 79
August, 90
"*Autet e bas,*" 85
Ave maris stella, the star of the sea, 110

345

Ballad of Dead Ladies, The, 117
Barbara Frietchie, 218
Baroness Mu impeded in her wish to help famine victims in Wei, 7
Be kind, good sir, and I'll lift my sark, 11
Beyond the sphere which spreads to widest space, 99
Birks of Aberfeldy, The, 197
Bitwene Mersh and Averil, 100
Blow, blow, thou winter wind, 159
Bob Southey: You're a poet—Poet-laureate, 201
Bonnie lassie, will ye go, 197
Bonnie Lesley, 198
Bookmark, 127
Borough, The, from, 182
Brereton Omen, The, from, 210
Brown is my Love, but graceful, 142
But *Bacchus* was not so content: he quyght forsooke their land, 58
But do not let us quarrel any more, 242
But give them me, the mouth, the eyes, the brow!, 255
But how shall we this union well express?, 172
By the flat cup and the splash of new vintage, 35

Can it be right to give what I can give?, 215
Canterbury Tales, The, from, 102-105
Cantico del Sole, 86
Canzone: Donna mi priegha, 93
Canzone: Of the Gentle Heart, 88
Carnival Songs, from, 118
Celebration of Charis, A, from, 173
Centenarian's Story, The, 265
"Chkk! chkk!" hopper-grass, 3
Chou and the South, from, 3
Classic Anthology, The, from, 3-14
Cold Heaven, The, 289
Come away, come away, death, 164
Come live with me and be my love, 147
Come unto these yellow sands, 148
Complaint of Rosamond, The, from, 143
Complaint of the Fair Armouress, The, 111
Complaint of the Morpethshire Farmer, The, 314
Conversations in Courtship, from, 278
Creeper grows over thorn, 11
Cyclops, 62
Cymbeline, from, 165

Daedalus, 43
Darling, you only, there is no duplicate, 278
De Consolatione Philosophiæ, from, 68
De Rerum Natura, from, 32
Dead shalt thou lie; and nought, 18
Dear Son, Leave Thy Weeping, 109

Death's Jest Book, from, 213-14
Deer Sing, from, 13
Description of Sir Geoffrey Chaucer, The, 141
Dirce, 200
Dirge, 139
Don Juan, from, 201-206
Done to death by slanderous tongues, 150
Down by the salley gardens my love and I did meet, 287
Downe to the King's most bright-kept Baths they went, 16

Efficient Wife's Complaint, The, 5
"*Ein feste Burg ist unser Gott,*" 120
Enchantment, The, 25
Endymion, from, 211-13
Envoi (1919), 310
Epigram, 127
Epitaph, 133
Epitaph in Form of a Ballad, The, 114
Even such is Time, which takes in trust, 133
Exile's Letter, 72

Face, A, 252
Faintheart in a Railway Train, 286
Fanny, from, 207-209
Fanny was younger once than she is now, 207
Fear no more the heat o' th' sun, 165
First time he kissed me, he but only kissed, 217
Flower of this purple dye, 153
Fo' a yeah or mo' on this roof I'se layed, 19
For August, be your dwelling thirty towers, 90
For I will consider my Cat Jeoffry, 179
For my part, I'le not meddle with the cause, 18
Fra Lippo Lippi, 231
Fragment on Death, A, 115
Fraternitas, 13
From fairest creatures we desire increase, 166
From her bed's high and odoriferous roome, 17

Garden Fancies, 227
Gin the Goodwife Stint, 313
Give me your hand old Revolutionary, 265
Go, dumb-born book, 310
Go, lovely Rose!, 175
Go, soul, the body's guest, 133
Good-by er Howdy-do, 276
Graceful as acorus or lotus flower, 13
Gratitude, 124
Green grow the rashes O, 199

Half close your eyelids, loosen your hair, 289

Happy too much, the former age, 68
He Remembers Forgotten Beauty, 288
He Thinks of Those Who Have Spoken Evil of His Beloved, 289
Hep-Cat Chung, 'ware my town, 10
Her Triumph, 173
Heredity, 283
Here's the garden she walked across, 227
Hierusalem, my happy home, 77
High Bridge above the Tagus River at Toledo, The, 307
Hill-billy, hill-billy come to buy, 8
His Mother's Service to Our Lady, 115
His stature was not very tall, 141
Holly, The, 123
House of Life, The, from, 271
How do I love thee? Let me count the ways, 217
How fair is youth that flies so fast! . . . , 118
How It Strikes a Contemporary, 221

I am poor brother Lippo, by your leave!, 231
I am the family face, 283
I could have painted pictures like that youth's, 225
I had over-prepared the event, 308
I hate and love. Why? You may ask but, 33
I have been here before, 271
I only knew one poet in my life, 221
"I Shall Not Die for Thee," 305
I sing the body electric, 256
I walked along a stream for pureness rare, 146
I wanted to harness and go, 7
I wot full well that beauty cannot last, 131
I would set all things whatsoever front to back, 306
I would to heaven that I were so much clay, 201
Idylls, the, from, 25
If all the world and love were young, 132
If I, like Solomon . . . , 311
If one could have that little head of hers, 252
If she be made of white and red, 151
If the scorn of your bright eyne, 161
If this our little life is but a day, 128
If thou must love me, let it be for nought, 216
In chariot like an hibiscus flower at his side, 10
In Praise of the Sun, 138
In shards the sylvan vases lie, 256
In the South be drooping trees, 3
It once might have been, once only, 250
It was a lover and his lass—, 161

Jubilate Agno, from, 179

King Henry V, from, 171

King Midas, 58
Kupris bears trophies away, 22

Lady of Heaven and earth, and therewithal, 115
Lark, The, 81
"*L'aura amara,*" 84
Let nothing disturb thee, 127
Lie, The, 133
Light do I see within my Lady's eyes, 92
Likeness, A, 253
Lonely Beauty, 143
Lover to His Lady, The, 131
Love's Labour's Lost, from, 151

Maesia's Song, 141
Maid, where's my *Lawrel?* Oh my rageing Soul!, 26
Marsh bank, lotus rank, 12
May I for my own self song's truth reckon, 69
Meleager, 46
Men, brother men, that after us yet live, 114
Merchant of Venice, The, from, 162-63
Merciles Beaute, 105
Meseemeth I heard cry and groan, 111
Metamorphoses, the, from, 38-66
Midsummer Night's Dream, A, from, 152-57
Moods, The, 288
More whyght thou art then Primrose leaf my Lady *Galatee,* 62
Most high lord, 86
Much Ado About Nothing, from, 150-51
My girl, thou gazest much, 131
My Lady's face it is they worship there, 92
My thoughts do harbour with my Silvia nightly, 149

Never more will the wind, 311
Nosce Teipsum, from, 172
Not marble nor the gilded monuments, 168
Not mine own fears, nor the prophetic soul, 170
Nothing to do but work, 277
Now have I brought a woork too end which neither *Joves* fierce wrath, 65
Now high and low, where leaves renew, 85
Now in this while gan *Dædalus* a weariness to take, 43
Now my charms are all o'erthrown, 149
Now the hungry lion roars, 155
Now *Thebes* stood in good estate, now *Cadmus* might thou say, 38
Now welcom somer, with thy sonne softe, 107
Nymph's Reply to the Shepherd, The, 132

O mistress mine, where are you roaming?, 163
O saw ye bonnie Lesley, 198
O To Be a Dragon, 311

O woman, shapely as the swan, 305
Odes, the, from, 35-37
Odi et Amo, 33
Odyssey, the, from, 16-18
Of His Lady's Old Age, 128
Of The Months: Twelve Sonnets, from, 90
Old Menalcas on a day, 139
On Heaven, 290
On the up-platform at Morpeth station, 314
One night i' th' year, my dearest Beauties, come, 174
One Times One, from, 316
One-Way Song, from, 306
Orpheus and Eurydice, 255

Palmer's Ode, The, 139
Pardon, goddess of the night, 151
Parlement of Foules, The, from, 107
Passionate Shepherd to His Love, The, 147
Past ruin'd Ilion Helen lives, 200
Pastime with good company, 122
Pedlar, 8
Philemon and Baucis, 54
Pictor Ignotus, 225
Pirithous being over hault of mynde and such a one, 54
Plain Language from Truthful James, 274
plato told, 316
Pleasure it is, 124

Ravaged Villa, The, 256
Roma, 67
Roundel, 107

Sans Equity and Sans Poise, 6
Say good-by er howdy-do—, 276
Say what you will in two, 178
Schools (Letter XXIV), 182
Seafarer, The, 69
See the chariot at hand here of love, 173
Sequaire, 75
Shall I compare thee to a summer's day?, 166
Shao and the South, from, 3, 4
Sigh no more, ladies, sigh no more!, 150
Signal Fire, The, 19
Simplicity sings it and 'sperience doth prove, 143
Simplicity's Song, 143
So he won't talk to me when we meet?, 11
Some people hang portraits up, 253
Song Set by John Farmer, 142
Song Set by Nicholas Yonge, 142
Songs of Ch'en, from, 12, 13

Songs of Cheng, from, 10, 11
Songs of T'ang, from, 11
Sonnet to Heavenly Beauty, A, 128
Sonnets, the, from, 166-70
Sonnets from the Portuguese, from, 215-18
Soul and the Body, The, 172
Splendour recurrent, 13
Spring, 108
Stand close around, ye Stygian set, 200
Sudden Light (Song IV), 271
Suddenly I saw the cold and rook-delighting heaven, 289
Sum of Life, The, from, 277
Sweet are the thoughts that savour of content, 141
Sweet Love, mine only treasure, 136

Take Time while Time doth last, 142
Tell me now in what hidden way is, 117
Tell me, where is fancy bred, 163
Tempest, The, from, 148-49
Thank Goodness, the moving is over, 304
That day the sunlight lay on the farms, 290
That she hath gone to Heaven suddenly, 97
That time of year thou mayst in me behold, 169
The batalis and the man I will discrive, 34
The bitter air, 84
The doubt of future foes exiles my present joy, 129
The face of all the world is changed, I think, 215
The fire seven times tried this, 162
The golden sun that brings the day, 138
The night, say all, was made for rest, 137
The old house of Flanders, 304
The Pharisee murmurs when the woman weeps . . . , 75
The ploughland has gone to bent, 313
The seven white peacocks against the castle wall, 303
The woosel cock so black of hue, 153
The year has changed his mantle cold, 108
There was the sonne of *Ampycus* of great forecasting wit, 46
These Gothic windows, how they wear me out, 286
These women all, 125
This monument will outlast metal and I made it, 36
Three stars, five stars rise over the hill, 4
Through the forest have I gone, 152
Through the house give glimmering light, 156
Thus far, with rough and all-unable pen, 171
Time drops in decay, 288
Tir'd with all these, for restful death I cry, 169
To a Poet, Who Would Have Me Praise Certain Bad Poets, Imitators of His and Mine, 289
To Delia, from, 145
To every Class we have a School assign'd, 182

To His Friend, 131
To His Lady, 123
To His Lovely Mistresses, 174
To Mr. Henry Lawes, 176
To So-Kin of Rakuyo, ancient friend, Chancellor of Gen, 72
To the Marchesana of Pescara, 119
To the States or any one of them, or any city of the States, *Resist much, obey little*, 270
Triumph of Bacchus and Ariadne, 118
Twelfth Night, from, 163-64
Twelve Herds of Oxen, no lesse Flockes of Sheepe, 17
Two Gentlemen of Verona, The, from, 149

Under the greenwood tree, 158
Under the lindens on the heather, 82
Under the Waterfall, 284
Up and down, up and down, 154
Up from the meadows rich with corn, 218
Upon Visiting His Lady by Moonlight, 137

Verse makes heroic virtue live, 176
Villanelle: The Psychological Hour, 308
Vision of Piers Plowman, The, from, 101
Vita Nuova, La, from, 96-99

War Song, A, 80
Webster was much possessed by death, 312
Weep, weep, ye woodmen, wail, 139
Wei Wind, from, 8
Well pleaseth me the sweet time of Easter, 80
Western wind, when will thou blow, 126
Whan that Aprille with his shoures soote, 102
What greater torment ever could have been, 143
What has this bugbear death to frighten man, 32
What is your substance, whereof are you made, 168
What shall he have that kill'd the deer?, 160
What the Orderly Dog Saw, 303
When I see the lark a-moving, 81
When I was fair and young, and favor grac̀ed me, 130
When, in disgrace with Fortune and men's eyes, 167
When in the chronicle of wasted time, 170
When my arms wrap you round I press, 288
When the hounds of spring are on winter's traces, 272
"When the World Was in Building . . . ," 304
When to the sessions of sweet silent thought, 167
When winter snows upon thy sable hairs, 145
When you are old and grey and full of sleep, 287
When you are very old, at evening, 128
Whenever I plunge my arm, like this, 284
Where His Lady Keeps His Heart, 136

Where neither King nor shepheard want comes neare, 16
Where the bee sucks, there suck I, 148
Whereto should I express, 123
Which I wish to remark, 274
Whispers of Immortality, from, 312
Who is she that comes, makyng turn every man's eye, 91
Who would list to the good lay, 79
Why should this a desert be, 159
Wind o' the East dark with rain, 5
Within the gentle heart Love shelters him, 88
Women, 125
Women of Trachis, from, 22

Ye pilgrim folk advancing pensively, 98
Yes! hope may with my strong desire keep pace, 119
Yes! I have seen the ancient oak, 210
Yet but three? Come one more, 154
Yet, love, mere love, is beautiful indeed, 216
You say, as I have often given tongue, 289
Young Glass-Stainer, The, 286
Your yën two wol slee me sodenly, 105
Youth and Art, 250
Yung Wind, from, 6, 7